LOST WISDOM

Rethinking Modernity in Iran

by

ABBAS MILANI

MAGE PUBLISHERS
WASHINGTON, D.C.
2004

Copyright © 2004 Abbas Milani

Library of Congress Cataloging-in-Publication Data

Milani, Abbas.
Lost wisdom : rethinking modernity in Iran / by Abbas Milani.
-- 1st ed.
p. cm.
ISBN 0-934211-89-2 -- ISBN 0-934211-90-6 (pbk.)
1. Iran--Intellectual life. 2. Islamic fundamentalism -- Iran.
3. Islamic modernism -- Iran. 4. Islam and politics -- Iran.
5. Secularism -- Iran. 6. Culture conflict -- Iran. I. Title.
DS266.M484 2004
306.6'97'0955--dc22
2003021327

First Edition
Printed in the USA

HARDCOVER ISBN 0-934211-89-2
PAPERBACK ISBN 0-934211-90-6

MAGE BOOKS ARE AVAILABLE AT BOOKSTORES OR DIRECTLY FROM THE
PUBLISHER VISIT MAGE ON THE WEB AT WWW.MAGE.COM OR CALL
1 800 962 0922 OR E-MAIL INFO@MAGE.COM

CONTENTS

For my teacher, mentor, and friend,
Michael Shapiro

And for my brother,
Hassan Milani

MODERNITY
In the Land of the Sophy*

Some twenty-five hundred years ago, when Herodotus was writing his *Histories*, Iran, or Persia as it was called then, was the West's ultimate "other." Today, that otherness has once again reared its divisive head. A central theme of the essays in this collection is that Iran and the West have more in common than in difference. The crucial link of their unity is their common, albeit historically disparate, quest for human ideals like democracy and freedom.

The other connective thread of the articles is a radical reappraisal of Iran's experience with modernity. I propose that we heed Descartes' call to skepticism, and doubt much of what has been accepted as gospel in the nature and historiography of modernity in general, and of Iranian modernity in particular. Such a reading will, I suggest, demonstrate that Iran has had three crucial encounters with modernity—the first commencing long before the Renaissance in Europe—and each has been thwarted by a small, radical group using religious obscurantism and Islamic fundamentalism to frustrate the evolution of modern ideas like rationalism and the rule of law. Developments in Iran today are only the most recent examples of this historic pattern.

I offer the essays collected here as elements of a new discourse—one that is in dialogue with Iran's past, present, and future, woven with the warp of local history and the woof of universal knowledge and global developments.[1] Such a discourse is essential if we are to understand the fateful question of modernity in Iran—and by extension, in other Islamic countries. This new kind of vision is also indispensable if Iran is to succeed in its thousand-year-old struggle toward a genuine modernity.

---

* In *The Twelfth Night*, Shakespeare refers to Iran as "the land of the Sophy."

1. Many critics and theorists have written about the necessity for knowledge to be "local." See for example Clifford Geertz, *Local Knowledge: Further Essays in Interpretive Anthropology*, (New York, 1996). Others have emphasized the necessity of combining local knowledge with global awareness. See for example, Walter D. Mignolo, *The Darker Side of the Renaissance: Literacy, Territoriality, and Colonialization* (Ann Arbor, 1995).

It has been a common belief of scholars that modernity began in the West, and is by its philosophical nature, economic underpinning, and cultural exigencies a uniquely Western phenomenon. All "other" cultures, those who have lived on the "darker side of the Renaissance,"[2] must emulate the Western experience, if they want to be modern. From Max Weber to Milan Kundera,[3] many Western scholars and writers have argued that everything from representative democracy and rational thought to the art of the novel and the essay are not only Western in origin but also uniquely suited to its culture, and native to its temperate climes.

In Iran, an interesting confluence of conflicting ideologies have joined forces to foster the same Eurocentric idea. Some intellectuals, awed and inspired by the West, became advocates of this Eurocentric vision. Their social perspectives, even their personal demeanors, had much in common with the Russian "Westophil" intellectuals so brilliantly described in nineteenth-century novels like Dostoyevsky's *The Possessed* and Turgenev's *Fathers and Sons*. The essay on Shadman in this collection describes the morphology and consequences of this viewpoint and offers a critique of the role it has played in Iran's culture wars. A number of other writers discussed in this volume—particularly Ebrahim Golestan and Houshang Golshiri—have also criticized this Eurocentric vision, and offered different views of Iran's history.

With a few individual exceptions Iranian Marxists have been the second group advocating this self-deprecating view of modernity. By mechanically and uncritically applying to Iran Marx's description of European historical development, and by insisting that his historical schemata[4] is universally—and uniformly—valid, they too have helped

---

2. As the Renaissance was enjoying what it self-righteously called the process of "discovering" the world, the inhabitants of these newly "discovered" territories experienced "the darker side of the Renaissance." An elegant discussion of this question can be found in Walter D. Mignolo's *The Darker Side of the Renaissance*.

3. Max Weber makes the case for modernity as essentially Western in the preface to his book on Protestantism. See *The Protestant Ethic and the Spirit of Capitalism*, trans. Talcott Parsons (New York, 1992), 13-31. For Kundera's intervention in the debate, see The Art of the Novel (New York, 1984).

4. Iranian Marxists were particularly fond of the idea that all societies go through the same five stages of development, beginning with primitive communism and slavery, on to feudalism, capitalism and of course socialism and communism. Stalin was the chief architect of this banal historical construction. He was worried that Marx's reference to the "Asiatic Mode of Production" and its inherent despotism might be construed as a reference to precisely the kind of despotism that existed in Stalinist Russia. He thus ordered the potentially messy concept of Asiatic Mode banned from the lexicon of "orthodox" Marxism. The "five stages of history" became gospel, and it was this Procrustean model that was favored by the majority of Iranian Marxists.For an interesting discussion of this vision and its consequences for historiography, see Abbas Vali, *Precapitalist Iran: A Theoretical History* (London, 1993), 1-20.

sustain the myth that modernity is European in nature, and came to Iran only with colonialism.

The third group to champion the idea of Western modernity has in fact been the enemies of modernity in Iran. Religious forces bent on halting the march of secular humanism have systematically tried to equate modernity with unsavory colonial and Western influences. They helped develop a "nativist"[5] response to modernity that hides its inherently anti-democratic sentiments in the garb of a fuzzy and eclectic anti-colonial rhetoric. It was precisely this beguiling rhetoric that convinced many secular democrats, in Iran and the West, that Ayatollah Khomeini was a "progressive" critic of modernity and colonialism. The essay on *Kafi* in this book offers a glimpse into the textual sources of a fundamentalist religious response to modernity.

The power and prevalence of this Eurocentric vision has meant that in the last hundred years Iranian advocates of modernity have had to fight the charge of being conscious, or inadvertent, tools of Western domination. A surprisingly wide array of secular writers and Islamist clerics—from Sheikh Fazlollah Nouri and Ayatollah Khomeini to Jalal Al Ahmad and Noureddin Kianouri[6]—have all denigrated democracy and modernity as a Western ruse, a veritable Trojan Horse used by "colonialists" to undermine Iran's "genuine" cultural or political nature. But these pundits and ideologues misunderstand or misrepresent what is culturally specific about Iran, and historically universal about modernity.

Persia, later renamed Iran, has more than two thousand years of recorded history. Though in recent times, its politics have caused it to be often maligned in the Western media, a new impartial, albeit critical, look at its history will, I submit, show not just its impressively rich and varied cultural legacy, but its formative, now forgotten, role in shaping Western consciousness itself.

To begin at the beginning, the Bible is replete with profuse praise for Persia and its kings. In the book of Ezra, the Lord of the Old Testament speaks through the proclamations of Cyrus, King of Persia, who declares,

---

5. Boroujerdi defines nativism as the call "for the resurgence, reinstatement or continuance of native or indigenous cultural customs, beliefs, and values" while decrying others as inauthentic. See Mehrzad Boroujerdi, *Iranian Intellectuals and the West: The Tormented Triumph of Nativism* (Syracuse, 1996), 14-10.

6. Nouri was a cleric and an enemy of the constitutional revolution of 1905-06; Khomeini needs no introduction; Al Ahmad was a well-known author generally thought to have been influential in paving the way for rapprochement between the clergy and the middle class and intellectuals; and Kianouri was a leader of the pro-Soviet Communist Tudeh Party of Iran, an architect by training who lived much of his adult life in exile. After the revolution, in spite of his avid support for clerical despotism he was arrested and forced to confess to spying for the Soviet Union.

"The Lord God of heaven hath given me all the kingdoms of the earth, and he has charged me to build him a house in Jerusalem." Cyrus, as we know, acceded to this lordly edict and thus was the second Temple in Jerusalem built. In other parts of the Old Testament, Cyrus is often referred to as God's "anointed" and the "chosen" ruler. This fulsome praise was partially in recognition of his role in freeing the Jews from their Babylonian captivity; of equal importance was the fact that the vast Persian empire of the time was a paragon of religious and cultural tolerance.[7] There is something of a consensus among historians—with the glaring exception of Sheikh Sadeq Khalkhali, if he can be called an historian[8]—that Cyrus was in fact the first ruler to issue a declaration of human rights. It predates the Magna Carta by more than a millennium. Cyrus was also the first ruler to create a truly multi-cultural empire by affording his conquered peoples the liberty to maintain their own linguistic, religious, and cultural autonomy. So ubiquitous was his reputation that songs in his praise have reached as far away as Iceland and formed an important part of Icelandic sagas.[9]

Many Biblical scholars have further shown that a plethora of theological concepts, from the notions of Satan and hell to those of angels and heaven, and most importantly, the idea of the resurrection of the body, have all been the result of Persian—or more specifically, Zoroastrian— influences on the Bible. Some scholars have suggested that Zarathustra was the first prophet of a monotheistic religion; others maintain that the idea of a millennium—the significance afforded to thousand-year cycles in history—found its way to Christianity through the Zoroastrian religion.[10]

Hegel, the nineteenth-century German philosopher, whose writings are considered by many as the apex of the Western philosophical tradition, uses superlatives in praising the role of Persia and Zarathustra in history. "Persians," he writes, "are the first Historic people…. In Persia first arises that light which shines itself and illuminates what is around….

7. For a fascinating account of the biblical Persia see Edwin M. Yamauchi, *Persia and the Bible* (Grand Rapids, 1996). The book's extensive bibliography is rich in sources about many aspects of Persian history, culture, religions and languages.

8. Khalkhali, known to the world as the infamous "Hanging Judge," dabbled in what he called scholarship, and in one of these tragicomic forays, he attacked Cyrus as a pederast and a liar. See Sadeq Khalkhali, *Kourosh-e Doroughin-e Jenayat-kar* [The false and criminal Cyrus] (Tehran, 1370/1990).

9. Jakob Jonson, "Cyrus the Great in Icelandic Epic: A Literary Study," *Acta Iranica* (1974): 49-50

10. Mary Boyce has written a scholarly introduction to the beliefs, practices, and influence of Zoroastrianism. In her view, "Zoroastrianism is the oldest of the revealed credal religions, and it has probably had more influence on mankind, directly or indirectly, than any other single faith." See Mary Boyce, *Zoroastrians* (London, 1979), 1

11. Georg Hegel, *The Philosophy of History*, trans. J. Sibree (Buffalo, 1991), 173.

The principle of development begins with the history of Persia; this constitutes therefore the beginning of history."[11]

Hegel wrote these lines around the time Nietzsche was writing his magnum opus, *Thus Spoke Zarathustra*. Nietzsche's book offers a radical critique, almost a total debunking, of the whole Western tradition of philosophy. It is no mere accident that Nietzsche chose to articulate his critical views in the name of Zarathustra. Of course the end of the nineteenth century was not the only or the last time Zarathustra played a prominent role in shaping Western consciousness and philosophic discourse. Indeed, in the 1990s, Persian influences on the millennial fever, and on other New Age themes, were so strong that Harold Bloom, the eminent American critic, suggested that the last decade of the twentieth century should in truth be called "a return to Zoroastrian origins."[12]

Zarathustra was not the only Persian prophet to play an important role in the development of Judeo-Christian theology. Scholars like Carl Jung have traced some of the ideas and rituals of Christianity, particularly the notions of a messiah sent from heaven, the ritual of baptism, and sharing in the body and the blood of Christ, to Mithraic rites. Even the architecture of the Christian church, with its hallowed chancel, seems inspired by the designs of Mithraic temples.

Western art, no less than history and theology, bear testimony to the ubiquity of the Persian presence in antiquity. Of all the extant works of Greek tragedy, for example, the only one that is about a non-Greek subject is Aeschylus' play *The Persians*.[13]

Persian influences continued long after the days when Christianity was born. St. Augustine's *Confessions*, written a good three centuries later, affords clear evidence of the immense influence Persian ideas, including those of Mani, exerted on Augustine's intellectual development, and through him, on the evolution of Christian theology and culture. In fact, some scholars have suggested that Augustine's strict admonishments against bodily pleasures and his dualistic vision of the world as a place riven between good and evil, are evidence that he appropriated many of Mani's ideas for Christianity. Indeed, Persia can be held at least partially accountable for what has come to be called pejoratively the Manichean view: A vision that reduces the infinite complexities of reality into a simple duality of good and evil. Even well into the twenty-first century, the

---

12. Harold Bloom, *Omens of Millennium: The Gnosis of Angels, Dreams, and Resurrection* (New York, 1996), 221.

13. Fouad Rouhani has translated *The Persians* into Persian. See *Parsiyan* [The Persians], trans. Fouad Rouhani (Bethesda, 1998).

14. In his book and television interview, *The Power of Myth*, Joseph Campbell talked of the mythological underpinnings of such popular works as the *Star Wars* movies.

cosmology and ethics of such popular films as *Star Wars* and *Lord of the Rings* continue to resonate with Manichean perspectives.[14]

Interesting and important as these religious influences are, Persia's role in the development of the Greco-Roman or Western sense of cultural identity is no less significant. It would be no exaggeration to suggest that the West's consciousness of itself as a unified civilization, distinct from the culturally different "other," was first shaped in opposition to Persia. More than four hundred years before the birth of Christ, Herodotus, often called the father of Western history, and himself born within the confines of the vast Persian empire, wrote his seminal work to chronicle the wars between the Greeks and the Persians, and described the genesis of this sense of identity and difference. Ironically, one of the catalysts for the recognition of this "difference" was the question of young women and what to do if they were abducted. Persians apparently took "the seizure of the women lightly enough, but not so the Greeks: The Greeks, merely on account of a girl from Sparta, raised an army," and invaded the abductors.[15] Women, in other words, were in those days a key element of Greek "honor." Today, the wheels have changed, and this time, for Iranian Muslim men, not just their identity but their very honor and "manhood" depends on their ability to protect "their" young women from others.

In the opening paragraphs of his *Histories*, Herodotus writes, "In this book, I hope to do two things. To preserve the memory of the past by putting on record the astonishing achievements both of our own and of the Asiatic people. Secondly and more importantly, to show how the two races came into conflict."[16] He goes on to explain that by Asia he means both Persians and the lands dominated by them. He writes, for example, of Darius as the discoverer of much of Asia, as the king who mapped for the first time many of the seas and rivers of the world, and as the far-sighted monarch who even attempted to build a waterway where twenty-four hundred years later the Suez Canal was constructed. Darius is, of course, also the king who helped build the great city of Persepolis. The ruins of that once great city are still considered one of the most important historic sites in the world; its architecture, combining eclectic influences from many corners of the globe, exemplifies the genius of the Persian

---

15. Herodotus, *The Histories*, trans. Aubrey De Selincourt (London, 1954). Herodotus writes that "From that root sprang their belief in the perpetual enmity of the Grecian world towards them—Asia with its various foreign-speaking people belonging to the Persians, Europe and the Greek states being, in their opinion, quite separate and distinct from them" (14). For a clever and insightful fictional rendition of Herodotus' life and his divided loyalties, see Gore Vidal, *Creation* (New York, 1981).

16. Herodotus, *The Histories*, 13.

spirit. Persians freely adopted aspects of other cultures, but always did so only after creatively transforming what they wanted to adopt into something that was uniquely Persian. The library at Sarouye—located near where the city of Isfahan is today—was another clue to this Persian openness to "others." Though only a few random pages of its vast holdings have survived, we know of its grandeur through the testimony of its contemporaries, who compared it, in terms of the awe it inspired, to the Egyptian pyramids.[17] The famous Jondishapur medical center in pre-Islamic Iran was also open to scholars and doctors from other religions and nationalities of the world. Persians were not only open to other cultures, but freely adopted all they found useful from them. Indeed, an eclectic cultural elasticity has been said to be one of the key defining characteristics of the Persian spirit and a clue to its historic longevity. This fascinating trajectory can be traced in everything from the way Persians prepare tea and rice to the way they build colonnades and domes.

The Arab invasion, in the seventh century, radically altered the contour of Iranian history.[18] After a prolonged period of bloody battles, Persians finally succumbed and at least ostensibly accepted the new creed. But once again, the quality of eclectic assimilation began to manifest itself; many pre-Islamic ideas—like the expectation of a messiah—simply took on an Islamic façade and survived. A number of Persian and European scholars have found myriad elements of the classical Persian culture that survived this way and even shaped the post-Islamic history of Iran. For example, in a monumental four-volume study of what he calls the Iranian Islam, Henry Corbin, the renowned French philosopher and Orientalist, has parsed, in some detail, Zoroastrian, Mithraic and Manichean ideas, which were reformulated by Persian artists and thinkers to make them amenable to the conquering Arabs and their new creed.[19]

---

17. A brief account of the library and its wonders is available in *Dehkhoda's* encyclopedia of the Persian language.
18. Muslim historians, both Arab and Iranian, have long offered the idea that Iran, on the verge of the Arab invasion, was a society in decline and decay and thus it embraced the invading Arab armies with open arms. Mohammad Mohammadi Malayeri's erudite four-volume study of the question of the nature of Iranian society's response to the Arab invasion uses mostly Arab sources to show clearly, and convincingly, that contrary to the claims of the Muslim apologists, Iranians in fact fought long and hard against the invading Arabs. Moreover, once the Persians accepted political defeat, they began to engage in a culture war of resistance and succeeded in forcing their own ways on the victorious Arabs. See Mohammad Mohammadi Malayeri, *Tarikh-e Farhang-e Iran* [Iran's Cultural History], four volumes (Tehran, 1372/1982).
19. Henry Corbin, *En Islam Iranien: Aspects Spirituels et Philosophiques* (Paris, 1971-1972). Mohammad Moin has made much the same argument in his classic book, *Mazdeyasna va Adab-e Farsi* [Mazdeyasna and Persian letters] (Tehran, 1355/1976).

With the conquest of Iran, Islam was well on its way to becoming an empire. Within two hundred years, what is generally acknowledged as the "Golden Age" of Islam commenced. Scholars like Ehsan Yarshater and Mohammadi Malayeri have shown the important role Persian theologians, philosophers, mathematicians, linguists and scientists played in the creation of this Golden Age.[20] Concurrent with this Golden Age—in fact a crucial link in its genesis—was the advent of an early, albeit aborted, modernity in Iran.

As Iran was undergoing these changes, the West's image of Iran continued to hint of grandeur and enduring mystery. Persia was, after all, the land where Prestor John was reportedly guarding the Holy Grail. The legend of the Grail itself was probably inspired by the Persian myth of Jamshid and his famous cup. Other indications of Persian influence can be seen in everything from Dante's *Divine Comedy* to Chaucer's *Parliament of Fowls*.[21] Conversely, the temptations of the West, particularly the Hellenic philosophy of Plato and Aristotle, continued to be a topic of considerable interest for Muslim thinkers in Persia. By any measure, eleventh-century Iran, with its great cities like Nishapur and Rey,[22] was in no way inferior to any of the numerous principalities strewn throughout Europe. In fact, Europe continued its medieval slumber as Iran was caught up in the throes of change.

Soon, however, for reasons that continue to vex historians, the West took off on its path to the Renaissance that was to change, irrevocably, not only the face of Europe, but of the world. Iran, on the other hand, began to gradually slip into almost eight hundred years of internecine wars, famines, and obscurantism. The only short respite in these benighted years came during the reign of Shah Abbas. Sixteenth-century Isfahan, with its grand mosques, sumptuous bazaars, tree-lined boulevards, and splendid gardens, was the impressive metaphor of this short-lived, ill-fated, and native "modernity" in Iran. It is the splendor of this city and its court that is reflected in the many favorable references to Persia in the

---

20. Ehsan Yarshater, *The Persian Presence in the Islamic World* (Cambridge, 1998). The extensive bibliography of this monograph is a tour de force of learning and erudition and includes an impressively long list of articles and books on the topic of Iran's role in shaping Muslim culture and the "Golden Age" of Islam.

21. For a remarkable chronicle of the influence of Muslims in Spain, and through Spain in the rest of Europe, see Juan Vernet, *Ce que la Culture Doit Aux Arabes d'Espagne* (Paris, 1978).

22. For an account of the glories of the city of Nishapur, see Richard Bulliet, *The Patricians of Nishapur: A Study in Medieval Islamic Social History* (Cambridge, 1977). Three years ago, Shafi-e Kadkani published an annotated edition of a book called *Tarikh-e Neyshapour* that covers much the same era as Professor Bulliet's book. See *Tarikh-e Neyshapour*, ed. Shafi-e Kadkani (Tehran, 1379/2000).

Western literature of the Renaissance. From Sir John Mandeville's best-selling—and altogether fabricated—tales of his world travels[23] to the plays and poems of Shakespeare,[24] Persia appears as the land of opulence and culture—and altogether different from the rest of the Muslim world.

The third stage in Iran's long and complicated encounter with modernity took place in the nineteenth century, when Iran was already enfeebled by Oriental despotism and Western colonialism. The essay in this book on Nasir al-Din Shah and his travels to Europe recounts some elements of this encounter and the king's response to what seemed like the inevitability of modernity. In his narrative of modernity, democracy and freedom had no role to play. They were European in genesis and useless in Iran.

Nonetheless it was during the reign of Nasir al-Din Shah that early signs of what eventually became the constitutional revolution first appeared on the horizon. By 1905 a coterie of intellectuals, mostly from the embryonic middle class, united with some of the more enlightened clerics of the time, and forced the king to sign into law a new constitution that limited the power of the monarch and moved Iran in the direction of creating a modern democratic system. But democracy is more than just ideas; it requires an intricate network of institutions; it needs a civil society to act as a buffer between the power and the people. It is, as Jean Jacques Rousseau never tired of reminding his readers, a highly sensitive organism, in need of constant monitoring and mentoring; it requires a citizenry conscious of the perils that threaten democracies and willing to show the patience and tolerance necessary to sustain a democratic polity.

Democratic laws, grafted from the Belgian constitution, were enacted in 1905. Thus, political modernity was willed into law. Yet the social institutions and political habits necessary for democracy's survival were simply wanting. The result was almost two decades of chaos, and chaos, history teaches, is a fertile ground for the growth of despots and Caesars

---

23. Sir John Mandeville is one of the most fascinating characters of fourteenth-century Europe. His Travels was easily the "most popular secular book in circulation" at the time, and claimed to be a chronicle of travels to the East. In fact, it was a hoax, but it represented many of the "facts and fictions" of the era. His representation of Persia is of a land of mystery and wealth, where Hermes came and built Hormose. See Mandeville's Travels, ed. M.C. Seymour (Oxford, 1967).

24. For a brief discussion of some of Shakespeare's references to Iran see Sami Gorgon Rudi, "Sophy and the Persian Prince: Shakespeare and Persia," http://www.iranian.com.

who deliver peace at the price of liberty. Reza Shah (1925-1941) and his son, Mohammed Reza Shah (1941-1979) both assumed a king's mantle and undertook to modernize the Iranian economy and much of its infrastructure; both believed in the indispensable role the state must play in changing the fabric of society; both believed that despotism was the necessary price of modernization. And for both, democracy was a political Achilles' heel. To them, as to Nasir al-Din Shah, democracy and freedom were Western concepts, not applicable to Iran.

The case of Mohammad Reza Shah and his nemesis, Ayatollah Khomeini, is an interesting example of how opposing political forces have used the same argument to dismiss democracy as something foreign to the Iranian landscape. The Shah was often pressured by the US government to democratize the Iranian polity and share power with the technocratic middle classes. He generally refused and the harvest of his refusal was a revolution that ended his reign. To the recurring suggestions of US administrations, and to the constant jabs of the Western media, he offered the same evasive response. Democracy is the invention of the "blue-eyed world," he would say, and does not fit the Persian political landscape.[25] Ayatollah Khomeini used much the same argument, albeit in the lexicon of a defiant Islamic piety, to dismiss any criticism of his Islamic regime's despotism.

But as I have tried to show in a number of the essays in this book, these Eurocentric arguments are based on a misreading of the nature of modernity, and Iranian history. Between the tenth and thirteenth centuries, many of the ideas we now consider the quintessence of modernity—rationalism, secularism, individualism, urbanism, limited government—began to evolve in Iran and helped shape a native "Renaissance." Modernity is, in the words of Hans Blumenberg, a secular form of critical cultural Gnosticism.[26] Yet such critical self-scrutiny has only just begun in Iran: the most important texts of the country's "Golden Age," from the works of the now best-selling poet Rumi, to the less known historical narrative of Beyhaghi, still await to be read critically. An interrogation of these texts will show many of them to be a rich repository of the very ideas that have been assumed "Western" since the nineteenth century. The essay in this book on "Sa'di and the Kings" offers a glimpse into the possible results of such a reading. Ironically, Sa'di, long dismissed as a panegyrist to kings,

---

25. I have discussed these pressures and the shah's response to them in *The Persian Sphinx: Amir Abbas Hoveyda and the Riddle of the Iranian Revolution* (Mage, 2001). The paperback edition of the book has just been published by Mage.

26. Hans Blumenberg, *The Legitimacy of the Modern Age*, trans. Robert M. Wallace (Cambridge, 1983), 126.

emerges in the first chapter of his *Golestan* as an advocate of a surprisingly democratic theory of monarchy.

Such a re-reading will, I submit, show that at an early juncture, long before the advent of the Renaissance in the West, Iranian thinkers and writers developed the rudiments of a democratic theory, a rational historiography and cosmology, a kind of embryonic empiricism, and widely accepted norms about the necessity of writing simple, precise and parsimonious prose. In the West, the Copernican revolution is considered the pivot of the scientific revolution, and the central component of the Renaissance. Scholars have argued that the Copernican revolution would not have been possible without the pioneering work of Biruni and Tusi, both shining lights of Iran's early Golden Age. During this aborted modernity, the observatory in Maragheh, in Northern Iran, was renowned throughout the world and scholars from as far away as Sweden traveled there to learn the newest theories and discoveries in astronomy. Like Biruni, Avicenna, an Iranian scientist of that era, was no less a pioneer in the field of medicine than in using Aristotle to understand and solve the problems of the world.[27]

Another sign of modernity is the emergence of a new kind of historiography. *Tarikh-e Beyhaghi,* a work of seminal significance, written almost a thousand years ago, is a fascinating instance of an unseasonably modern Iranian history. The Turkic conquest of Iran, coming on the heels of the Arab invasion, had created a forced cultural hybridity. While Ferdowsi's *Shahnameh* was a paradigmatically defiant rejection of the realities of this dual conquest, *Tarikh-e Beyhaghi* embodies the cultural paradigm of accommodation. More importantly, Beyhaghi's method is refreshingly innovative. While other historians at the time, both Persian and Western, were essentially writing royal or religious hagiography, Beyhaghi came close to what we call social history. The simplicity of his prose, the care he showed in citing and critically indicating and appraising his sources, the privileged position he afforded to firsthand narratives and empirical observation, his careful attention to the details of the lives of common people, his attempt to maintain an impartial vista, his propensity to preserve and use original documents

---

27. Toby Huff's informative book on the rise of early science is fascinating for two opposing reasons. On the one hand, it chronicles the incredible accomplishments of Iranian and Arab scientists during the tenth to twelfth centuries. On the other hand, the chapter dealing with these developments is called "Arabic Science and the Muslim World." Many of the crucial scientists he refers to are Iranian; the observatory where they worked—Maragheh—was in Iran and its "creator," Tusi, was a Persian. See Toby E. Huff, *The Rise of Early Modern Science: Islam, China and the West* (New York, 1993).

of the time, and his attitude that history could be studied most accurately using rational and critical faculties,are all elements we commonly associate with modern historiography.[28]

One of the most important aspects of modernity—in both the East and West—is the change it brings to the lives of women. Though Iran's aborted Renaissance shows little by way of serious change in the social status of women—the rare ascent of a couple of women to the throne, and the dominating role of a couple of other royal mothers notwithstanding—twentieth-century Iran has seen radical changes in this arena. Some of the essays included here, particularly "Modernity and *Blue Logos*" and "Houshang Golshiri and the Janus Face of Tradition," attempt to shed light on aspects of this development.

The misreadings have not been limited to the distant past. Indeed a serious confusion about the meaning of the concepts of modernity, modernism and modernization, and the common propensity to treat them as interchangeable synonyms, has resulted in some seriously questionable categorization of writers like Sadeq Hedayat, and Houshang Golshiri.

If the question of modernity and democracy can be historically and theoretically disentangled from the question of Western desires and designs for domination, and if its diverse cultural roots can be unearthed, then we can begin to talk of a new global modernity that celebrates and underscores difference rather than forced assimilations. Furthermore, despots will be henceforth denied their age-old use of cultural difference as a license for denying people their democratic rights, for they have long claimed that freedom and democracy are Western in origin and essence, and a mere ruse to conquer the East. Mining the past, and uncovering the native roots of ideas like freedom, can pave the way for a more democratic future in Iran. The notion of democracy in Iran will be seen as a genuine renaissance of an idea that is at once deeply Persian and universal.

In these textual excursions into the past and present, I have tried to excavate history through a focused gaze on a few select texts. My methodological point of departure has been the notion that all texts are woven from the fabric of history; conversely, history is itself a text written by certain authors. The most sophisticated articulation of this complex relationship has been offered by Stephen Greenblatt. He calls it "the poetics of culture."[29] Another critic has called this dialectic the historicity of

---

28. See my "Tarikh dar Tarikh-e Beyhaghi" [History in Beyhaghi's history] in *Tajaddod va Tajaddod Setizi dar Iran* [Modernity and its foes in Iran] (Tehran, 1382/2003), 26-51.
29. For Greenblatt's pioneering work in the poetics of culture see his *Learning to Curse: Essays in Early Modern Culture* (New York,1990),146-161.

texts, and the textuality of history.[30] The history of modernity has also been a much-contested text shaped by authors who in the recent past seem to have had at least an unwitting stake in establishing the supremacy of Western values. The same history, written from a different vantage point, will surely lead to different results.

In writing or thinking about Iran, finding a theoretical vista that is free from the self-congratulating swagger of Eurocentrism and the self-deluding slumber of nativist thought continues to be a vexing problem. As I argue here in the essays on Golestan and on "The Purgatory of Exile," the emotional, epistemological, even geographical distance that comes with the "bitter bread of banishment" might well be the most suitable perspective for a fresh re-reading of Iranian history and its encounters with modernity. Texts are particularly suitable subjects for the scrutinizing gaze of exiles. They are suffused with the realities of their contexts. They are, in this sense, similar to artifacts found in archeological excavations. Knowledge of the context allows us to "date" and place the artifact, and in return, details of the new artifact enrich our understanding of the context.

The goal of such an archeology is of course not to find new trophies for the mantles of nationalists or religious zealots who already claim that all that has ever been of value in the world has come from Iran, or from Islam. Instead, I hope to show that democracy, rationalism and the rule of law are not strange and alien ideas to Iran, but have deep native roots in the intellectual soil of this old, enduring, and now beleaguered land.

---

30. Louis Montrose, writes that, "By the historicity of texts, I mean to suggest…the social embedment of all modes of writing…. By the textuality of history, I mean to suggest firstly, that we have no access to a full and authentic past…and secondly, that those textual traces [of the past] are themselves subject to subsequent mediations." See "The Poetics and Politics of Culture" in The New Historicism, ed. H. Aram Veeser (New York, 1989), 20.

KAFI IS KAFI[*]

Textual Sources of Shia Fundamentalism

*When God was Shepherd, there
was no political constitution*
—PLATO

Power usually needs to justify itself; oftentimes it uses a "legitimating narrative." Such narratives afford legitimacy either by invoking divine rights or by claiming to represent popular will and sovereignty.[1]

In Europe, secularism fostered modernity, the notion of a social contract and the idea of progress. Popular will became the only legitimate narrative for power. But just as these ideas were on the rise in the West, in Safavid Iran, Shiite clerics were achieving political prominence. In Europe, Shakespeare, Bacon, Machiavelli and Cervantes were harbingers of a new humanism; in Iran, Mullah Mohammed Bagher Majlesi and his large coterie of clerics were shaping an ideology/theology that was, in almost every detail, inimical to modernity. Their ideology fosters a divinized and ritualized world—an "enchanted world," to quote Max Weber— where God is the shepherd, and the Utopian polis is not a human construct in some distant future but a divine gift moored to the pristine prophetic past. In fact, since the sixteenth century, one of the defining characteristics of Iranian politics has been the claim by some clerics that their rule is the sole legitimate form of government. They have offered their theocentric paradigm as an alternative to the rational and secular model of modernity. The Islamic Revolution, too, was, at least in its architect's mind, an attempt at halting the march of modernity.

Searching for the genealogy of this form of Islamic power and its legitimizing discourse leads one to Kulaini. He is one of the sources for what in journalistic jargon is called Shiite Fundamentalism, an approach to religious exegesis that denies any interpretive license, and opts instead for a

---

* *Al-Kafi* is an anthology of Shiite *hadith*, collected by Abu Ja'far Kulaini, who lived around 900 A.D. In Persian and Arabic, the word *kafi* means "that which is sufficient."

1. Jean Francis Lyotard, "Notes on Legitimation," *Oxford Literary Review*, vol. 9, nos. 1-2, (1987): 107.

strict adherence to the letter of a divine, inerrant, and totally self-sufficient canon. For fundamentalists, such adherence is the key to salvation
in the other world, and for happiness in this temporary abode on earth.

For the Shiites, divine wisdom, or the small fraction to which man
has been made privy, has found textual manifestation. As the American
philosopher and social critic Norman Brown reminds us, in Islam, *logos
is* the Book.[2] While the holy Qur'an is the foremost repository of divine
guidance, the wisdom embodied in a "reliable" hadith is the other major
component of these sacred scriptures.

Hadith is a form of "traditional narrative."[3] For the Shiites, it recounts
the words or the deeds of the prophet or of an Imam as narrated by reliable sources. The authority and legitimacy of each narrative rests on its
content—and specifically its compatibility with the Qur'an and other reliable hadiths—and the reliability of the narration lineage. If the lineage is
reliable, if every narrator in the chain of narration is deemed reliable and
pious, then the narrated deed or word becomes part of the canon. As can
be expected, and as is readily admitted by Islamic scholars, hundreds of
thousands of hadiths have been fabricated to legitimize different claims
within the Islamic community. The question of delineating an "authentic" hadith, as opposed to a "fabricated" one, has thus become a highly
politicized game that cuts to the core of sectarian politics in Islam.[4] At the
same time, these attempts to find methodologies for comparative analysis lead to the development of complex modes of textual analysis in Islam,
where nuances of syntax and other literary tropes are used to categorize
and judge different narratives, and their supposed veracity. Furthermore,
a whole field devoted to the biographical studies of narrators evolved, in
which people's lives are studied from the sole perspective of their piety
and their fidelity to the teachings of the Imams and the prophet.[5]

2. Norman Brown, *Apocalypse And/Or Metamorphosis* (Berkeley, 1997).

3. For a discussion of "traditional narrative" and how it differs from modern forms of narrative see Jean Francis Lyotard, *The Post-Modern Condition: A Report on Knowledge*,
trans. Geoff Bennington and Brian Massoumi (Minneapolis, 1984).

4. For a pioneering discussion of hadith in English, see Ignaz Goldziher, *Muslim Studies*, ed.
S.M. Stern, vol. 2 (London, 1971), 17-255. It must be remembered that his account, as
well as most studies of Islam in that period focused, almost entirely, on Sunni texts. The
Islamic revolution in Iran changed that. For a general bibliography on hadith, see Munowar
Ahmad Anees, *Hadith and Sura Literature in Western Languages: A Bibliographic Study*
(Bloomington, 1989). For a critical, almost satirical portrait of hadith and its role in Iranian
history, see Shoja al-Din Shafa, *Towzih al-Masa'el* [Answer to Questions] (Paris, 1982).

5.These biographies are radically different from our common conception of this genre.
Here "the biographer had little incentive to document his subjects' idiosyncrasies; thus
tabaghat [as compendiums of these biographies]do not fail to take account of individ-
uality; they succeed in excluding it." For a discussion of these types of biographies, see
Interpreting the Self, Autobiography in the Arabic Literary Tradition, Ed. by Dwight F.
Reynolds, (Berkeley, 2001), 20-24.

During the Crusades, Europeans learned of this sophisticated Oriental methodology, and the newly acquired methods helped the rise of Occidental scientific discourse.[6] Textual rigor, paired with critical and skeptic rationality, created the modern scientific paradigm. Within the Shiite tradition, however, the same method sustained a theocentric vision that kept cannibalizing a few sacred texts at the expense of an active reason.

Amongst these sacred texts, Shiites believe four to be the most authoritative and authentic canonical collections of hadiths. And *Usul Kafi* is certainly the most important book of this select group.[7] In fact, it is claimed that after the Qur'an, *Usul* is not only the most important source of divine wisdom, but that no less an authority than the Twelfth Imam himself, the Expected Messiah, saw the book before his occultation and said of it, "For our followers [or literally our "Shiites," the Arabic for "follower" or "partisan"] *Kafi* [Arabic for "sufficient"] is sufficient."[8]

Usul Kafi is part of a larger work entitled *Ketab-e Kafi*, compiled by Abu Ja'far Kulaini. He is one of the most esteemed scholars of the Shiite pantheon.[9] Not much is known about his life, save that he was born in the village of Kulain and began his studies in the first decade of the tenth century. From 913 to 923, he studied in Qom—a small sleepy town in those days, and now, next to Najaf, one of the centers of Shiite radicalism in the Middle East. He then went to Baghdad and spent the remainder of his life compiling his magnum opus.

The era in which Kulaini lived was one of great turmoil for Shiites. When the eleventh Imam died in the ninth century, some Shiites declared that he had fathered no son. Others began to worship newly claimed messiahs and Imams. Rationalism was on the rise, and Sufi sects had received unprecedented acceptance amongst the populace.[10] In this context the "Twelver" Shiites emerged. They believed that the eleventh Imam had indeed left behind an infant son and that the son had gone into two occultations: a minor one, lasting but a few years, and the major one that still continues

6. Gustav E. Von Grunebaum, *Medieval Islam: A Study in Cultural Orientation* (Chicago, 1996).

7. *Encyclopedia of Islam*, ed. M. H. Houtsam, vol. 2, (1927), 193. Nearly every discussion of Shiism includes some discussion of these four canonical books. See for example, Hussein Tabatabai, *Shia dar Islam* [Shiism in Islam] (Tehran, 1969).

8. Kulaini, *Usul-e Kafi*, trans. Seyyed Javad Mostofi (Tehran, 1969), 1.

9. Western scholars had often ignored most aspects of Shiism, including such topics as Kulaini and his life. Important changes have begun to occur. For example, in the first edition of *Encyclopedia of Islam* (Leiden, 1927) Kulaini is only mentioned in passing in an article on hadith. In the new edition, there is a whole article devoted to him. See *Encyclopedia of Islam*, new edition, vol. 5 (Leiden, 1986), 362-363

10. For a general discussion of this period, and the origins of Shiism in Iran, see Abbas Eghbal Ashtiyani, *Khandan-e Nobakhti* [The Nobakhti Dynasty] (Tehran, 1978).

today and shall last until his reappearance. And when he returns as the twelfth and last Imam, and as the expected Mahdi, justice and salvation will come to humankind, or more accurately, salvation will come to the pious Twelver Shiites, and the rest of humanity will face bloody revenge.[11]

The ambiguities surrounding the question of the Imam's succession—a perennial problem for Shiites—and the dangerous rise of Sufism (at best exemplified in the prominence of the Christ-like Hallaj),[12] along with other political pressures, led to the necessity of canonizing Shia theology and jurisprudence. *Kafi* is the key element in this effort.

The sixteenth century was another moment of epochal significance for Shiism. The temptations of Hellenism, this time in the form of new contacts with Europe, were again on the horizon. Furthermore, Shiism was about to become the state religion of Iran. Majlesi, the beloved cleric at the court of the last Safavid Kings, set out to fashion a Shiite ideology that would become the legitimizing discourse of clerical hegemony. Even the King's power was made dependent on clerical approval. To underscore this fact, Majlesi broke with a long tradition and "anointed" the new King, giving him the crown and scepter on the day of coronation.[13] In forging this new ideology, Kulaini, particularly his *Kafi*, proved to have seminal significance. Indeed, Majlesi's many volumes of collected hadith are an expanded rendition of Kulaini's opus.

The third moment of crisis for Shiism came in the latter part of the twentieth century and saw the "resurgence" of Kulaini's brand of Islam under the charismatic leadership of Ayatollah Khomeini. The Shah's modernizing program, begun in the early sixties, threatened to undermine what remained of the Shiite clerics' claim to power. Their "purse," as the key source and symbol of their power, was jeopardized by the continuous secularization of Iranian society, and by the nature of the economic policies pursued by the Shah. The traditional bazaar, historically the key source of revenue for the clerical "purse," was being increasingly overshadowed by the rise of a new Western-oriented, capitalist class schooled in the ways of modern industry and commerce. The fact that this class often had Western companies as partners gave the bazaar's complaint against them a nationalist tone. Furthermore, other policies pursued by

---

11. For a general discussion of Shia messianism as well as the English translations of some of the most important hadiths about the return of the Imam, See Abdulaziz Abdulhussein Sachedina, *Islamic Messianism: The Idea of Mahdi in Twelver Shiism* (Albany, 1981).

12. Hallaj is one of the most colorful figures in the history of Sufism. Shia clerics were instrumental in accusing him of heresy and bringing about his death. See Louis Massignon, *The Passion of Hallaj: Mystic and Martyr of Islam* (Princeton, 1982).

13. For insightful and detailed discussions of many aspects of Safavid history, see Jean Calmard, ed., *Etudes Safavides* (Paris, 1993) and Charles Melville, ed., *Safavid Persia: The History and Politics of an Islamic Society* (London, 1996).

the "modernizing monarch"[14]—from the government's close ties with Israel and the regime's tolerance for the Baha'is to its consistent attempt to aggrandize pre-Islamic Persia—also added to the ire of the traditional segments of the Iranian society, particularly among some of the merchants of the bazaar and poorer segments of the urban poor who, as a rule, were recent immigrants from the countryside. Ayatollah Khomeini and his brand of Islam emerged as the dominant force of this movement of discontent. Once again, Kulaini and his *Usul* emerged as a crucial source for the new regime's legitimizing discourse.

Usul is composed of four volumes and a total of 3,785 hadith. Despite the book's aphoristic style and apparently disjunctive structure, the narrative is unified by its underlying epistemology and political philosophy.[15] At the heart of the book, and I would suggest at the core of this particular Shiite vision, lies a peculiar notion or concept of truth. Only if one accepts this particular conception can one find any coherence in the ontological, epistemological, and political vision of people like Kulaini and Ayatollah Khomeini and, ultimately, their fundamentalist followers.

For Kulaini, Majlesi, Ayatollah Khomeini, and their disciples, hadith are not instruments for ascertaining the truth; they *are* the truth. In the realm of this epistemology, truth is not understood along lines familiar to the tradition of philosophic discourse. In other words, the validity of a hadith resides not in its "truth content," but in its origin. A proposition is "true" simply because of the sanctity, the divine inspiration, of its source. The Prophet and the Imams have become privy to parts of the infinite wisdom of the Lord. The best that the mortal, finite mind of humans can do is to unquestioningly submit to this revealed truth.

This truth is "decreed" and "revealed," not "discovered" or "created" (as in modern science and art). Thus, all the cardinal questions of philosophy—from the meanings of truth, justice, happiness and freedom to questions about the methods for defining or discovering each—are reduced to a literal and limited exegesis of one or a few antiquarian texts. Collections of hadith establish rules of conduct in all realms of human action, using only a closed circuit of heavenly edicts and divine traditions. Indeed, the legitimizing discourse for this notion of "truth" is

---

14. The title appears in a dispatch from the US embassy in Tehran. See US Embassy, Tehran, Iran, "Iran's Modernizing Monarch: A Political Assessment," January 1, 1971, National Security Archives, Washington, D.C., document number 1060.5.

15. For a discussion of the relationship between aesthetics of a text and its political posture, see Michael Shapiro, "Literary Production as a Politicizing Practice," in *Language and Politics*, ed. Michael Shapiro (New York, 1984), 215-255.

ultimately self-referential. A few hadith legitimize the validity and the "truth content" of other hadith.[16]

If we accept the notion that rationalism is a cardinal element of modernity; if we agree that skepticism, along with a Sisyphean, individualized quest for an ephemeral truth, is an inseparable part of modernity's epistemology or theory of knowledge; and finally, if we concur that the modern notion of progress posits that happiness, and the knowledge necessary to actualize it, are functions of our own actions and not fate, or as Shakespeare puts it, if we accept that "the fault lies not in our stars but in ourselves," then it becomes evident why Shiite Fundamentalism and the certitude it promises can appear as a critical response to, or a remedy for, the anxious incertitude of modernity. If Dostoyevsky's Grand Inquisitor, and later writers like Erich Fromm and Hannah Arendt,[17] are right that people fear freedom and choice, and prefer magic, mystery and authority, then the rise of fundamentalism in recent years can be understood as a balm to the "unwanted" freedoms of modernity.

At the same time, to anyone who has read St. Augustine, such notions of "truth" are not strange or new. What is important about the Islamic version—first articulated by Kulaini, then again by Majlesi in the seventeenth century, and finally by Ayatollah Khomeini in the twentieth century—is the fact that it gained and regained political ascendancy in Iran precisely at the time when such ideas were being discarded in the West. Just as the rise of the Renaissance in the West was eclipsing Augustinian ideology, in Iran, under Safavid rule, an Islamic version of this ideology became the dominant language of politics. The same anachronism repeated itself in Iran in 1979. Just as the last vestiges of totalitarian regimes, based on ideologies that promised "truth," were about to disappear, and just as the "Third Wave" of democracies began

---

16. It is important to remember that this strange, self-serving and self-referential notion of "truth" is shared not just by other fundamentalists of other faiths and religions, but also by twentieth and twenty-first century totalitarian ideologies. In the case of Iran, for example, the dominant paradigm of Marxism—with its roots and branches, and much of its nourishment, in Soviet Marxism—shares its notion of "truth" with religious fundamentalists. Marxists' "sacred" books are, of course, the "canonized" writings of Marx, Lenin, Stalin, and Mao. It is, I think, this crucial shared epistemology that accounts for two important facts of modern Iran: The relevant ease with which the Soviet version of Marxism all but eliminated other varieties of Marxism from the Iranian intellectual landscape, and the unusual "unholy" alliance that has existed between advocates of Soviet Marxism and Islamic Fundamentalists. They are Siamese twins, joined at the epistemological hip.

17. Dostoyevsky in The Brothers Karamazov, Fromm in Escape From Freedom, and Arendt in Origins of Totalitarianism have argued that humans are, as a general rule, averse to the burden of choice. They prefer the comfort of a false and enslaving certitude to the anxiety of making choices by themselves.

to appear around the world, Ayatollah Khomeini and his new interpretation of Kulaini came to power in Iran.[18]

Contrary to modernity's idea of progress, for Shiism the course of temporal history invariably leads to the degradation of the human spirit. Only with the reappearance of the now hidden Imam will salvation—not liberation or happiness—come to humans. The key to this salvation lies in the hidden truth of the hadith and of Qur'anic verses.

Not everyone, of course, has access to the wisdom of these Holy Scriptures. Indeed, the common stock of humanity can only perceive the literal and superficial meaning of the holy writ. Only God has access to the ultimate and complete meaning of these texts. Every hadith, and every verse in the Qur'an, has infinite layers of meanings. In this labyrinth of meanings, the devout Shiite can at most grasp the outermost, superficial layer. The inner layers, and the true meaning, are a domain only the Prophet and the Imams are privileged to enter. In one hadith, it is claimed that on his deathbed the prophet Mohammad recounted one thousand hadiths to Ali, his son-in-law and, according to the Shiites, the prophet's divinely designated successor. It is further claimed that each of these hadiths was itself the key to another one thousand hadith and that mere mortals can, at best, be privy to one or two of these nuggets of heavenly wisdom.[19] In fact, the two concepts of *tafsir* and *ta'wil* (or simple and allegorical interpretation)[20] serve to denote two ways of deciphering sacred text. Only the Prophet and his progeny are empowered to find the allegorical meanings of the text and unravel the mysteries of its inner layers. Since salvation only comes from this sacred fount of wisdom, it is incumbent upon the majority to assume a posture of total submission to the will of these select interpreters. Georges Bataille, the French philosopher, correctly sees Islam as the religion of submission, and one can hardly find a more concise articulation of this aspect of Shiism than the hadith that says, "You shall find salvation only if you accept, and you shall not accept unless you submit."[21] In another hadith, we learn, "There is no salvation other than obedience."[22] Furthermore, if the content of a hadith seems to defy the limits of what is deemed reasonably acceptable, then a devout Shiite, according to *Kafi*, should suspend critical judgment, and

---

18. Many scholars studying the transition to democracy have written about the "third wave" commencing in the mid-seventies. The last decades of the nineteenth century saw the rise of the first wave; the years after the end of the Second World War brought about the second wave, and the mid-seventies heralded the advent of a third wave.

19. *Kafi*, vol. 3, 58.

20. For a discussion of *tafsir* and *ta'wil*, see Hamid Enayat, *Modern Islamic Political Thought* (Austin, 1988), 23-33.

21. *Kafi*, vol. 3, 37.

22. Ibid., 110.

wait for the day when someone chosen to decode the divine semiotics can explain the anomaly.[23] In short, in a method opposite to the Cartesian call to skepticism, the Kulaini vision suggests that one should doubt everything except one's faith in the infallibility of the Qur'an, a reliable hadith, and the ability of the Imams to know the "truth."

In a sense, of course, this cult of obedience emanates from the Islamic concept of the relationship between humans and God. If, in Christianity, man is the Son of God, the Qur'an is replete with the image of man as "the slave" of God. Echoes of this curious relationship can be found in *Kafi*. The opening lines of the book clearly betray the implied structure of authority: "Praise be upon God who is praised for his offerings, worshiped for his power, and is the King of his Kingdom, feared because of his magnanimity."[24]

To posit a text (or a few texts) as the sole embodiment of a self-sufficient and eternal truth requires a discourse to legitimize these texts and empower those who hold the key to their inner treasures. At the same time, it demands action to discredit other potential sources of truth. *Kafi* does a masterful job of providing ample hadiths to accomplish both of these goals.

Many hadiths in *Kafi* reassert the notion that the Qur'an and reliable hadiths are the sole repositories of truth. Furthermore, lest there be doubts about the veracity of these claims, other reliable hadiths prove the existence of rather mysterious parchments and tablets. One is called *Jame'* and is "a long parchment dictated by the prophet and written in Ali's handwriting." The second is *Jafr*, "a box made of leather, in which is posited all known knowledge of the past." Finally there is *Moshef-e Fatemeh*, "a book three times the size of the Qur'an, in it is written the inner meaning of the Qur'an."[25] It is even claimed that there exists a letter from God to the Prophet wherein God has written the names of the twelve Imams.[26] And if Europeans coped for centuries with the question of God's preferred language and the "perfect language" of Paradise,[27]—or more practically, the language God used to talk with Adam and Eve—Shiite Fundamentalists harbor no doubt that not only God, but all angels and prophets, from Adam to Mohammad, including Moses and Jesus Christ, spoke Arabic. Some even claim that all the 124,000 prophets were "closet" Muslims. In further describing the

23. One example of such a temporarily incomprehensible hadith is quoted in the translators' preface to the book. The hadith itself appears on page 341 of the second volume of *Kafi*. It recounts the nocturnal visits of angels with the imams and how on occasions the angel's feathers would be found all over the backyard in the morning.

24. *Kafi*, vol. 2, 471.

25. *Kafi*, vol. 1, 1.

26. *Kafi*, vol. 1, 345-347.

27. Umberto Eco, *The Search for the Perfect Language*, trans. James Fentress (New York, 1997).

singularly divine place of the Shiite Imams, Imam Sadeq (the sixth Imam) is quoted as having said, "Because of us, trees bear fruits; through worshipping us, God can be worshiped…. We are God's reason; we are the gate to God; we are God's language; we are God's eyes amongst his people; we are the guardian's of God's cause amongst his slaves."[28]

Thus the select are custodians of a heavenly library, as well as the guardians of the *polis,* whose only source of salvation is in those sacred texts. For this very reason, the longest chapter in *Kafi* deals with the lives of the Imams, wherein many relevant tales, some fantastic even by hagiographic standards of the Middle Ages, are recounted. In one hadith, for example, ten qualities are said to be the common characteristics of all Imams. They include the facts that, "he is born clean and circumcised…upon birth, he puts his hands on the floor and recites [Qur'anic verses]. He never has wet dreams.… He does not yawn or stretch…his feces are fragrant."[29] Fascinating stories about the life of the Twelfth Imam—reminiscent of magic realism in their ability to disregard reason, logic, and temporal or physical laws—abound in the book. In recent years, modern writers like Golshiri have begun to read these stories as literature (not sacred texts) and have found in them a rich reservoir of nimble narrative tropes.[30]

Kafi is replete with hadiths that claim that the sole legitimate power humans have ever known—or will ever know—is the rule of the Imam, a saintly creature, devoid of all sins and free from all temptations. All other governments are inherently illegitimate. Such insistence on divine legitimacy, and its incumbent dismissal of all other sources of authority, can be seen as an important source of the dynamic tension between the Shiite vision and political modernity, a vision that accepts only the "social contract" and the will of the people as the source of legitimacy.

Shared and common belief about a community of interests between the state and the masses, between "we" and "they," is essential for the creation of civil society and democracy. Shiites, on the other hand, claim that such a community of interest exists only with the Imam as the sole legitimate ruler. This community they call *omat*; all other forms of alleged community are, according to *Kafi*, sacrilege. That is why, almost a thousand years later, Ayatollah Khomeini dismissed democracy and "nationhood" as colonial ploys intended to undermine the unity of Islam's spiritual

---

28. *Kafi*, vol. 1, 199. In another hadith, the imam announces that if he were to ever meet Moses, "I would tell him I am more knowledgeable than you…you are only knowledgeable about the past, but through inheritance from the Prophet, I have knowledge about everything up to the day of reckoning." *Kafi*, vol, I, 388.
29. *Kafi*, vol. II, 388.
30. See the chapter in this book entitled "Golshiri and the Janus Face of Tradition."

community (or omat). In their place he offered his rather unique theory of *velayat-e faghih*, or the rule of the juriscouncil.[31]

While the bliss of heaven, according to *Kafi*, awaits those who accept only the legitimacy of an Imam's rule, hell is the punishment for all others; these "others" have always been the majority. In fact, *Kafi* conveniently quotes a hadith to the effect that "true believers" and good Shiites are forever a minority: "People are generally like beasts...with the exception of a few believers, and a believer is a rarity."[32] Another hadith assures this perpetual minority that "gold loves minorities...only a few of God's slaves are thankful."[33]

In a number of other hadith, people are divided into three classes, as one of the Imams is reported to have decreed, "We are the learned; our Shiites are the learners; and all the other people are the dust floating atop water."[34]

Obviously, the learners can only learn of this wisdom through the grace of the learned, who are themselves graced by God. Any individual attempt to negotiate a private path to salvation outside the hierarchy of authority and knowledge is sure to lead the seeker into ignominy and hell. Again, modernity individualizes the relationship between God and humans. It obviates the need for a "spiritual middleman." Shiism, particularly in the version fostered first by Kulaini and then by Ayatollah Khomeini, is inseparably linked to the idea that the majority must emulate the pious few or face perdition.

It is not hard to see that such a perception is contrary to the very idea of a liberal democracy and the notion of a social contract. Democracy is founded on the assumption that the collected wisdom of a majority is ultimately more reliable than the views or preferences of a minority or an individual. The Shiite vision thus has more in common with the Jacobin vision, which grew out of the French Revolution, and advocated the cult of a righteous minority. This Jacobin proclivity can, at least partially, account for the fact that in recent history, Shiite attempts to create a "modern" state have shown a great propensity towards totalitarianism—the evil child of modernity.

A convenient strategy to preserve these eternally outnumbered righteous believers is also discussed at length in *Kafi*. It is called *taghiyeh*, or dissimulation—similar to what Shakespeare dismissively calls "Jesuitical equivocation." It permits true believers to use all tactics of concealment

---

31. For an English translation of Ayatollah Khomeini's tract on the rule of the juriscouncil, see R. Khomeini, *Islamic Government*, trans. Hamid Algar (Berkeley, 1981).
32. *Kafi*, vol. 3. 340.
33. *Kafi*, vol. 1, 17.
34. *Kafi*, vol. 1, 42.

or deceit to confuse the foe and preserve themselves. One hadith, in fact, claims, "nine-tenths of our religion is taghiyeh. Taghiyeh is prohibited only in two things: 'drinking wine and ablution of the feet while wearing shoes.'"[35] As a mode of social behavior, taghiyeh is inimical to the idea of trust, and again trust is an essential component for the creation of civil society and of the modern state. At the same time, taghiyeh may be a culprit in bringing about the circuitous discourse, dissimulation, and ambiguity that have become intrinsic components of a large part of public discourse in the Persian language.

Kafi is also rich in hadiths that delegitimize other sources of wisdom and alternative methodologies of accessing and arriving at the truth. In one hadith, the Prophet first limits valuable knowledge to that which comes from the Qur'an, the correct performance of religious obligations, and a reliable hadith, and then goes on to add, "...all else is superfluous; those who know them, don't benefit from them; and those that don't won't suffer on account of this ignorance."[36] Again if we accept Blumenberg's idea that "theoretical curiosity" is at the core of modernity, then Kulaini's constraining vision is clearly ill-fitted for the kind of curiosity modernity begets and requires.

More importantly, Kulaini in the tenth century, Majlesi in the seventeenth, and Ayatollah Khomeini in the twentieth, all argue emphatically against any attempts by mortals to establish laws and morality. To them such attempts are ill-advised tampering with a realm divinely monopolized. In one hadith, Imam Sadeq is quoted as having said, "If you face a problem the answer to which you do not know, you should do no other than refer it to one of God's Imams."[37] Furthermore, many hadiths in *Kafi* prohibit the use of one hadith to infer what the divine teaching should be on a similar problem. The Prophet is said to have admonished against analogies: "Those who engage in analogies only destroy themselves and others around them."[38] In another hadith, Imam Sadeq warns that Islamic rules do not lend themselves to analogical reasoning. In justification he points to the rather curious paradox that the religious rules on fasting and praying for a menstruating woman are not the same. Had mortal souls attempted to construe from the rules on fasting what the probable rules on praying should be, they would have surely gone astray.[39]

If analogical reasoning is forbidden, if the canon is deemed as totally self-sufficient, one could then expect that canon to have rulings on

---

35. *Kafi*, vol. 3, 307.
36. *Kafi*, vol. I, 37.
37. Ibid., 63.
38. Ibid., 54.
39. Ibid., 74.

each and every major and minor aspect of man's private and public life. *Kafi* more than fulfills this expectation. Two of the book's four volumes are filled with hadith on such mundane topics as where to give a kiss on a friend's face, how to keep a secret, how to sneeze, the dangers of laughter, and how to use a whole array of incantations to cure any and all diseases. Other collections of hadith, particularly by Mohammed Bagher Majlesi in the seventeenth century, have come to fill any lacunae Kulaini might have left. Later scholars have searched and found the proper hadith to deal with some of the most bizarre and esoteric problems imaginable. For example, should a believer wonder what he should do if he were hungry and stranded on an island with only some pork, some wine and a cadaver available, *Sharia*,[40] a much respected book of Shia jurisprudence, will come to his aid. The hungry islander is ordered to discard the wine and the pork; there follows advice on which part of the cadaver he should eat first, lest he be led astray by beginning with the wrong part.

Such "holy" edicts afford a numinous aura to even the most mundane problems. In a sense, they provide a solution to what Weber calls modernity's problem of a "disenchanted world," a world bereft of ritual and sacred solemnities. On the other hand, this kind of "enchantment" betrays a shockingly low estimate of human beings, deeming them incapable of solving even the simplest problems of the quotidian. Advocates of this form of "enchantment" see themselves justified in intruding into all aspects of social and individual life. That is why, in one hadith, the Imam talks of his desire to inculcate the correct religious vision with the power of a whip.[41] Such attempts at forced "enchantment"—reminiscent of Lenin's promise to take the Russian people into the Communist promised land "in chains," if necessary—turns the Kulaini-Khomeini vision of politics into a dangerous form of "soul-craft." Democracy and civil society, in contrast, are predicated on a vision that sees politics as no more than "state-craft." Rather than attempting to create a "model" citizen, as totalitarian advocates of "soul-craft" are wont to do, a liberal polity tolerates the weaknesses and the impurities of the citizenry.[42]

---

40. Mohaghegh-e Helli, *Sharia al-Islam*, trans. Abu Ghassem ibn-Mohammad Yadi (Tehran, 1981).

41. *Kafi*, vol. 1, 35.

42. Sheldon Wolin, in his now classic study of political philosophy, writes of two kinds of theories: Those that engage in soul-craft and want to create a "new man and woman," and those happy with state-craft, and the task of making the best possible society with the existing "crooked timber of humanity." Isaiah Berlin, too, in many of his books writes of the dangers of the kind of utopian politics that are based on some "perfect" notion of society and/or humanity. See Sheldon Wolin, *Politics and Vision* (Boston, 1960) and Isaiah Berlin, *The Crooked Timber of Humanity*, ed. Henry Hardy (New York, 1991).

If we accept Richard Rorty's notion that contingency of truth is the *sine qua non* of democracy, if we accept his view that democratic societies must not only respect the private realm but must strive to expand the arena they leave to individual initiative,[43] then it can easily be seen how the visions articulated by Kulaini, Majlesi and Khomeini are ominously antithetical to modernity.

Kulaini's vision is of course not the only Islamic narrative in Iran. Historically, many other schools of Shia thought have tried to replace this kind of exegetic intransigence with a more rational and dynamic approach. Indeed, from the early advent of Islam, there has been a struggle between two schools of thought know as *Motazeleh* and *Ashari*, the first advocating a marriage of theology and rational philosophy, and the latter insisting that all philosophy is a prelude to apostasy. More recently, around the time of the Iranian Constitutional Revolution (1905), the struggle between the two factions called *Akhbari*, advocating a limited and strictly literal understanding of the text, and *Usuli*, supporting a more open and liberal interpretation of the Word, was another moment in the history of this struggle.

In the years since the Constitutional Revolution, Kulaini and Majlesi's brand of exegetic intransigence has been subjected to critiques from a variety of secular as well as Shia perspectives. Voices of Shia modernism, going all the way back to Ayatollah Na'ini and including such personages as Sangalaji and Mahmud Taleghani, both open-minded clerics, and Ali Shariati and Abdulkarim Soroush, both Western-educated professors and pundits, have all decried the anachronism of this kind of literal interpretation. Na'ini advocated accommodation to such modern political concepts as constitutional government and popular sovereignty.[44] Hakamizadeh, in his controversial monogram called *Secrets of the Millennium,* rebuked the anachronism of Shiite Fundamentalism. Taleghani, a cleric of liberal persuasion, often insisted on creative and contemporary readings of religious texts.[45] Shariati, albeit superficially and eclectically, attacked what he called "Safavid Shiism," and attempted to mold traditional Shia thought into an ideology rid of all remnants of obscurantism and acceptable to an

---

43. Richard Rorty, *Contingency, Irony and Solidarity* (New York, 1980).43. For a discussion of this among Shiites, see Hamid Algar, *Religion and State in Iran, 1785-1906: The Role of Ulama in the Qajar Period* (Berkeley, 1969), 6-36.

44. For discussion of Na'ini's views see Abdul Hadi Haeri, *Shiism and Constitutionalism in Iran: A Study of the Role Played by the Persian Residents of Iraq in Iranian Politics* (Leiden, 1977).

45. Mahmud Taleghani, *Society and Economy in Islam: Writings and Declarations of Ayatollah Seyyed Mahmud Taleghani,* trans. R. Campbell, ed. Hamid Algar (Berkeley, 1982).

intelligentsia under the sway of the scientific spirit of modernity.[46] And finally, in recent years, a number of clerics, and religious intellectuals like Soroush and Baghi, have argued that a distinction ought to be made between the essence of divine teachings, which are by definition primordially valid and inerrant, and man's understanding of such teachings, which is, also by definition, prone to error and inadequacy. Out of this dualism, they argue, arises the need to constantly renovate and reinterpret an era's understanding of divine teachings. Each era must come to its own interpretation of this font of wisdom and each reinterpretation must not only be imbued with the most recent discoveries of science but should, at the same time, attempt to help resolve each era's pending practical and theoretical problems. They have argued that science and theology are both accepted modes of inquiry in the search for truth.[47] Some, erstwhile advocates of an "Islamic Republic," have gone so far as to valiantly call for a completely secular new republic. Ali Akbar Ganji, the well-known journalist who still languishes in prison, is a fitting example of these new advocates of a secular republic.

Fresh as these ideas are in the context of Shiism in Iran, they are in essence no more radical than St. Thomas Aquinas' pronouncements seven hundred years ago. Furthermore, as powerful as these critiques have been, Fundamentalism's biggest foes are the stubborn facts of a constantly changing social, historical and economical reality. Such realities have in fact been changing at an ever-rapid pace. They refuse to fall into the kind of stasis the Fundamentalist mind posits and demands. Coping with these pulsating realities entails coping with their dynamic nature. Nietzsche had it right when he wrote, "The snake which cannot shed its skin shall perish. It is the same with minds, which are prevented from changing their opinions. They cease to function as minds."[48]

---

46. For a selection of Shariati's writings in English, see, A. Shariati, On the Sociology of Islam, trans. Hamid Algar (Berkeley, 1982). For an account of his life that nears a hagiography in its infatuation with the subject see Ali Rahnema, An Islamic Utopian: A Political Biography of Ali Shariati (London, 1998).

47. For a sample of Baghi's views, see Elizabeth Rubin, "The Millimeter Revolution," New York Times, Magazine (April 6, 2003) 38-43, and Baghi's own Do Pendar dar Tarazu [Two Ideas on a Balance] in Aftab, (Esfand 1380/2001). For Soroush's ideas, see his "Theoretical Expansion and Contraction of Sharia," Kayhan-e Farhangi, no. 12, col. 5, (March 1989), 11.

48. Friedrich Nietzsche, Daybreak: Thoughts on the Prejudices of Morality, trans. R.J. Hollingdale (Cambridge, 1982). Hollingdale's translation is slightly different from Solome, which I have used here. See Lou Solome, Nietzsche, trans. Siegfried Mandel (New York, 1988).

SA'DI & THE KINGS*
A Twelfth-Century Source of Modernity

Sa'di, they say, is the soul of Persia. As Shakespeare is the center of the "Western canon"¹ so too is Sa'di, in prose and poetry, the pivotal core of Persian letters. He is the master of mirth and melancholy; his eulogies and his satirical poems are peerless. While his bawdy verse is still considered too raw to be published in twenty-first century Iran, the parsimony, precision, power and beauty of his prose continue to be the measure and ideal for all who write in the Persian language. In all he wrote, there is a beguiling simplicity that appears easy to emulate, but is impossible to imitate. For Sa'di, simplicity in style is not just an aesthetic commitment; it is also part of a necessary and complicated strategy of concealment. Those who speak openly, he often reminds us, lose their lives at the hands of despots.² The "word within [his] word" is a poignant, witty, and exquisitely executed labyrinth of hints and allusions.

The simplicity of his style is in sharp contrast to the complexity of his thought. It has often been said that the ability to hold two opposed ideas at the same time is a sure sign of intelligence. By this measure, Sa'di is surely a first rate mind, one which probed deeply into many facets of the subjects he wrote about. In a culture that created Manichean philosophy, he was the enemy of dogma and false certitudes, and the champion of the notion of the contingency of our thoughts. At a time when travel was dangerous, and hardly a favorite avocation of Persian society, he was a world traveler, spending almost forty years on jour-

---

* For Professor Jalal Matini, a Persian patriot and scholar.
1. Harold Bloom, *The Western Canon* (New York, 1994). In a later book, Bloom takes the argument one important step further and suggests that Shakespeare was responsible for the modern notion of the human. See his *Shakespeare: The Invention of the Human* (New York, 1998). Some critics have accused Shakespeare of excessive "bardolatry."
2. The first story of the first chapter of his *Golestan*, in fact, repeats this point and seems to be Sa'di's way of offering a map for a more accurate reading of his words. Later in this essay, the story is discussed at greater length.

neys exploring places as far away as Europe and China, North Africa and India.[3] For these reasons, and many more, Sa'di represents the epitome of Iran's aborted "Renaissance."[4]

From the tenth to the twelfth centuries, a large group of Persian writers and poets, historians and philosophers, astronomers and mathematicians—from Khayyam and Kharazmi to Beyhaghi and Biruni—created what has been called "the most glorious era"[5] in the history of Persian culture. The intellectual hallmarks of this era included many of the ideas that usually herald the advent of modernity in a society. Rationalism, empiricism, skepticism, pluralism of ideas, secularism, the idea of a "social contract," development of a national language, the evolution of a simple prose tailored to the contours of Ockham's famous razor,[6] and finally, the emergence of individual sensibility in works of art are some of the essential building blocks of modernity. Sa'di's opus was not just a window to the soul of Persian culture, but embodied many of Iran's early but short-lived "modern" accomplishments.

Critics have long recognized Sa'di's significance in Persian letters. Some have in fact suggested that he was more than just an accurate "echo" of his era; he was, they argue, the very architect of the modern Persian language. "Experts wonder at the fact that Sa'di wrote in our language some seven hundred years ago, but the truth is that after seven centuries, we speak the language we have learned from Sa'di."[7] Another critic elevated Sa'di to the realm of the divine, comparable to the prophet of Islam, Mohammed. "Sa'di is the prophet of the Persian language," he writes, "and his miracle is his language."[8]

---

3. Mohammad Mohit Tabatabai, "Nokat-i dar sargozasht-e Sa'di"["Some Points on Sa'di's Life"], in Zekr-e Jamil-e Sa'di [In Praise of Sa'di], vol. 3 (Tehran, 1366/1997), 185-213.

4. For the literary aspect of this Renaissance, see E.G. Browne, Literary History of Persian People, vol. 2.

5. Mojtaba Minovi, Naghd-e Hal [Contemporary Critique] (Tehran, 1351): 288.

6. Also spelled Occam's razor, it is sometimes referred to as the law of parsimony. It was articulated by William of Ockham who lived from 1285 to 1347 or 1349, and is partially the historic basis for the popular character of William of Baskerville in Umberto Eco's novel, The Name of the Rose. (In the film version William's character is played by Sean Connery.) Ockham suggested "pluralitas non est sine necessitate", or that "Plurality should not be posited without necessity." The theory based on this proposition indicates that in all heuristic endeavors, precedence should be given to the shorter, simpler version and nothing that is not necessary should be added to the explanation. In Hamlet Shakespeare would later offer a brilliant synopsis of this theory, writing, "Brevity is the soul of wit." Hamlet, 2.2.96.

7. Quoted in Zia Movahed, Sa'di (Tehran, 1373/1994). The book is an erudite introduction to Sa'di and his work. What makes the small book particularly valuable is the fact that Mr. Movahed is well-versed in both the traditions of Persian literature and in modern theories of criticism.

8. The words are those of Habib Yaghma'i. I have jotted the quotes in my notebook but somehow forgot to indicate the exact details of where the quote comes from.

Persians have not been the only ones waxing eloquent about Sa'di and the brilliance of his mind. Emerson, who read Sa'di only in translation, compared his writing to the Bible in terms of its wisdom and the beauty of its narrative.[9]

In spite of these exuberant words of praise, little work of serious scholarship has been hitherto published about Sa'di and his place in Persian history. The shortage of such works by Persian critics is particularly glaring. A reliable Persian biography of him has yet to be written. In fact, it is only in the last four decades that annotated critical editions of his two masterpieces—*Golestan* and *Bustan*[10]—have been published. Furthermore, all too often he has been chastised, even ridiculed, as a mere panegyrist to kings, a greedy wordsmith who sold his "craft" to the highest bidder. Others have accused him of lacking a cohesive vision. His work, they claim, is a literary "grab bag," hurriedly collated in a few days. It lacks, Dashti pronounced, "what the Europeans call a system. In other words, there is no dominant and uniform methodology around which all of his books and views can be arranged."[11] Henri Masse, the French Orientalist who wrote the first serious book-length study of Sa'di, suggests that any attempt to "create a logical construct out of the fragments of Sa'di's thought," will be in conflict with the method of the poet himself.[12] Kasravi, the iconoclastic Persian nationalist historian, goes one step further, suggesting that *Golestan* is "yet another historic proof of the mental mendacity of the [Iranian] people." According to Kasravi, Sa'di does nothing "other than concoct sonnets, lament of love, offer panegyrics to the rich and give stupid advice."[13] Masse, along with other "progressive" Persian literary critics, asserts that, "Sa'di was obviously a monarchist"; the essence of his teaching, they say, can be found in his aphorism, "obedience is the secret of greatness."[14]

---

9. For a detailed discussion of Emerson's views on Sa'di, see Farhang Jahanpour, "Sa'di va Emerson" ["Sa'di and Emerson"], *Iran Nameh*, no. 1 (Summer 1985/1364), 691-704.

10. Both editions were prepared by Gholam-Hossein Yousefi, (Tehran, 1368/1989; Tehran, 1359/1980).

11. Ali Dashti, *Dar Ghalamro-ye Sa'di* [*In The Realm of Sa'di*] (Tehran, 1364/1985), 231.

12. Henri Masse published his *Essai Sur le Poete Saadi* in 1919. The book was translated into Persian by Gholam-Hossein Yousefi and Mohammad Hassan Mahdavi Ardabili. The Persian version is called *Tahghigh dar Bareh-ye Sa'di* [*Research on Sa'di*] (Tehran, 1369/1990). The quote is from the Persian version, page 261.

13. Ahmad Kasravi, *Sufigari* [*Sufism*] (Tehran, 1339/1960).

14. Masse, *Tahghigh dar Bareh-ye Sa'di*, 178.

In recent years, apologists for the Islamic regime in Iran have further confused the picture by claiming Sa'di as an early advocate of an "Islamic Republic."[15]

It is high time to ask whether these critics are right in their dismissive judgments of Sa'di. Is the nature of their readings, or misreadings, itself a revealing chapter in the tormented history of Persian modernity? Should their attitudes be construed as another example of the mindless dismissal of all Persian tradition that came to be the hallmark of some early Iranian advocates of modernity? Is there truly no cohesive vision beyond, or beneath, the fragmented nature of Sa'di's prose and poetry? Is there no unifying vision, a *Weltanschauung*, in his writing? If in fact there is such a vision—as I contend—what are its main components, and do they bear any relationship to the question of modernity in Iran?

Nearly all the early Iranian advocates of modernity believed that disdain for Persian tradition, a nihilist negation of its value—much like the character Bazarov's nihilism in Ivan Turgenev's *Fathers and Sons*—was the first step in building a truly modern polity. When in his greener days Seyyed Hassan Taghizadeh suggested that Iranians must shed all that is Persian and in its place become, through bone and blood, Western, he was articulating the callow views of this group. Of course he had the wisdom to realize quickly the fallacy of his argument and moved to amend it. A close and critical reading of Sa'di will demonstrate the obvious dangers of this kind of cultural nihilism. Specifically, I will read the first chapter of Golestan, dealing with "The Manner of Kings,"[16] and deduce from its form and content Sa'di's political philosophy, particularly as it relates to kings and the nature of their rule. We will, I think, discover that in this chapter, Sa'di was, contrary to the accusations of his detractors, a harbinger of political modernity and a thoughtful critic of kings and their despotic rule.

In the West, the rise of modernity and its incumbent individualism led to the concomitant rise of new literary genres, among them the novel and the essay. Montaigne[17] is credited with discovering the form of the "essay"

---

15. In recent years, some critics have offered strange, and hard-to-fathom interpretations of some of Sa'di's words as proof of his allegiance to the idea of the rule of clerics. For one such attempt, see Ali Sheikh al-Eslami, "Velayat dar Asar-e Sa'di," [Guardianship in the works of Sa'di] in Zekr-e Jamil-e Sa'di [In praise of Sa'di], vol. 3, (Tehran, 1364/1985): 1-21.

16. There are more than one translation of Golestan. I have decided to use Sir Edwin Arnold's translation which appeared in 1899. See The Gulistan, Being the Rose-Garden of Shaikh Sa'di, trans. Sir Edwin Arnold, (London, 1899).

17. Montaigne, whose full name was Michel Eyguem de Montaigne, was born on February 28, 1533 in Chateau de Montaigne, near Bordeaux, and died in the same place on September 23, 1592. For a brief account of his life, see The Complete Essays of Montaigne, trans. Donald M. Frame, (Stanford, 1957).

wherein he wanted to try—"assay"—rendering one aspect of reality from the point of view—or perspective—of one individual. He put into practical and discursive use what Descartes would later summarize in his *cogito ergo sum* postulate. Montaigne wanted to shape each essay from his concrete, individual and personal experience. For him, in other words, the essay was a form of self-assertion. Indeed, he wrote that his original urge to write an essay arose out of his grief at the death of a dear friend. He could no longer communicate with the friend, and the essay, he wrote, was a surrogate and a substitute for that aborted connection.[18]

In other passages, Montaigne writes more clearly about the essay as an instrument to fight the contingent nature of our existence, something to cling to in our despair over the material and transient nature of life. Sa'di, too, was both keenly aware of the tragic nature of existence, and unabashedly self-assertive in his work. Examples of this self-assertion abound in his famous preface to *Golestan*. There he asserts that his fame has reached all corners of the world, and that his words are all around the world "as sought after as gold."[19] Another side of this sense of self-importance can be seen in the pejorative way he refers to those he has praised in his panegyrics. He calls them mere "so and sos" (*felan*) and informs them in no uncertain terms that they should consider it a sign of their great good luck to have been born during the "age of Sa'di."[20]

At the same time, like Montaigne, he is also concerned about the contingency of life. In a passage remarkable for its pith and modern echoes, he writes of this world as a brief hiatus "between two nothingnesses." Furthermore, in describing his reasons for writing the book, he suggests, "philosophers have said that impermanent phenomena are not worthy of our attachment…and thus I decided to create a *Golestan*"[literally a "rose garden"] that could withstand the ravages of time."[21]

Montaigne did not, of course, invent the essay *ex nihilo*.[22] The genealogy of this new genre can be found in a medieval form of narrative that combined poetry and aphorism. Sa'di's formal strategy in the first book of *Golestan* also creates—assays—something new.

---

18. For a brilliant philosophical inquiry into the works of Montaigne, see Jean Starobinski, *Montaigne in Motion*, trans. Arthur Goldhammer (Chicago, 1984); an earlier analysis of the essay and its foundations can be seen in Erich Auerbach, *Mimesis: The Representation of Reality in Western Literature*, trans. Willard Trask, (New York, 1957), 249-273.

19. The words appear on page 57 of Yousefi's edition of *Golestan*.

20. Sa'di, *Kolliyat-e Sa'di* [Collected works of Sa'di], ed. Mohammad Ali Foroughi (Tehran, 1357/1979), 9.

21. Yousefi, *Golestan*, 58.

22. Auerbach, *Mimesis*, 240-273.

In the first chapter on the "Manner of Kings," he uses a genre of writing that owes its genealogy to the Arabic *maghameh*. In its Arabic origin, the genre was known for its purple prose and obtuse and often repetitious imagery. The intent was to show the author's erudition and mastery of form by conjuring the ostentatious phrases of other authors and maintaining the purity of the literary language. That is why one critic in fact called maghameh a case of "verbal exhibitionism."[23] Sa'di took of this ancient form all that he found useful, discarding the cumbersome elements and forging out of the remaining tropes a unique style that was "modern," beguilingly simple, poetically parsimonious, and descriptively precise.

The old genre was known for its rigid rules and strictures about length and narrative style.[24] Sa'di broke with tradition and made the length of every piece a purely aesthetic decision. In the aesthetics of modernity, the artist's sensibilities—and not dictates of tradition—are the sole criteria for executing a work of art. Sa'di, too, made of maghameh a varied and varying instrument of the author's self-expression. Furthermore, he occasionally creates imaginary heroes and places them at the center of the narrative; other times he himself enters into the story as Sa'di. Here too we can detect an early sign of one of modernity's most important aesthetic developments. In modern works, concrete and complex individuals and characters, and not one-dimensional social types or abstract Platonic Forms, are at the center of narrative. Individualism, and the recognition of each person's singularity and immutability, is a cardinal element of modernity. The emergence of character as the focal point of literary narrative is the aesthetic manifestation of the rise of individualism.[25] In Sa'di we can discern early attempts at recognizing and empowering the individual. In fact, his effort to shape his narrative only through the prism of individual sensibility started long before these developments begin in the works of such Western masters as Shakespeare.[26]

An example of the early rudiments of character development in *Golestan* can be found in the story of the king who had, "passed a whole night of pleasure, and being full drunken, was singing, 'Never to me came a rosier hour than this, / Who care not whether good is, or bad is, / And let no

---

23. Movahed, *Sa'di*, 148.

24. Jalal Matini, "Maghaleh-ye Manzum be Zaban-e Farsi" ["An Essay in the Language of Poetry"], *Iran Nameh*, no. 4 (Summer 1364/1985), 704-732.

25. For a discussion of the rise of character, see Ian Watt, *The Rise of the Novel* (Berkeley, 1957); and Wayne C. Booth, *The Rhetoric of Fiction* (Chicago, 1961).

26. For the consequences of this kind of subjectivity on poetry and Shakespeare's pioneering role in its evolution, see Joel Fineman, *Shakespeare's Perjured Eye*, (Berkeley, 1986).

meddler plague my perfect bliss.'"[27] Soon, a "darweesh, who was sleeping naked in the snow outside" called out to the king, "Oh Happy Prince! Of state unequalled see / 'Tis well for you, but what say you of me?" The king was "tickled by this snatch, and flung a bag containing a thousand dinars out of the window."[28]

Before long, the darweesh "ate up, or otherwise wasted, all his money" and came back for more. But this time the king was in no mood for philanthropy, and "became enraged and turned away a frowning face."[29] He ordered the man beaten and driven from the palace.

In this pithy anecdote, we learn much about the character of the king. Though a Muslim, he drinks, following a tradition of fast-drinking kings; though a king, he is often oblivious to the fate of his subjects; though generous, he is also inconsistent. In fact, we learn more about his character from the ruminations of his mind than any other aspect of his reality. Interiority, or the artist's commitment to showing the reader as much about the inner anxieties and dialogues, fears and sentiments of the characters as about their outer appearance, is another element in the aesthetic of modernity. The closer we come to our time, the more novels and short stories, even poems and paintings, have tried to map out the inner world of the artist or the characters they depict.[30] Early signs of interiority can be seen in parts of Sa'di's *Golestan*. For example, in one story, Sa'di tells us about one of his friends, "Bewailing to me the hardness of the times, saying how that he possessed such small means and many children, and knew not how to face penury."[31] The friend reveals his plans "to go to some other land" where oblivion would come to his rescue. Yet, he confesses that he is "in dread of the malignity of enemies, who will mock at me…and blame my conduct."[32] The fascinating story goes on to discuss the fickle quality of kings, whose service "is like a voyage upon the sea: profitable yet perilous."[33] In the course of the narrative, we learn about the character of the narrator and of his interlocutor essentially through their inner thoughts and anxieties. It is not too far fetched to argue that the famous sections of *Golestan*, where Sa'di ostensibly engages a highly intelligent adversary in a debate about the virtues and vices of wealth, is in fact an interior dialogue conducted by the author with himself.[34]

27. Arnold's *Gulistan*, 29.
28. Ibid., 30.
29. Ibid.
30. Milan Kundera talks about this evolution in *The Art of the Novel*, trans. Linda Asher (New York, 1988).
31. Arnold's *Gulistan*, 36.
32. Ibid., 37.
33. Ibid., 43.
34. In his book *Montaigne in Motion*, Starobinski argues that the essay is ultimately a kind of a dialogue of the author with herself or himself.

Another sign of modernity is the gradual appearance of the vernacular in the hitherto rarified realm of literary language. This linguistic turn is in fact a concomitant part of the democratic change in society. From egalitarian linguistics, or the recognition of the necessity of polyphony in art (and society), to political democracy is but a short step. In Europe, Dante, with his *Divine Comedy* and his essays on the virtues of a simpler language, was the first advocate of the vernacular in literature.[35] A good two hundred years later, Cervantes and Rabelais incorporated the vernacular into their stories and helped create the genre of the novel. Furthermore, Cervantes entered into the second half of the narrative as himself, and gave his novel a precociously "postmodern" flair. Sa'di explored and experimented with both these ideas as early as the first decades of the thirteenth century. He discarded maghameh's literary language, and its attempt to create ever more complicated and convoluted constructs, in favor of the vernacular and simplicity. Furthermore, other Persians who wrote maghamehs sometimes wrote them in Arabic. Sa'di, on the other hand, insisted on writing in Persian, and using a language close to the vernacular.[36] Even when he used Arabic phrases, he tried, as much as possible, to use Persian syntax.[37] Because of these accomplishments, Sa'di is usually praised no less than Ferdowsi[38] for his role in preserving the Persian language and allowing it to become a great bastion of the Persian identity.

It is a sad irony of Persian history that two hundred years after Sa'di, just as the West was beginning to take off on its road to the Renaissance, Iran began to move—or to fall—in the other direction. Sa'di's simple, supple and parsimonious prose was supplanted by a new style characterized by frivolous complexity, tiresome repetition and troubling imprecision. In the mid-nineteenth century, when modernity was once again Iran's central problem, the obfuscations of this pompous and ponderous prose were finally discarded in favor of a new style, once again directly inspired by Sa'di.[39]

---

35. For a translation of Dante's controversial essay on the subject and the historic condition of its publication, see Marianne Shapiro *De Volgari Eloquantia* (Lincoln, 1990).
36. Mohammad Jafar Mahjoob, "*Zaban-e Sa'di va Payvand-e on ba Zendegi*" ["Sa'di's Language and its Connection to Life"], *Iran Nameh*, no. 4 (Summer 1361/1985): 595.
37. Movahed, *Sa'di*, 150-151.
38. It is a common adage of Persian history that a key to its ability to withstand the Arab onslaught and maintain its cultural identity has been the power of the Persian language, and that Ferdowsi, in his monumental *Shahnameh*, with his conscious effort to avoid Arabic words, helped preserve Persia and the Persian identity. There is now an emerging consensus that Sa'di too belongs to the pantheon of guardian angels of the Persian language.
39. A key text of the nineteenth century generally thought to have commenced the movement of a return to Sa'di and the classics is Ghaem Magham Farahani, *Monsheat-e Ghaem Magham* [Ghaem Magham's writings] (Tehran, 1357/1978).

The kind of new democratic linguistics advocated by Sa'di in Iran and Dante in Europe has two other important consequences. In the West, one of the most important early signs of the Renaissance was the Bible's translation into a variety of emerging national languages. Reformists like Luther forsook Latin and delivered their sermons in languages understandable to the masses.[40] Furthermore, as the hold of Augustinian theology[41] on church and society began to wane, so did Augustine's admonishments against the celebration of the body and its pleasures. One of the important characteristics of Renaissance art was the rediscovery of the human body and its beauty. In medieval times, the frank enjoyment of bodily appetites, as well as bawdy narratives and erotica, had been relegated to the subversive cultural underground. The Renaissance brought them into the open, and afforded them the legitimacy they had enjoyed during the early "golden" days of Greek culture.

The end of this kind of bodily asceticism had another corollary as well. The cult of poverty, long preached by the church, and the promise that the poor shall inherit the earth and have easier access to heaven, was replaced by the novel idea that wealth itself is a sign of grace, and that the wealthy are indeed God's favorite children. These changes took place in Europe during the sixteenth-century Reformation. Sa'di experimented with carnal literature and an embryonic "reformation" at least three centuries earlier.

Sa'di was truly revolutionary in his celebration of carnal pleasure as a principle, freely admitting to his own enjoyment and "indiscretions." Indeed, his prose and poetry dealing with this kind of erotica—accounts of his many love escapades, his love of young boys, and the hypocrisy of society in denying the pleasures of the flesh—were so open that even twentieth-century editors in Iran refuse to publish them. Other critics consider them a sure sign of the "depravity" of his character and of his arrogance in admitting "engaging in inhuman behavior."[42]

Sa'di's views on the question of wealth were no less iconoclastic. He lived in an era when Sufism, with its cult of poverty and "other-worldliness,"

40. For a discussion of the role of language in shaping national identities in the modern age, see Benedict Anderson, *Imagined Communities: Reflections on the Origins and Spread of Nationalism* (London, 1991).

41. As Augustine makes clear in his *Confessions*, he was deeply influenced by the ideas of Mani, who saw the world in terms of a duality of good and evil, and who relegated to the realm of evil all that had to do with bodily pleasures. For him, as for Augustine, denying the body its appetites, particularly those of a carnal nature, is the *sine qua non* of salvation.

42. Foroughi writes that "we omitted [parts that were] obscene and unpleasant." *Complete Works of Sa'di*, 183; Ali Dashti accuses Sa'di of depravity: Dashti, *In the Realm of Sa'di*, 272.

was rapidly on the rise. Some scholars have even found Sufi influences in Sa'di himself. Nevertheless, in one of the most often quoted parts of *Golestan*, he offers bold and "modern" answers to the age-old question of wealth and poverty. One cannot but be impressed with his uncanny ability to concurrently hold and defend—with equal vigor and vitality—two opposing views. On the one hand, he suggests that the "owners of worldly wealth are graced by God." He even hints at "supply side" economics in suggesting that the livelihood of the poor is a function of the power and wealth of the rich. On the other hand, no sooner has the reader accepted these arguments in favor of the rich than Sa'di turns the table, and suggests that the rich are "arrogant," "self-righteous," idle human beings, selfishly obsessed with wealth and possession.[43]

Sa'di's attempt at moderation in this crucial question is not an isolated instance but part of a persistent pattern of his aversion to extremes and his proclivity for the golden mean. In fact, in his moderation, Sa'di has been compared to Erasmus, the quintessential humanist intellectual of the Renaissance.[44]

Sa'di's form is not all that is "modern" in him. The essence of his philosophy and political vision, as they manifest themselves in the first book of *Golestan*, are equally unusual for their advocacy of ideas we generally consider quintessentially modern and Western. Furthermore, these ideas are incongruent with the common perception of Sa'di as a panegyrist to the kings.

The first book of *Golestan* is composed of forty-one short parables and stories. Of these, at least twenty-seven are unambiguously critical of kings. The result would be even more revealing if we treat all of the first book as a single text[45] and then deconstruct from it the character of the king. In other words, in such a reading, different stories of the first book will be treated as episodes in the life of a hero called the king. The image that emerges in such a reading is disconcerting. Here we find a king who gives the "order to put to death" a captive wretch. He is so attached to his power that even "a hundred years after death, when all his body had moldered into garments and become dust," he is still angry and worried because someone else "might sit on his throne." He is shallow and vain in demeanor, rash and cruel in his

43. Yousefi's *Golestan*, 160-168.
44. Masse, *Research on Sa'di*. 345.
45. Shakespeare's sonnets, as well as the Old Testament, have been read in precisely this manner, and the results have been fascinating. For example, for the image of god as the central character of the Old Testament see Jack Miles, *God: A Biography* (New York, 1997).

judgments. His cruelty is such that a holy man's best prayer for him was that he should sleep, "every day at noon; for so doing, there will be a moment when thou wilt not be oppressing thy people." He spends a whole "night's pleasure, being fully drunk." He is negligent of the affairs of the state and even keeps "his army short of supplies." He is defined by his "inconsistency"; one moment he is unpredictably "offended by compliments," another moment he is gratefully granting a prize for an "actual abuse." This inconsistency and the fickle quality of character is serious enough that wise and learned men are averse to the idea of serving the king, for "fear of death." His ministers readily "ruin the dwelling of the subjects," in order to fill "the treasure-chamber of their prince." When afflicted with a sickness and told that his remedy is "the gall of a male child," he bribes the parents of the innocent child and forces his mullah to issue a fatwa indicating that spilling the blood of a peasant "for the purpose of restoring health to his Majesty" is lawful and just.[46] It is hard to see how anyone could read the first book of *Golestan* and still believe that Sa'di was just a panegyrist of kings.

There are of course a few kings about whom Sa'di has, albeit faint, words of praise. Interestingly, all except one of these kings either belong to the pre-Islamic period of Persian history or are characters from the *Shahnameh*. Such love of old Persia is neither unusual in the history of Persian culture nor is it incongruent with Sa'di's modernity. In the West, modernity began with a "rebirth" of classical heritage. Sa'di and his clear affinity for the pre-Islamic kings is a failed attempt at just such a Persian Renaissance. Furthermore, scholars like Henry Corbin and Mohammad Moin have argued that a defining characteristic of Persian culture has been its ability to maintain its pre-Islamic values and divine pantheon by giving them an Islamic veneer. Sa'di then is one poet among many whose ubiquitous love of old Persia appears in his work in a variety of guises.

A clear indication of this love of old Persia is that, of the thirty-two different characters mentioned in his *Golestan* and *Bustan*, thirteen belong to Persia's mytho-historic past. Like Dante and his controversial decision to make Virgil his guide in the *Divine Comedy*, Sa'di defiantly places Anoushirvan, "though alleged to be an infidel," in heaven.[47] He deserves to be in heaven, declares Sa'di, because he was a just king, and never took anything, "not even a handful of salt," from the people without their

---

46. All quotes are from the first chapter Arnold's *Gulistan*, "The Manner of Kings."
47. Yousefi's *Golestan*, 58.

consent.[48] The contrast between Muslim kings, often unjust and cruel, and the pre-Islamic rulers, wise and just, is underscored in the very first story of the first book. After describing the cruel behavior of the king, the story ends with the lines, "On the porch of Feridun's [a king from the *Shahnameh*] palace was written: 'This life's show, my brother, endureth for none.... When the soul is a-flitting, what difference is found / Twixt the King on his throne, and the hind on the ground!'"[49]

A close reading of the first book of *Golestan* also clearly undermines the recent claims of Islamic critics about Sa'di's alleged affinity for an Islamic regime. In the forty-one stories of the first book, Sa'di only makes three passing references to verses from the Qur'an and one to a hadith. He uses many more secular and pre-Islamic poems and aphorisms than Qur'anic verses. When, for example, he writes of a king who had "put forth the hand of oppression" and exploited his subjects, Sa'di offers him advice not from the Qur'an but from the *Shahnameh*, "relating to the downfall" of another kingdom. Indeed, in the whole of the first book, Sa'di makes no direct or indirect reference to the rule of mullahs or even to the king's supposed duty to rule by the dictates of Islam. In some of his other writings, Sa'di in fact clearly advises kings to keep religion and politics apart. In the first chapter of *Golestan*, such advice is implied by the glaring omission of any reference to the role of religion in shaping the "manner of kings."

Sa'di's advice to men of letters and learning—and surely clerics must be considered part of that group—is to avoid proximity to the king. Kings, he says, are fickle and fiendish. Their love and anger have usually no rhyme or reason. Neither can they be anticipated. Such inconsistency begets danger to those around the king. The first words of the first chapter hint at this menace. The chapter begins declaring, "I had heard of a certain king, who had given orders to put to death one of his captives. The hapless wretch, in that hour of despair, began to curse his Majesty...." Our first impression of the king is of a man who casually orders the death of a "hapless wretch."[50]

---

48. Sa'di's rendition of pre-Islamic kings is often a romantic and idealized image. The best example is his much beloved Anoushirvan who is praised "for not even taking a handful of salts" but brutally put the sword to the Mazdaki movement, and by one account killed forty thousand of them. Even many *Shahnameh* kings are far from ideal models of kingship. The only exception is Kay Khosrow—a genuine democrat who resigns his post when he gets old and allows for young blood to take over. For a discussion of his character, and his usefulness as a model of democracy, See Fereydoun Hoveyda, *The Shah and the Ayatollah: Iranian Mythology and the Islamic Revolution* (New York, 2003).

49. Arnold's *Gulistan*, 5.

50. Ibid., 3.

Sa'di's democratic bent is also evident in the numerous references he makes to the common people in *Golestan*. In the West, one of the first signs of the Renaissance was the entry of the common folk into the realm of aesthetics. Painters like Brueghel began to paint peasant faces, and tried to capture them in their daily lives. Idioms and mores of the non-aristocratic classes figure largely in the novels of Cervantes and the plays of Shakespeare. In *Golestan*, we see the first steps of the same process at work some three hundred years earlier than Cervantes. In Golestan, there are references to 339 different characters and professions. Kings are mentioned forty-seven times, and religious figures a mere thirty-nine times. Common people, on the other hand, are referred to eighty-six times.[51]

This wide-ranging diffusion of references is no accident but reflects Sa'di's democratic tendency and his aversion to traditional notions of kingship where the people are "subjects" and live and die at the mercy of an omnipotent king. In some parts of the first book of Golestan, one can even discern early hints at a "social contract" theory of law. Sa'di clearly believed in the fundamental equality of all humans. In what is probably his most often quoted line of poetry, he writes, "limbs of a body are we, son of men,/Made from the same clay, born of same origin." Furthermore, he suggests that the power of the king is directly "dependent on the support of the people—a king must be just in order to attract the support of the people."[52] He advises a prince, "infamous for his oppression," that if he wants to withstand the attack of powerful enemies, he must heed the needs of his weakest subjects. "Show mercy to the humble," he says, "if thou wouldst not be in terror of the strong."[53] Another parable is even more pregnant with suggestive ideas about democracy. Sa'di writes, "the king needs his subjects more than the subjects need the king, for whether there is a king or not, the subject remains the subject, while it is impossible to imagine a king without the existence of the subjects."[54] Sa'di's depiction parallels, in many key ideas, Hegel's famous theory about the dialectic of master and slave, where every slave eventually comes to dominate his master. According to Hegel, slaves have an autonomous existence, but masters need a "slave" in order

51. Jalal Matini, "Ashkhas-e Dastan-e Golestan," ["Characters in the story of *Golestan*"], a paper delivered in a 1971 conference on Sa'di, held in Shiraz, Iran. The author kindly provided me with a copy of the article.
52. Sa'di, *Complete Works of Sa'di*, 805.
53. Arnold's *Gulistan*, 27.
54. Sa'di, *Complete Works*, 820.

to assert their masterly identity. Sa'di offers the poetic gist of this elegant philosophical principle in exactly twenty-eight words.[55]

As intriguing as many of these ideas are, it is of course important to ask why Sa'di offered them in the guise of parables and aphorisms. Here, too, Sa'di uses the text of the first book of *Golestan* to tell any careful reader why he had to disguise his political views. He even offers some guidelines on how to get to the meaning of his metaphoric discourse. In the first story of the first book, he writes, "Whoever has washed his hands of living / Utters his mind without misgiving."[56] In other words, under despotism, only those who have "washed their hands of living" can talk openly and freely. Everybody else, including Sa'di, talks, perforce, in metaphors.

Lest his early hint goes unnoticed, Sa'di ends his book with another, even more clear, indication of the metaphoric structure of his narrative. He writes that some have criticized him for only writing light and insubstantial verse (and by this reference, he makes it clear that he and others were, at the time, concerned with the "social responsibility" of the artist, itself a particularly modern idea.) He points out that in fact his narrative is anything but a collection of frivolous stories and light verse. Clever readers, he suggests, are not going to miss the real intent and content of his narrative. They will notice how he has "suffused the bitter pill of advice in the sweet syrup"[57] of a narrative that is frivolous in appearance, but serious in intent. In other words, the very oppressive kings he was fighting in the first book of *Golestan* also forced him into a metaphoric language. More importantly, Sa'di clearly wants to rely on the imagination of his readers to infuse the metaphors with their intended meaning. Such reliance on the reader is in itself a sign of modernity. Umberto Eco has convincingly shown that modernity begins when the text is "opened,"[58] and the reader's role in infusing a narrative with its meaning is recognized. But Sa'di's metaphors of concealment proved too clever for many generations of his readers. As the story of Iran's aborted modernity remained buried in history, so too the soul of Sa'di's writing, itself long considered a window to the soul of Persia, remained undiscovered as well. The renewed interest in his work over the last decade is a promising harbinger of his "rebirth."

---

55. The dialectics of master and slave is a central component of Alexander Kojeve's famous study of Hegel. See Alexandre Kojeve, *Introduction to the Philosophy of Hegel* (New York, 1993).

56. Arnold's *Gulistan*, 3.

57. Yousefi's *Golestan*, 91.

58. Umberto Eco in *The Open Text* writes of the new "openness" and its methodological elements. In his *Interpretation and Over-Interpretation*, he points out to the perils and promises of this openness. (Bloomington, 1990).

NASIR AL-DIN SHAH IN FARANG
Perspective of an Oriental Despot[1]

Nasir al-Din Shah ruled Iran for nearly half a century. He came to power in 1848, when he was only seventeen years old. An assassin's bullet ended his reign in 1896. His death was the first sign of incipient crisis in the institution of monarchy in Iran. After him, only one king died peacefully in Iran and on the throne. His name was Mozaffar al-Din Shah, and he was the king who signed the new constitution, limiting the power of despotic monarchs. After him, every king died in exile, driven from office. The last to meet this fate was Mohammad Reza Shah, who left Iran in 1979 and took with him the twenty-five hundred year-old tradition of monarchy in Iran.

Iran's encounters with Western modernity began under Nasir al-Din Shah's long rule. His coterie of courtiers included both zealous reformers and incorrigible advocates of despotism. The tremors that ultimately erupted in Iran's Constitutional Revolution (1905-07) began under his reign.

The onslaught of modernity shook to the core the existing Iranian sense of cultural identity and community. What critics have called "the fixity and fetishism"[2] of cultural identities began to crack. A new "cultural hybridity" seemed unavoidable.

In this context, new competing and conflicting cultural "strategies of self-hood" began to emerge. Religious forces, suspicious of change, advocated social and spiritual isolation. Only a culture enveloped in divine wisdom, they argued, could survive the satanic verses of modernity. On

---

1. An earlier draft of this chapter appeared in *Challenging Boundaries: Global Flows, Territorial Identities*, ed. Michael Shapiro and Hayward R. Alker (Minneapolis, 1996), 219-232. I am particularly grateful to Michael Shapiro for his many insightful comments on the earlier draft of the paper.
2. Homi K. Bhabha, *The Location of Culture* (New York, 1994), 199.

the opposite extreme were the advocates of "cultural transubstantiation," who encouraged a total submersion of Iranian culture into the paradise of European civilization.

And thus, the primitive despotic machine of Nasir al-Din Shah was faced with a serious crisis. It knew the winds of change were in the air; new political desires and designs were on the horizon. The king also knew that if he was to survive, he had to domesticate modernity into a servile tool of his despotism. Nasir al-Din Shah's European travelogues are an early testimony to this quixotic effort.

The king's idle curiosities, his insatiable desire for frivolities, his "addiction"[3] to travel, his attempt to consolidate his relationship with European powers, his greed for gold, his reformist courtiers' designs to "enlighten"[4] the king, and finally the colonialists' attempts to enlist his favors, led to the Shah's decision to travel to Europe. Out of a labyrinth of these conflicting desires and designs came a project that began as a journey of discovery, and ended as a narrative of despotic machinations.

On three occasions, in 1873, 1878, and 1889, each time for about four to five months, the king, along with nearly all of the country's political elite, traveled to Europe. All the customary pomp of the exotic "Oriental" surrounded his entourage.[5]

As was his habit in nearly all his trips, Nasir al-Din Shah decided to write an account of his travels.[6] In their form and content, these travelogues are a fascinating arena in which different cultures and sensibilities cohabit. The tensions and pretensions of the text can be seen as a metaphor for the historical dilemma and the strange contour of modernity in Iran. Indeed, the texts of the travelogues, as well as the context and the subtext of their production and dissemination, betray a fierce battle between competing visions of power and their incumbent political and aesthetic discourses.

---

3. Ehsan Yarshater, "Observations on Nasir al-Din Shah," in *Qajar Iran: Political, Social and Cultural Change*, edited by Edmund Bosworth and Carole Hillenbrand (Edinburgh, 1983), 8.

4. Fereydoun Adamiyat, *Andisheh-ye Taraghi* [The idea of progress] (Tehran, 1972), 259.

5. Vita Sackville-West describes how Nasir al-Din Shah "used to startle Europe by his arrival in her capital with his Oriental accoutrements and the black mustachios like a scimitar across his face." See Vita Sackville West, *Passenger to Tehran* (New York, 1992), 138. See also Zeynep Celik, *Displaying the Orient: Architecture of Islam and Nineteenth Century World's Fair* (Berkeley, 1992), 334-36 and 120-122.

6. See the following titles, all authored by Nasir al-Din Shah: *Safar Name-ye Nasir al-Din Shah* [Nasir al-Din Shah's travelogue] (Tehran, 1342/1963); *Name-ye Farangestan* [Letters from Europe] (Tehran, 1342/1963); *Ruznameh-ye Khaterat Nasir al-Din Shah dar Safar-e Sevvum Farang* [Nasir al-Din's Shah's travelogue of his third trip to Europe] (Tehran, 1370/1990).

In a sense, every political discourse is also an attempt to displace (or to "dis-course") alternative claims (or structures) of power. The narratives of the royal sojourns to Europe were no exception. They became part of Nasir al-Din Shah's strategy for maintaining power. At the same time, like all texts, they betrayed more than he intended. They have what has been called a "political unconscious."[7] In his case, the narratives' "unconscious" betrays his anxieties and his fervent desire to find and put into practice aspects of modernity amenable to the needs of his despotic rule.

Confounding this individual battle was the peculiar problem of the new stage of modernity in Iran. If in the West the battle between the ancient and the modern was a bipolar struggle, in nineteenth-century Iran the fight was, every step of the way, overshadowed by the enormous complexities of the colonial question. In those days, Russia and England fought for influence in Iran, while lesser European powers each struggled for a smaller piece of the pie. On the one hand, the ferocity of this colonial fight ensured at least nominal independence for Iran. On the other hand, all aspects of what Hannah Arendt calls "the Social Question"[8] —all the social issues modernity hurls into the public domain—were invariably ensnared with colonial politics. In Nasir al-Din Shah's convoluted vision of Europe, in his mutilated narrative of discovery, in his peculiar acts of omission and commission, we see the perils and the paradoxes of this entanglement.

In the place of the "will to know" or possess—the engines of modernity's "discourse of discovery"[9]—here we find in his travel writing the will to pleasure and the will to contain. Instead of "theoretical curiosity," a cardinal element of modernity's epistemology, we have here, at best, a politically neutered and often frivolous inquisitiveness. His narrative is shaped by his desire to hide some truths about the modern West and contain the subversive potentialities of others. A key element of this dual strategy is to emulate some so-called modern forms while eliding their democratic content. The narrative's own manner of production and dissemination is itself the best example of the "modern" Oriental despot's elective affinity for modernity.

---

7. Frederic Jameson, *The Political Unconscious: Narrative as Socially Symbolic Act* (Ithaca, 1981), 77.

8. Hannah Arendt, *Between Past and Future: Eight Exercises in Political Thought,* (New York, 1983), 41-80.

9. Stephen Greenblatt's *Marvelous Possessions* is a brilliant look into the two medieval and modern types of curiosities or wonders and their corresponding ways of representing and "possessing" the objects of marvel. *See Marvelous Possessions: The Wonder of the New World* (Berkeley, 1991).

Before Nasir al-Din Shah, Iran's despots were often oblivious, even disdainful, of the West. We read of Iranian kings who, less than one hundred years before Nasir al-Din Shah, received Western envoys in their pajamas and exhibited a defiant, if not grandiose, sense of superiority over the West.[10]

With Nasir al-Din Shah, the tide began to turn. Colonial cultural and political hegemony was on the rise. Iranian despots were now more often than not in awe of the West; their sense of political security was dependent on the pulse of Western powers, and not the will or opinion of their own "subjects." At great cost, they usually tried to cultivate a "modern image" of themselves in the eyes of the West.[11] Early signs of this development can be seen in the fate of Nasir al-Din Shah's royal narrative. Their intended reader, what Umberto Eco calls their "model reader,"[12] was more European than Persian. In fact, the travelogues were immediately ordered by the king translated and published in English. Throughout the last decade of the nineteenth century, they were read and discussed in English intellectual circles far more than in Iran itself.[13]

But every narrative, regardless of its avowed intention, is never "merely a neutral discursive form...but rather, entails ontological and epistemic choices with distinct ideological and even specifically political implications."[14] What then is the way of political life insinuated in the Shah's narrative?

In the West, modernity privileged written over oral discourse, and created a nearly fetishistic preoccupation with memory and archives.[15] In traditional Iran, there was a glaring dearth of autobiographies and

10. Rostam al-Hokama, *Rostam al-Tavarikh* [*History According to Rostam*] (Tehran 1972).

11. At the turn of the nineteenth century, many Oriental despots were caught in the frenzy of appearing modern. The Egyptian ruler went so far as to build an opera house and commission a special opera for its opening. Egyptians never took to opera, but the world has since enjoyed the grandeur and pathos of *Aida*. See Edward Said, *Culture and Imperialism* (New York, 1993), 110-134.

12. Every text, according to Umberto Eco, has at the moment of its conception a "model reader" in mind. The relationship between the text and this reader is reciprocal. The text at once shapes and is shaped by the model reader. Eco writes that "every text is a syntactic-semantic-pragmatic device, whose foreseen interpretation is part of its generative process." See Umberto Eco, *The Role of the Reader: Explorations in the Semiotics of Text,* (Bloomington, 1979).

13. Sackville-West, *Passenger to Tehran*, 130-140.

14. Hayden White, *The Content of Form: Narrative Discourse and Historical Representation,* (Baltimore, 1987), ix.

15. For a discussion of modernity's impact on historical narrative and on the discipline of history, see Michel De Certeau, *The Writing of History*, trans. Jay Conley (New York, 1988). Foucault, too, in his *Archeology of Knowledge*, (New York, 1972) discusses historiography in light of modernity.

travelogues and a nearly complete absence of archival official records. Nasir al-Din Shah, on the other hand, had a fervor to write and record his trips. But in fact we can speak of him as the "author" of these logs only with some caveats. He was their author only in the sense Foucault desribes in his controversial essay on the "death of the author." For Foucault, it is no longer possible to talk of the person who "pronounced or wrote a text"; rather, every text is conjured up and shaped by an endless array of overt and covert structural influences on the author.[16] The texts Nasir al-Din authored were only in a titular sense his writing. For him, the act of writing was more royal theater than a simple, individual discursive practice; it embodied what Certeau calls "scriptural operations," wherein words are orally performed in the "presence of officially sanctioned recorders."[17] Such is the king's description of his own "scriptural operations":

> Bashi was holding the inkwell; Akbari the candelabra; Amin Khabar holding a notebook, ready to write; Etemad al-Saltaneh holding a Western newspaper, ready to read; Mirza Mohammad Khan holding a candelabra for him; Majd al-Dowleh, Abol Hassan Khan, Mardak, Mohammad Ali Khan, Mohammad Hassan Mirza, Adib Jujeh, Karim Khan, Agha Dai all standing, Taghi Khan holding water.[18]

With such a large constellation of courtiers in attendance, some enjoying their aristocratic titles (like Etemad al-Saltaneh, "the trustee of the king"), others suffering belittling, diminutive labels (Mardak, "little man" or Akbar Jujeh, "Akbar the little chick"), the king strutted around dictating entries that he hoped supplicant scribes would accurately transcribe into a text. Only on rare occasions would the Shah deign to jot down a few words himself. Serious textual differences between various "editions" of the logs indicate a certain degree of expected scribal corruption.

The king not only had strange ideas about "writing"; his sense of the mimetic principle implied by the travelogue as a genre is equally ambivalent. For instance, we read, "I said my prayers in the Kremlin, then I had the photographer take a portrait of me, then we went and visited the museum. Now that Abol Hassan Khan is writing these words, I haven't taken any pictures yet, nor have I visited the museum. Maybe there won't even be a picture-taking or a visit to the museum."[19]

---

16. Michel Foucault, "What is an Author," in D.F. Boncard, ed., *Language, Counter-Memory, Practice* (Ithaca, 1977), 125-127.

17. De Certeau, *The Writing of History*, 210.

18. Nasir al-Din Shah, *Ruznameh-ye Khaterat*, 17.

19. Ibid.,138.

The epistemic contract implied in this passage, with repercussions for the whole of the text, seems at once unusually avant-garde and dangerously despotic. The form of the narrative is in some complex and confusing way "modern." It resembles moments in modern novels when the novelist, in the process of writing, engages in a deconstructive act by exposing the fictive nature of the narrative. Like Chaucer's Pardoner, the king exposes the tricks of his narrative; he shows the potentially fictive quality of his narrative. Yet he wants us to read his fictions as facts. Whereas in the hands of novelists, the deconstructive act serves to demonstrate the permeable boundaries between what Vladimir Nabokov calls the facts of fiction and the fiction of facts, the tone of the king's narrative leaves no doubt that he expects the reader never to doubt the "facticity" of his fiction.

From what the narrative betrays, the king travels not just to discover the West as the dreaded and desired "Other," but also to reinvigorate his own waning powers at home. In almost every page, we are treated to elaborate, repetitious details about the pageantry of his visit, the charisma of his presence among powerful Western politicians and kings, and the "unbelievable, uncontrollable" surge of popular enthusiasm for His Majesty. On all such occasions, the narrative is suffused with the kind of familiar honorifics that commonly studded Iranian courtly discourse. If it can be said that the fundamental difference between genuine art and kitsch is that kitsch traffics in false familiarities, whereas art "defamiliarizes"[20] reality, then the Shah's travelogues are perfect examples of kitsch. They desperately try to tame and traditionalize the dangerously modern and unfamiliar. Repeatedly, the king insinuates the vocabulary of despotic power and traditional forms of authority into descriptions of the unfamiliar world of Western European politics.

The point is nowhere more evident than in the king's narrative of his trip to England during Queen Victoria's reign. In spite of common diplomatic rules of decorum, the queen did not go to meet the visiting king at the port of entry, but forced the Shah to travel to Windsor Palace. For political reasons the king makes absolutely no mention of this clear diplomatic slight. Instead he waxes eloquent about the respect afforded him during the visit.

But there was an even more serious problem. Victoria was a woman. To circumvent what the Shah felt to be the embarrassing and potentially dangerous idea of a ruling woman monarch, he chose essentially to hide

---

20. For a discussion of "defamiliarization" see Victor Shklovsky, "Art as Technique," in *Russian Formalist Criticism*, trans. Lee T. Lemon Maron (Lincoln, 1965), 13.

from any but his most astute and informed readers Victoria's gender. Instead of using the word *malekeh*, Persian for "female ruler," to refer to Victoria, throughout the text he repeatedly refers to her using the Persian word *padishah*, a word that usually implies a male ruler. In writing about the sixteenth century, he had no such compunction in referring to Elizabeth as *Malekeh*.

In fact, the question of women permeates, often in a tragicomic manner, much of the fiber of the text. The king was renowned for his insatiable libido. By the time he died, he had legally wed at least eighty-five women. To be bereft of female companionship for the duration of the trip was for him simply unthinkable. To take all (or even some) of his harem proved logistically impossible, religiously complicated, and politically embarrassing. Improvisation was necessary.

On one trip, he took Malijak along, a young boy with whom he had fallen in love. Throughout the three travelogues, the only time the language of the text becomes emotionally charged and resonates with human passion is when the king discusses this young beloved. During that same trip, he ordered his ambassador to the Ottoman court to dispatch to him a fourteen-year-old white slave girl. The scene of the arrival of the girl evokes a Shakespearean comedy of errors.

The king's description of the affair at the same time poignantly reveals his own disturbed sense of self. In this passage, we get a rare glimpse of this mutilated self-perception, as the pompous political persona he uses to hide a pitiable insecurity falls away. In describing the episode with the girl, he writes:

> I had asked for a girl from Istanbul. Last night when we were asleep, she arrived. Agha [the eunuch of the entourage] broke the good news of her arrival. We had ordered that her hair be cut so that she could look like a man.... When I saw her today, she smiled. From her laughter, I gathered that when they told the girl that we are taking you for the Persian King, she must have had strange ideas in her mind. She must have thought: What kind of a creature is this King of Persia? Does he have horns? In her mind, she conjured the image of a man with heavy, long pointed beard, with seven manes reaching the earth, a thick moustache curled around his head, a lanky jaundiced face, shining, bulging yellow eyes, big mouth, rotten teeth, with a couple of ugly canine teeth protruding, a foul-smelling mouth, long hat on his head, and so short-tempered that whomsoever he meets he slaps so hard that blood gushes from their nostrils.[21]

---

21. Nasir al-Din Shah, *Ruznameh-ye Khaterat*, p.206.

Aside from the fact that the image bears a frightening resemblance to actual pictures of the Shah's father and grandfather, the passage is particularly significant for what it reveals about the damaged identity the king harbors beneath the façade of royal hauteur. This ambivalence of identity is at the core of his problematic relationship with Western powers. Whereas xenophobic nationalists and religious fundamentalists harbor narcissistic illusions of ethnic or religious grandeur, some advocates of modernity foster a cult of self-denigration and illusory notions about the "perfect West."[22] To fashion a self free from both grandiosity and abasement is one of the most daunting tasks facing the once-colonized peoples of the world.

As despots are wont to do, Nasir al-Din Shah tried to turn necessity into virtue and to transform his constant preoccupation with women as sexual objects into a natural and positive quality. He claims in fact to have discovered the key to Europe's success: "I met the Foreign Secretary of Holland," he writes, and "It has become apparent to me that all these Westerners are whoremongers and lechers. The Foreign Secretary was constantly looking at women. The reason the Westerners are so powerful is that they are constantly in pursuit of pleasure."[23]

Delusive distortions are not of course the only revealing textual strategy employed by the monarch. Implicit in every text is an epistemic hierarchy that helps categorize certain facts as relevant and important, and thus a necessary part of the narrative, and dismisses others as irrelevant. A crucial element of this implicit taxonomy is the presumed boundaries between the realm of the public and the private. If we accept the notion that modernity transforms politics from the private arena monopolized by the elite to the public theater wherein the masses are the necessary and legitimate players, then Nasir al-Din Shah's narrative of "discovery" seems archaically traditional. Page after page of the text are given to descriptions of zoos and hunting trips, yet there is scant allusion to the political structure of Europe. He writes repeatedly of his desire "to buy" the beautiful women he meets. His crude flirtations with a Russian woman—whom he has to give up because he finds out she is a Jew[24]—is treated with far more fanfare and in far more detail than the famous London, Paris, and Moscow world exhibits he visits. Indeed, in writing about the exhibit in Moscow, he comments only on "the beautiful women visiting the exhibit," lamenting the fact that he "could not get his hands on any of them."[25]

---

22. For a more detailed discussion of this vision, see chapter nine of this book, "Shadman and Modernity."
23. *Ruznameh-ye Khaterat,* 286.
24. Ibid., 128.
25. Ibid., 162.

Every day's entry begins with a repetitious reference to the fact that His Majesty woke up, ate, and went out, but there is hardly any reference to the political discussions that took place throughout his trip. Nearly all references to such discussions are limited to the same curt refrain. "Some good discussions were held," he deigns to inform the reader. In all such cases, the implicit tone is one of disdain; it implies in no uncertain terms that politics is not the business of the public, and, by extension, of his readers.

While the king insists on preserving his privileged monopoly of politics, he accepts no responsibility for the consequences of his political decisions. In parts of the three narratives, he uses an eerily cool and distant language to describe the miseries he witnesses in the cities and villages of his own domain. With no sense of shame, remorse, or responsibility, he writes of emaciated, hungry faces, derelict buildings, and bad roads. In one instance, traveling through one of Iran's villages, he muses, "It is as if the Mongol hordes have ravaged the land."[26] The tone resembles that of an innocent tourist in a benighted land, not of its absolute monarch from a dynasty that had ruled Iran for nearly a century.

By the third trip, Nasir al-Din Shah was clearly disdainful of the political atmosphere of Europe. Describing a meeting with Bismarck and the Kaiser, he writes:

> I came down into the room and sat down. The Kaiser came too. We would sit, stand up, walk around, eat something, sit down again. The generals were also walking around. Some sat down. There was freedom. There stood one general, smoking, with his ass to the Emperor. Another was sitting yonder with his ass also to the Emperor. One of them had his ass toward me. In a word, there was freedom.[27]

Of course not all aspects of modernity were as disturbing to him as his strange concept of "freedom." His eclectic affinity with certain aspects of what he saw in Europe seems emblematic of many other "third world" leaders' piecemeal appropriation of modernity. Modernity's neverending fever for global expansion fit perfectly with Nasir al-Din Shah's insatiable personal greed. He was more then willing to auction off Iran's sovereignty for paltry personal gains. Indeed, during his reign, eighty-three concession treaties and economic pacts were signed with European powers. Of these, thirty-five were signed by the Shah before he had even looked at the details. As a recompense for his blind trust, he received payoffs from these European powers.

---

26. Ibid,. 70.
27. Ibid., 220.

After his first two trips, he engaged for a while in a frantic, often ludicrous search for gold in Iran. He also appreciated Europe's system of tax collection. With glee he writes about the system of income and property taxes he saw there, and adds "even animals are taxed separately."[28] He approved of the militarist air of Bismarck's Prussia. "There even children," he reports, "wear military uniforms and learn the habits of army life."[29] He relished the stores filled with commodities—and the enormously long list of his purchases is as impressive in size as in its depressing vulgarity. He also liked Western guns. But most of all, he liked modernity's system of social control.

During his first visit, he hired an Austrian count to establish a modern police force for Iran. The blueprint the count prepares, after becoming Tehran's chief of police, reads like pages from Foucault's *Discipline and Punish*.[30] The Count suggests a new regime of surveillance, the permanent registration of the population, standardization of weights, and crowd-control techniques. Every teahouse, the traditional hub of neighborhood life and political gossip, was to have a police detachment. The Shah immediately approved the blueprints and ordered their implementation. They heralded the dawn of a new age that combined the despotism of tyrannical authority with the presence of panoptic surveillance.

There is yet another gradual change evident in the progression of the three narratives. Between the first and third trips, a definite linguistic change creeps into the texts. When talking about Iran, the king uses increasingly hostile and disparaging adjectives and metaphors: Iran looks more arid, the faces of its people more vacuous, its cities more decrepit. On the other hand, descriptions of Europe are more ebullient. The metaphor of "paradise" is repeatedly invoked to describe a European garden or a forest. In fact, by the third trip, the word *Farangi*, the Persian word for the "Franks" or Europeans, had become for the king synonymous with higher and nobler qualities. For example, on the eve of his third trip, Tehran, the capital city, was festooned with flags and decorations. In praise of the city, Nasir al-Din Shah writes, "the streets had so much glamour that they hardly looked like Tehran. They looked like European cities. There was grandeur to them."[31]

The royal lexicon is also transformed in the course of his accounts of the three trips. In later writings, the king peppers his discourse with French words. Sometimes these words are by necessity used to refer to concepts

---

28. Nasir al-Din Shah, *Safar Name-ye Farangestan*, 190-191.
29. Nasir al-Din Shah, *Safar Name-ye Nasir al-Din Shah*, p, 75.
30. Michel Foucault, *Discipline and Punish: The Birth of the Prison*, trans. Alan Sheridan (New York, 1977), 190-202.

then still alien to the Persian language. Oftentimes, however, he seems to derive a sense of personal pride in his newfound linguistic prowess. His linguistic proclivity has all the characteristics of what Pratt calls "autoethnography," or more specifically "a partial collaboration with and appropriation of the idioms of the conqueror." Other accounts left by his courtiers support this perception. The king was wont to pretend more comprehension of foreign languages than was warranted by his abilities.

Colonial hegemony usually entails a sharp decline in the prestige of the native tongue, and a near-magical legitimization of the colonizing language. Furthermore, with the rise of science, the colonial languages—particularly French and English—become the lingua franca of cultural, artistic, and scientific exchange. Learning French and English thus becomes all but mandatory. This transformation in the relative importance of the native language is a key ingredient in the sense of undermined cultural sovereignty and damaged self-esteem so often found in colonized lands. The royal texts, too, reflect this transformation. The Shah becomes prouder and prouder of his newfound linguistic acumen. Like Shakespeare's Caliban, he has learned how to curse.

Sometimes metaphors of reality are more descriptively powerful than any theoretical construct. At the end of his first trip, in spite of his fear of the open seas, the Shah boards a ship on the Russian side of the Caspian Sea and heads home. If the sea can be mythically understood as a metaphor of change and utopia, then the Shah's fear of the sea poetically reflects his aversion to social change. Near the Iranian port, a storm sets in. He writes, "I descended from the deck. It was impossible to stand there. I went to my room, took off my clothes, and in melancholy, waited to see what Fate had in store for Us."[32] At the end of the second trip, once again near the same port, another storm threatens: "The horizons are bleak, winds are blowing, dark clouds appear. A storm seems imminent."[33] As Fate would have it, History, the Machiavellian Fortuna of modern times, had social revolution in store. The attempt to domesticate modernity proved ineffective. Not long after Nasir al-Din Shah survived those tempests at sea, political storms began to sweep the land.

31. Nasir al-Din Shah, *Ruznameh-ye Khaterat*, 18.
32. Nasir al-Din Shah, *Safar Name-ye Nasir al-Din Shah*, 250.
33. Nasir al-Din Shah, *Safar Name-ye Farangestan*, 257.

SHADMAN'S MODERNITY[*]
Integrating East and West

On a cold winter night, Seyyed Fakhr al-Din Shadman came to visit our house. I was ten years old. He was my mother's oldest brother, and in our house he was reverentially referred to as "Uncle Doctor." He and my mother sat near a Coleman wall-heater and began what soon became an animated conversation. My sister and I were playing in the next room. Occasionally we stole a glance in their direction.

Suddenly I heard my name called out. With fear and trepidation, I entered their room. As was the custom in our house, I kissed Uncle Doctor's proffered hand. His custom, in turn, was to receive such gestures with warmth and affection. He inquired about my school. In those days, I attended a small French private school named Madame Marica. It was one of Iran's few coeducational institutions. Our classes were conducted in French. For about an hour a day, we also studied the Persian language. My uncle asked me to fetch a copy of Sa'di's *Golestan*,[1] the ultimate masterpiece of Persian prose. He opened to its famous Preface and gently asked me to read it aloud. I read a few lines and made more than a few mistakes. I was nervous, and ashamed, and perspiring. He consoled me and reprimanded my mother. "It is a shame," he said, "that the son of a Iranian family would be more comfortable in French than in Persian." It took me twenty years to discover that in that gloomy winter encounter, one could find the contours of Shadman's intellectual odyssey.

In the long, tortured debate on modernity in Iran, his was a voice of uncommon erudition and prudence. Yet, in the pantheon of Iranian intellectuals, he has hitherto been relegated to a relatively obscure corner. He is an intellectual's intellectual, a man of little fame, but of sterling

---

*In memory of my mother, Zinat Shadman Milani.

1. For a discussion of the first chapter of *Golestan*, see the previous essay in this book, "Sa'di and the Kings."

reputation among his peers. He belonged to that generation of Iranians for whom culture and erudition did not necessitate a categorical disdain for all pragmatic politics. And his intellectual reputation clearly suffered because of his politics. He was a member of the "Coup Cabinet" that came to power immediately after the overthrow of the Mossadegh regime in August of 1953. And in modern Iran, the vagaries of politics have always cast a dark shadow on intellectual discourse. Shadman's acceptance of several ministerial portfolios in the Shah's regime was enough for some to seek his banishment from the republic of letters.

When he died in 1967, the opposition intellectuals kept silent, while many in the scholarly community praised his legacy in lavish terms. Iraj Afshar, a much-acclaimed editor and bibliophile, called Shadman "a scholar of much erudition, a writer of great power."[2] Habib Yaghmai, the renowned editor of a prominent literary journal, was even more unequivocal. "Iran," he wrote, "has lost one of its most outstanding and most noble children. In our day and age, finding someone else of Shadman's caliber is hard to imagine."[3] In the four decades since his death, almost nothing has been written about him and his views.[4] My purpose here is to try and fill part of this lacuna. I hope to discuss his views on modernity and Iran's relationship with the West.

Modern intellectual discourse on modernity in Iran has suffered from a kind of Manichean disposition. Some have been advocates of "de-modernization" and cultural isolation; others have suggested a self-loathing, submissive assimilation of Western culture. The two extreme positions have often emerged as the only two poles of this debate. Shadman proposed a new paradigm by offering a more subtle and sophisticated reading of modernity and Iran's tradition—in short, a new approach to Iran's encounter with the West, which he referred to as "*Farang*."[5]

Shadman was born in 1907, to a moderately prosperous family. His father was a cleric, his mother an enlightened woman, well versed in Persian classics and the Qur'an. Fakhr al-Din began his studies at one of Tehran's theological schools and received the kind of classical education

---

2. Iraj Afshar, "Seyyed Fakhr al-din Shadman," in *Savad-o Bayaz* [The rough and the final draft], vol. 2 (Tehran, 1349/1970), 539.

3. Habib Yaghmai, "Doctor Seyyed Fakhr al-din Shadman," *Yaghma*, no. 5 (5 Mordad 1346/1967,): 280.

4. One of the first attempts to analyze the entirety of Shadman's writings appeared first in a Ph.D. dissertation by Mehrzad Boroujerdi. See "Orientalism in Reverse: Iranian Intellectuals and the West"(Ph.D. diss. American University, 1990), 130-140. It was subsequently published as *Iranian Intellectuals and the West: the Tormented Triumph of Nativism* (Syracuse, 1996]

5. The term *Farang* was first coined during the Crusades, and thus something of a negative aura has always surrounded it. But in Shadman's hand, the word took on myriad meanings and new possibilities.

that was the staple of such institutions. He mastered Arabic, and Islamic jurisprudence. His passion for learning soon earned him a reputation as a young man of unusual erudition. Eventually, he enrolled at Dar al-Fonun, the first institution of modern learning in Iran, where he could more easily satisfy his passion for Persian letters and Western ideas. While there, he edited a journal called *Tufan Haftegi* ("Weekly Storm").[6]

After Dar al-Fonun, Shadman set out for Europe. In 1939, he received a doctorate in law from the Sorbonne. Four years later, he completed a second doctorate, this time in political science, from the London School of Economics. While in London, he married Farangis Namazi, a woman of high culture and the Persian translator of Shakespeare's *Macbeth* and Gibbon's *Decline and Fall of the Roman Empire*. In the same period, he helped create the Iran Society, where lectures and seminars on Iranian culture and history were organized. Such luminaries as Basil Grey, Sir Denis Wright and the now-famous translator of Rumi, Reynold Nicholson, were active members of the society.[7]

For a few years in Europe and America, and for many years in Iran, Shadman taught in various universities. He also held many important political positions, including ministerial posts in several cabinets. The most politically consequential of these appointments was his decision to join General Zahedi's cabinet in August of 1953. Zahedi came to power by overthrowing Mossadegh and thus his opponents disparagingly called his government the "Coup Cabinet." Shadman was named the Minister of National Economy. Late in 1955, he was given by the Shah the task of managing the vast endowments attached to the shrine of Imam Reza, the only Shiite Imam buried in Iran, and for centuries the recipient of the largess of the devout. Shadman abruptly resigned in 1959. The reasons for his resignation remain something of a mystery. Family gossip, naturally bent on lionizing him, said his action was a defiant gesture against the Shah, who was by tradition the chief trustee of Imam Reza's endowment. Every year, the Shah received some money as a fee for this titular role. The sum was not small. In 1975, for example, it was more than two million dollars. Shadman had argued that fiscal difficulties made it impossible for him to pay the fees in 1959, and the Shah was not happy. It was rumored that Shadman, in defiance, submitted his resignation not

---

6. A few years before his death, Shadman provided an Iranian journal a brief biographical sketch of his own life. See, "Dr. Seyyed Fakhr al-Din Shadman," *Rahnameh-ye Ketab*, no. 1. (Farvardin 1341/1962), 96-100.

7. Last year, Sir Denis Wright prepared a commemorative history of the Iran Society and kindly gave me a copy to read. It is, as far as I know, the most complete account of the history of the society and its activities.

to the Shah but to Ayatollah Boroujerdi, the Shiites' top cleric at the time. Whatever the real reason for his departure, managing the endowment proved to be Shadman's last political appointment. He spent the few remaining years of his life writing and teaching at Tehran University. He began to work on a treatise on the nature of politics in Iran. Only a small part of the manuscript was ever published, and it revealed his increasingly critical disposition toward the Shah and his regime. Shadman's research and writing came to a sudden halt when a metastasized cancer began to weaken him. Even doctors in his beloved England could not save his life. He died in 1967.

Shadman was a novelist, an essayist, a thinker and a translator. His most important work of translation was *The History of the Modern World* by Albert Malle and Jule Isak. He published three novels, widely different and uneven in terms of their formal structures and thematic cohesion. The longest, called *Darkness and Light*, was also his most widely read book. It was first serialized in one of Tehran's two semi-official dailies. His two other novels, *On the Road to India* and *The Nameless Book*[8] are more enigmatic in terms of their form and content. His most important essays were collected in two volumes, called respectively *Conquering Farangi Civilization* and *The Tragedy of Farang*.[9] He also published numerous letters and commentaries in Iranian and European journals.

If we accept Steiner's notion that to "read is to compare," and that the core of any hermeneutic exercise is "linguistic critical comparison," then Shadman was surely a competent reader. He rejoiced in his Persian heritage. He was, by critical acclaim, one of the masters of modern Persian prose. He was also at home in English, French and Arabic. Echoes of Hafez and Shakespeare, Browning and Sa'di, Homer and Ferdowsi are heard equally in his narrative. He was a rare Persian embodiment of the Goethean ideal of "world literature," one who "seeks to articulate ideas, attitudes of sensibility which belong to universalizing civilities of…Enlightenment."[10] Indeed, in the Iranian debate about the West and modernity, few Persians could match Shadman's privileged position of a considerable knowledge of both Western and Persian culture and literature.

---

8. For Shadman's books, see *Tariki va Roshanai* [Darkness and light] (Tehran, 1346/1965); *Ketab-e Bi Nam* [The nameless book] (Tehran, 1307/1926); *Dar Rah-e Hend* [On the road to India] (Tehran, 1335/1956). None of these books are available in English.

9. See *Taskhir-e Tamadon-e Farang* [Conquering Farangi civilization] (Tehran, 1326/1947); *Teragedi-ye Farang* [The tragedy of Farang] (Tehran, 1346/1967). It is a measure of renewed interest in Shadman's work that his *Conquering Farangi Civilization* was just republished in Iran (Tehran, 2003). I wrote a lengthy introduction to the volume and tried to place Shadman's works in a larger historical context.

10. George Steiner, *No Passion Spent: Essays, 1978-1995* (New York, 1998), 148. All quotations in the paragraph come from this source.

Beneath the formal diversity of his opus, one can discern a few thematic unities, some common threads that weave out of the diverse fragments a finely knit tapestry. The first book he wrote after his return from Europe, as well as his last book, are both about modernity. When an editor of a scholarly journal asked Shadman which of his own works he liked the best, he answered, "Of all I have written in Persian, I am most attached to the subject of the conquest of the *Farangi* civilization; I find the subject to be the most important topic in Iran today."[11]

Even his most enigmatic novel, *The Nameless Book*, published just before his sojourn to Europe, deals with the question of modernity and the crisis of identity it invariably entails. In the dreamy cosmos of the novel—reminiscent of *A Thousand and One Nights*—heroes and heroines seek to find, or fashion, an identity congruent with the new realities of the world. Ultimately, they recognize that the key to their salvation can only be found atop Mount Damavand. Damavand is, as any cursory reading of Iranian literature will indicate, the Mount Olympus of Iranian mythology. In other words, in fashioning a new self, Iranians must not, according to Shadman, relinquish their past. Only out of the solid earth of Iran's myths, history and culture can a new identity, at once rooted and dynamic, be nurtured. Just as the West recaptured its Greco-Roman heritage in the Renaissance, an Iranian Renaissance must begin by reclaiming the Persian past. It cannot, as some advocates of modernity had suggested, accomplish this through passive emulation of the European experience.

The second common characteristic of Shadman's opus is its rich and illuminating intertextuality. In a trope reminiscent of Cervantes' *Don Quixote*, and presaging the postmodern gesture of conflating the fictive and authorial personas, passages from Shadman's essays end up in his fiction. Other times, a hint of a question in a novel foreshadows a rigorous treatment of the same issue in an essay. There is a common subjectivity, a dominant theme, that permeates his oeuvre; it is that of a concerned Iranian intellectual using the tools of fiction and essay to disentangle the Gordian knot of cultural, epistemological, economical and religious changes that are together known as modernity.

Yet another common characteristic of Shadman's writing is the power, economy and beauty of his prose. In his writing he had a particular affinity for poetry. Few are his essays, even novels, in which poetry does not figure prominently. In his opinion, "Persian poetry embodies the height

---

11. Seyyed Fakhr al-Din Shadman, "*Kodam Asar-e Khod-ra Bishtar Mipasandid?*" [Which of your works do you like the most?] *Rahnameh-e Ketab*, no. 2 (Ordibehesht 1340/1961): 305.

of human wisdom and beauty." As one of the few who could make an informed comparison, he asserts "The world's best poetry is in Persian." It was, he proclaimed, part of his own *raison d'etre*. "I want to live longer," he wrote, "so I can read more Persian poetry. Persian is the world language of poetry."[12]

More than a simple aesthete's meticulous care was behind Shadman's love of Persian poetry and the clarity and rigor of his prose. His views on Persian language were in fact at the heart of his vision of modernity.

Recurrent images in his novels and repeated theoretical constructs in his essays both point to his view that Iran has been, for more than a century, in the throes of a serious crisis. The country has seen many calamities in her long history, he wrote, but the nature of the current crisis makes it "unprecedented in Iran's history." In stark terms, Shadman warned his countrymen, "Do not take the Farangi civilization too lightly...Farangi is not like the barefooted desert Bedouins or the blood-thirsty drunken Mongols."[13]

The essence of the crisis is cognitive and psychic confusion, and it cuts to the core of what it means to be a Persian. Its genealogy can be traced back to Iran's humiliating defeat at the hands of the Russians in the middle of the nineteenth century. "Until 150 years ago we, as a nation, had a mind of our own. Sometimes we were intellectually weak, sometimes strong, but always independent."[14] As a result of that debilitating defeat, "anxiety and despair permeated our soul. The independence of our mind began to falter in a way unprecedented in the country's two thousand five hundred year history."[15] All of the travails of the past, he warned, pale in comparison with the potential dangers of this new challenge: The identity of the nation is at stake.

Taking his cue from Herodotus, he noted that the current Persian crisis mirrors another moment of singular significance in human history, more than two thousand years earlier. Shadman wrote, "The history of Europe began with the wars between Greeks and Persians. The European identity appeared only after Greece stood up to the forces of Persian kings and safeguarded its own independence. Two thousand years later,

---

12. Jalal Matini prepared an anthology of the finest examples of Persian prose in modern times; a couple of pieces by Shadman where he waxes poetic about Persian poetry are included in the anthology. *Nemouneha-ye Nasr-e Fasih-e Farsi-ye Moaser* [Anthology of lucid modern Persian prose], vol. 2 (Tehran, 1357/1978), 104.

13. Shadman, *Taskhir-e Tamadon-e Farang* [Conquering Farangi civilization], 35.

14. Shadman, *Teragedi-ye Farang* [The tragedy of Farang], 193.

15. Ibid., 193.

this time, the survival—not the appearance—of Iranian identity depends on the country's victory in its encounter with Europe."[16]

Images of this crisis are the leitmotif of Shadman's two collections of essays, and of his novels. *Darkness and Light* is a case in point. The novel's title itself is an allusion to transition, to a liminal twilight stCate between the night of tradition and the dawn of the Age of Enlightenment. The opening lines of the novel are bristling with allusions to the transition of traditional, theocentric, feudal Iran into the secular world of modernity: "Tonight too there is only one light in the chancel (*shabestan*) of the mosque (*masjid*); a dim light barely capable of conquering the engulfing darkness. In its flight from light, darkness is trembling and pale, and the light cannot last until dawn. Half way through the night, it dies away."[17]

The Persian word for the chancel is *shabestan*, and its root word, *shab*, is Persian for "night." The language in the opening lines clearly implies that religion is ill-equipped to cope with the demands of this transition. We read about the "naked *manbar*," or pulpit, and how its top is "hidden beneath a cloud of darkness."

The crisis has also cast a shadow on the house of Mahmoud, the hero of the novel, whose life decidedly resembles that of Shadman himself. The house had been once "the place where Tehran's most beautiful flowers grew. It is now bereft of vitality. The flowerbeds of yesterday are now covered with weeds, and the leaves of its green hedges are covered with dust."[18] Even the cheap decoration in the sitting room is a portent of the impending crisis: "The canvas hangs over the fireplace," and on it, "the moon is shining just enough to show the frightened faces of shipwrecked passengers."[19]

Iranians, now "shipwrecked" in their tormented encounter with modernity and the West, have never been as despondent as today, according to Shadman. The encounter, he tells the reader, began in the sixteenth century, during the reign of the Safavid dynasty in Iran. But at the height of Safavid power, in the mid-sixteenth century, Iranians felt anything but shipwrecked. In the game of politics, and in the dialectics of cultural hegemony, they saw themselves as equals to the Farangi "other," and they demanded respect. Shah Abbas (1587-1627) was, in Shadman's opinion, the last scion of this soon-to-vanish Persian sense of pride, power and independence. Shadman quotes at some length from a letter the Shah

---

16. Ibid., 109.
17. Shadman, *Tariki va Roshanai* [Darkness and light], 16.
18. Ibid., 19.
19. Ibid., 20.

sent to one of his governors: "The Portuguese Farangis have now truly transgressed their limits, and begun to mistreat the functionaries of our state…. It has become necessary to eradicate these miscreants…so that the roots of the calamity might dry and die."[20]

But Shah Abbas, whose reign more or less corresponds to that of Elizabeth I in England, died "precisely at the moment when Europe was awakening from its thousand year slumber." It was the time, according to Shadman, when "the Renaissance, this phantasm of European light, with all its passion, pathos, and rationalism" began.[21] But as Europe was awakening, Iran was beginning to fall asleep. The narrator of *On the Road to India* asks, in a lamenting tone, "God knows what shall befall Iran after the death of Abbas!"[22] Apparently even the Shah himself, in the waning moments of his life, was tormented by the same historical angst: "The Shah closes his eyes. In the heart of darkness, he sees a stormy sea, and a ship, battered by soaring waves, about to be devoured. And in the midst of this darkness, the only dim source of light came from a small blinking star, and it too is about to be consumed by dark clouds."[23]

While the Renaissance placed Europe on the path to progress, Iran was thrown into two hundred years of civil war and social strife. Soon after Shah Abbas' death, Iran's sense of political and economic power, and concomitant self-esteem, began to vanish. In its place emerged a new insular and grandiose vision, one that deluded itself with false pride in either Iran's or Islam's past glory. This "vision" was also dangerously ignorant of all that was unfolding in the rest of the world. Mohammed Reza Beyk, Shah Sultan Hossein's emissary to the court of Louis XIV—and probably the historical source of Montesquieu's "Persian Letters"—embodied this sense of ignorant arrogance. In a narrative full of sarcasm, Shadman writes of Reza Beyk's "deep affinity for personal protocol. He never traveled without the pomp and ceremony of his personal guards. He showed respect to no one, and disdained everyone he met. He talked incessantly about the grandeur of the Iranian monarch, and of himself." While in Paris, "He had no curiosity to see the world. Instead he spent nearly all of this time in a room, reading the Qur'an and smoking his hooka."[24]

20. Shadman, *Dar Rah-e Hend* [On the Road to India], 11.

21. Matini, *Nemouneha-ye Nasr-e Fasih,*102.

22. *Dar Rah-e Hend,* 16

23. Ibid., 23

24. Accounts of Ayatollah Khomeini's life in Paris in 1979 are eerily similar to those of Reza Beyk's. There was of course one big difference: Ayatollah Khomeini was no fan of the hooka. For Shadman's account of the emissary's life in Europe, see "Sefarat-e *Mohammad Reza Beyk be Darbar-e Loui-ye Chahardahom*" [Mohammed Reza Beyk's embassy in the court of Louis XIV], *Mehr*, no. 4 (1312/1923): 291-292. As Shadman makes clear, his essay is in fact a synopsis of a French book he had read on the subject.

Mohammed Reza Beyk was not the only figure whose fixation on an imaginary past endangered Iran's real future. Dogmatic Islam was another serious obstacle to Iran's encounter with modernity. Shadman's views on religion and its relationship to modernity are an important part of his rather unique vision. He was a devout Muslim who had studied the history and practice of Shiism. Contrary to many Iranian advocates of modernity, he saw no irreconcilable contradiction between religion and modernity. The problem was not with religion per se but with its misinterpretation. Shadman had harsh words for "faithless mullahs…who misconstrue the words of the prophet,"[25] and are incessantly obsessed with lechery and monetary gains. He chastises them for their failure to bring innovation to their learning and curriculum, and for their obsessive reading and rereading of the same few texts.

In the nineteenth century, something more dangerous than this kind of ignorant pride emerged on Iran's cultural horizon. In apocalyptic terms, Shadman warns, "If the scourge survives, there will be nothing left of Iran." The embodiment of this scourge was described with his famous neologism, the *fokoli,* or literally, "the man with the bow tie."[26] If in Europe, the advent of modernity brought with it what Walter Benjamin calls the "flaneur,"[27] in Iran the new skewed modernity and its incumbent urbanity produced the fokoli.

For Shadman, the fokoli is Iran's mortal enemy. He is "that shameless half-tongued Iranian who knows little of a *farangi* language and even less of Persian, and claims he can describe for us, in a language he knows not, the farangi culture of which he is ignorant."[28] He is that dim-witted man who naively believes "all of Iran's problems will be solved if the Latin alphabet replaces Persian letters."[29] There is indeed much that makes this fokoli a kin of the colonized character so poignantly described by Franz Fanon in his *Wretched of the Earth.*[30] In both his

25. Shadman, *Taskhir-e Tamadon-e Farang* [Conquering Farangi civilization], 156.

26. Ibid. 4.

27. *Flaneur*, in Benjamin, is an urban wanderer, curious about the city, but unattached to it, idle yet in constant movement, a detective of infinite empathy for the subjects of his search and a romantic for whom the skyline of the city has replaced the natural landscape. See Walter Benjamin, *The Arcade Project*, trans. Howard Eiland and Kevin McLaughlin (Cambridge, 1999), 416-454.

28. *Taskhir-e Tamadon-e Farang*, 13.

29. Ibid., 41.

30. According to Fanon, colonialism is most dangerous, and successful, when it has convinced the colonized of their own inferiority. Gradually a damaged sense of the self, coupled with an exaggerated sense of the power of the colonizing "other" is internalized. This humiliated but internalized sense of self spells the moment of defeat for the colonized. Only through a radical psychological and political revolution can the syndrome be defeated and a new identity, free from both maladies of self-deprecation and over-infatuation with the colonialists, be fashioned. Such a new identity is the first necessary step toward genuine liberation.

novels and essays, Shadman offers a whole litany of criticism against the
fokoli. Like one of the central characters in *Darkness and Light,* a fokoli
is "an exhibitionist...who knows nothing of Iran, and whose knowledge
of Farang is limited to a few highfalutin words, impressive only to a
fool."[31] He is a fierce advocate of the "improvement" of the Persian language and its alphabet, "and what he understands by 'improvement' is
that his own altogether confused and error-ridden written and oral cre-
ations should replace the works of canonical authors of the Persian
language like Hafez and Ferdowsi."[32]

According to Shadman, unless the dangerous dilettantism of the fokol
is exposed, Iran as we know it will soon wither away. Yet in modern Iran,
the fokolis have been ensconced in power. In a critical tone more reminiscent of the radical rhetoric of the sixties than that of a Pahlavi minister,
he writes, "Our leaders are ignorant and nourish ignoramuses. They have
neither a Persian nor a farangi culture." He even claims that "for forty to
fifty years now the shortsighted leaders of the country have lied to the
people and gone out of their way to sell to the people pseudo-reform as
real change."[33] Readers are of course left to wonder why Shadman himself joined such a ruling elite. Never in his published writings does he
offer any explanation for his own involvement with the Pahlavi regime.

Fokoli advocates of a secular vision are not the only nemesis of genuine modernity in Iran. Shadman also warns of the emergence of a clerical
type of fokoli, no less superficial, and no less dangerous than its secular
counterpart. He is that "well-dressed cleric," with a handsome turban
and a finely trimmed beard, "who knows a few words of Persian and
Arabic and has read some thirty or forty books of some small-minded
but prolific Egyptian or Syrian writer, and has with great effort memo-
rized a couple of hundred philosophic and scientific words, themselves
lame translations of farangi terms, and augments it all with a few mis-
pronounced farangi expressions, and then with the kind of audacity one
can only find in Shia seminarians, he pontificates about every question
under the sun."[34] In retrospect, Shadman's pronouncements about this
type of "modern" clergy are prophetic; the political landscape of the
Islamic republic has, in recent years, become strewn with this kind of
pseudo-intellectual clergy.

---

31. Shadman, *Tariki va Roshanai* [Darkness and light], 192.
32. Ibid., 194.
33. Shadman, "Siyasatnameh-ye Iran" [Treatise on politics in Iran], *Khandaniha*, 26 (Tir
    1344/1965).
34. Shadman, *Taskhir-e Tamadon-e Farang*, 17.

The most fatal intellectual flaw of the fokoli, according to Shadman, is the belief that one can conquer the West, and modernity, without first learning about Iran. "In our odyssey toward conquering the farangi culture, the first stop is Iran, not Europe."[35] In this respect, fokolis are not the only culprits. Shadman castigates the Iranian masses for having limited their perception of the "Farangi civilization" to mere shadows. At the same time, they have failed to "master the Persian language and culture." Bereft of organic ties to their own tradition, they remain ignorant of the essence of Western civilization and modernity. On more than one occasion, he warns of the global nature of Western modernity, and asserts that its advent is inevitable. "The torrent of Farangi civilization will no doubt consume everyone," he proclaims, "It is best to learn about it and thus not allow it to take all you have."[36]

Only a special breed of intellectual can help Iran successfully navigate her way through this inevitable labyrinth. What is required in this encounter are Persians "whose spirit and intellect are filled with all the two thousand five hundred years' glory of Iran," and who have "mastered" the Persian language.[37] At the same time, they must also have mastered the culture of the West. Only such intellectuals are inured against the false temptations of the West, and equipped to help Iran take from modernity only those aspects that are desirable.

In the same spirit that Shadman considered the fokolis the Trojan horses of cultural enslavement in Iran, he believed that intellectuals like Foroughi, Iran's Prime Minister during the early days of World War II, and Ghazvini, a scholar of impressive erudition, could be harbingers of genuine Persian modernity. In *Darkness and Light*, there is a character of much charisma and erudition called Mirza Abolfazl Kermani. The contours of his life bear an unmistakable resemblance to Ghazvini's. In the novel, the narrator suggests that we must, by dictates of reason, encompass only gradually aspects of the new civilization into our culture, and that people like Mirza Abolfazl, who "have not estranged themselves from their own culture and know well enough the accomplishments of the Farangi civilization,"[38] can guide this process of gradual and selective adaptation.

But if we are to believe Shadman, mendacity and mediocrity have had the upper hand in Iranian politics, and consequently fokolis have usurped all levels of political and cultural power. A crisis of identity has

---

35. Ibid., p 104.
36. Shadman, *Tariki va Roshanai*, 410.
37. Shadman, *Taskhir-e Tamadon-e Farang*, 102.
38. *Tariki va Roshanai*, 564.

begun, and as is often the case, language is the best measure of it. In fact, as the result of the crisis, the Persian language is itself undergoing a profound change, and faces serious challenges.

As Shadman emphasizes, in the realm of language, Iran's experience is drastically different from that of the West. In Europe, the advent of modernity brought with it the emergence of national languages. Shakespeare and Chaucer helped establish English as the national language of what Anderson calls the newly emerging "imagined communities."[39] In Germany, Luther translated the Bible into German, and helped consolidate a new national language. The experience of Spain, too, points to an intricate relationship between the development of nationalism, modernity, and the vibrant birth of a national language.

The Iranian experience, however, was different. Long before the arrival of modernity in the West, Iranians identified themselves as a nation, and Persian was the dominant language of this long-fermenting sense of national identity. Nineteenth-century encounters with modernity and with the all-powerful West caused a crisis of identity, and as expected, the crisis soon manifested itself in language. A central theme of Shadman's writing was articulating the linguistic symptoms of this crisis and advocating ways of fighting it.

For Shadman, the Persian language is "the most important tool in any attempt to conquer the Farangi civilization."[40] It is the cement of an autonomous and self-assured identity. As he never tired of repeating, "Learning Persian is the first condition for our future progress."[41] Implied in his many forays into the field of linguistics was the notion—now accepted by most linguists—that language is not merely a tool of thought, but an essential component of it. A competent mind and a competent language are two sides of the same coin. Shadman often warned that mastering modernity is indeed "an intricate task and demands clear and precise thinking" and without "a clear and articulate" language, such progress is impossible to achieve.[42]

The development of such a language has, in his opinion, two foes—the "half-tongued" fokolis on one side and Islamic seminaries, or *madrasas* on the other. In Iran, traditionally, the dominant discourse on modernity has seen madrasas as bastions of reactionary Scholasticism. Shadman viewed these schools differently. On the one hand, he praised them as "Iran's oldest and first universities." In a thinly veiled allusion to the

39. Anderson, *Imagined Communities* (New York, 1991).
40. Shadman, *Taskhir-e Tamadon-e Farang, alef.*
41. Ibid., 70.
42. Ibid., *alef.*

dominant secular vision in Iran, he admonishes those "simple-minded ignoramuses" who saw such schools only as "training centers for *faghihs*," or "clerics," forgetting that Iran's "philosophers and physicians, astronomers and scholars, scribes and exegetes" were all trained in these schools.[43] At the same time, Shadman writes that most clerics in these schools seem to have forgotten that Persian, and not Arabic, is their native tongue. "And if they know this," he asks, "why don't they write their books in Persian?"[44]

Contrary to the opinion of nationalist zealots like Zabih Behruz, who waxed hyperbolically eloquent about the perfection of the Persian language, or Ahmad Kasravi, who championed the cause of linguistic purity, Shadman was no purist, nor was his praise of Persian exaggerated. He commended the poetic legacy of the Persian language, and posited that "a rich heritage of fictional narrative"[45] also exists in Persian. At the same time, he recognized that modernity would create and require changes in Persian language. "The best poetry in the world," he claimed, "is in our language, but we have never had a complete scientific language.... Our Persian is ill-equipped to convey scientific concepts and today, as we encounter different Western sciences and technologies, we must seek a solution."[46] He was, by temperament, against radical solutions and warned against them in the field of language as well. There is a need, he believed, for the creation of new words in the Persian language. At the same time, he was against the attempt, by Farhangestan—the Persian equivalent of the Academie Française—to rid Persian of all foreign words. He warned against futile attempts at linguistic social engineering. "In coining new words," he wrote, "We must make sure to continue following the path of Avicenna and Ferdowsi."[47] The sharp edge of his criticism in this area was directed toward the kind of fokolis who had been—and who continue to be even today—on a binge of coining neologisms. As later linguists have shown, of the more than thirty-five thousand words coined in the first few decades of Farangestan, only a few hundred have actually entered the vernacular.

An autonomous language, capable of conveying new ideas and old sentiments, connected to the cultural heritage of the country and capable of navigating in the waters of modern scientific narrative is, according

---

43. Shadman, *Teragedi-ye Farang* [The tragedy of Farang], 63.
44. Ibid., 87.
45. Ibid.
46. Seyyed Fakhr al-Din Shadman, "*Zaban Farsi Che Rahi ra Bayad Baraye Bayan-e Andisheha va Mafahim Tazeh Bargozinad*" [What should the Persian language do in order to express new ideas and concepts?], *Rahnameh-ye Ketab*, no 2 (Ordibehesht 1340/1961): 99.
47. Ibid.

to Shadman, a precondition of not only an autonomous identity but of a vibrant intellectual tradition. "Language…is the twin and symbol of thought."[48] Only with the help of a critical faculty, itself dependent on a subtle and supple language, can we come to know both Iran and the West, and appraise the positive and negative aspects of modernity.

For this critical faculty, curiosity is a prerequisite. In his magisterial study of modernity, Blumenberg has called "intellectual curiosity" a pillar of the modern sensibility.[49] Long before Blumenberg, Shadman, too, argued along similar lines. He called this kind of curiosity "the will to search," and defined it as "one of the most sublime of human qualities… a bewildering unity of opposites, at once in search of adventure and stability, with a keen and accepting eye for new ideas and new surroundings…a will to discover and invent and know the qualities of every atom of the universe and a will to uncover the secrets of the earth… Humans continue to search because they know their knowledge is incomplete and inadequate…. The will to search is the essence of humanity. It is the will to discover the covert and overt relationships that exist between humans and the world, between the realm of nature and that of metaphysics."[50] For Shadman, Mahmoud, the hero of the novel *Darkness and Light*, embodies this will to search. Fokolis, on the other hand, are altogether bereft of it. In them, the blind and pretentious desire to mimic the West has replaced the "will to search."

Skepticism is, according to Shadman, another necessary component of the kind of rationalism Iran needs to survive its encounter with modernity. Following in the footsteps of Descartes—who advocated doubting everything except doubt itself—Shadman was an avid proponent of skepticism. In a language that echoes the first lines of Descartes' *Discourse on Method*, Shadman writes, "For people of learning, no idea or theory is acceptable before its validity has been proven." He claims that, "Doubt was one of the reasons for the progress of the West. Farangi scientists began to doubt the movement of the sun around a stable earth…. They questioned the ideas of Socrates and Aristotle and thus enhanced the realms of science and philosophy. They questioned the right of kings to absolute power, and began to doubt the idea of divine right, and thus helped create the almost just and nearly faultless democratic system."[51]

48. Shadman, *Teragedi-ye Farang*, 198.
49. Hans Blumenberg, *The Legitimacy of the Modern Age*, trans M. Wallace (Cambridge, 1988). In his study of modernity, Blumenberg writes of this new kind of theoretical curiosity as the kernel of the modern attitude.
50. Shadman wrote an article on this question in *Teragedi-ye Farang*. In particular see pages 130 and 140.
51. Shadman, *Taskhir-e Tamadon-e Farang*, 47.

Such doubt clearly engenders and demands a new kind of religious belief, and some of Shadman's most innovative ideas belong to this sphere. He is acutely aware of the complicated relationship between modernity and religion. Contrary to many of the more radical advocates of modernity—in Iran and in the West—he is not a foe of religion as an institution. Instead, dogmatism and religious obscurantism are his bane. On the one hand, he advocates a rational and secular public and political domain. On the other hand, he believes humans to be, by nature, religious. For him religion is a necessary moral anchor for society; but its role should be limited to the private sphere. No sooner does it enter the arena of politics and policy than it becomes a blueprint for disaster and despotism. In unequivocal terms, Shadman claims, "Humans are forever caught in spiritual and physical quandaries and thus can never be free from the need to believe in a religion. Instead of the quixotic attempt to eliminate it, we must," Shadman suggests, "try to make religion, this constant companion of human sentiments, a tool of happiness and of the commonwealth."[52]

While critical of the obscurantism of many religious leaders, Shadman never considers Islam itself the cause of Iran's backwardness. Nor does he believe Christianity to have been the reason for Europe's successes. Dogmatism is the enemy of progress and it is not a unique quality of the Oriental mind. Shadman wrote of the days when, "in terms of science and philosophy, and absence of dogmatism, the Islamic civilization was far more advanced than the Christian."[53]

Shadman is clearly part of a tradition of thinkers, both religious and lay, who have long advocated the necessity of an Islamic Reformation. Clerics, in his view, must "become aware of new scientific and literary discoveries." He asks why Islamic madrasas, once bastions of science, "Pay no heed to modern sciences." Referring to those theological schools, he laments the fact "That our erstwhile universities have closed their doors to new discoveries."[54]

For Shadman, the progress of the West was the direct result of a new conception of politics, and had nothing to do with the nature of religious beliefs. He suggests that Iranian advocates of modernity must change tactics and vision. Instead of obsessively trying to undermine Islam, they must try to foster a new concept of politics. The ultimate focus of change must be the Iranian masses. Shadman is an advocate of

---

52. Shadmand, *Tariki va Roshanai*, 82.
53. Ibid., 158. In a lengthy section of the novel, Shadman offers a fascinating look at the progress made by Muslims during their early conquest of Spain and of Andalusia.
54. Shadman, *Teragedi-ye Farang*, 72.

structural cultural change and a critic of the concept of messianism that has been, in his opinion, an essential component of Iranian history. Waiting for the messiah has been one of the chief causes of Iran's backwardness. He asks, "How long should we wait for others to bring us into salvation? Why should a descendant of Avicenna be so simple-minded as to assume that a Dane, Dutch, American or Swiss citizen will come to Iran and build it for us?"[55]

Even in the technological sphere, Shadman advocates the idea that Iran can only be saved by Iranians. He writes of his days as the Minister of National Economy, when he "decided to establish a college of petroleum engineering…. The school was opened. A thousand candidates signed up…. I wanted Iran to become independent of foreign experts."[56] To achieve such technological autonomy, and indeed to foster modernity, Iran, according to Shadman, needs to embrace three principles. First and foremost is the idea and practice of freedom. "Europe's biggest discovery," he writes, "is freedom, and the continent's most sublime and sophisticated invention was the creation of a system that safeguards freedom and ensures that everyone enjoys the fruits of freedom and liberty and that this freedom does not become a license to trample on the rights of others."[57] Profuse in his praise of liberty, Shadman was no less unrelenting in pointing to the obstacles on the road to freedom in modern Iran. He warned that we must resurrect "the now half-dead" and "long-forsaken" ideals of a constitutional government.[58]

The second main tenet of modernity is, according to Shadman, the rule of law. Liberty is, in his view, coterminous with the rule of law. Lest this praise be construed as some kind of approbation for religious laws, he insists that, "Every astute observer knows that not every law is respectable, not every principle laid out by the law is useful. Only those laws founded upon rational principles can be deemed appropriate."[59]

From arguments about the virtues of the rule of the law, Shadman arrives at the principle of the necessity and legitimacy of a constitutional government. In the West, the advent of modernity changed the contours of political philosophy. "Statecraft" took the place of "soulcraft." In other words, beginning with Machiavelli, philosophers wrote not about how to create the perfect system, but instead about the workings of power, and the dialectics of civil society. Machiavelli did not seek a

---

55. Shadman, *Taskhir-e Tamadon-e Farang*, 96.
56. Shadman, "Dr. Seyyed Fakhr al-Din Shadman," *Rahnameh-ye Ketab* (1341/1962): 98.
57. *Taskhir-e Tamadon-e Farang*, 96.
58. Ibid., 164.
59. Ibid., 149.

utopia but a pragmatic republic. Shadman too is in search of an equitable and functional system of government for Iran. For him, the Platonic idea of the rule of the philosopher king is the best theoretically conceivable form of government. But such a system is, by its nature, unattainable, and thus "the rule of liberty," and in particular a "liberty nourished by rationalism,"[60] becomes for him the most desirable form of government. He believes that "The ultimate purpose of all these books and essays and speeches and revolutions has been to limit, by the force of law, the unbounded liberty of the despotic king and his men, and give a fair share of liberty to everyone."[61] He sees an inevitable tension between the dictates of individual liberty and the interests of civil society. It is only the rule of law that can mitigate this tension and ensure that a workable compromise can be found.

Along with the rule of law, Shadman was also an advocate of the rule of institutions in politics. His views in this area are reminiscent of Weber who argued that modernity heralds the "legal-rational" form of authority in politics and it, in turn, begets the dawn of bureaucracy. In such a society, legal and institutional relations irrevocably replace individual ones. In Shadman's own language, "Wise philosophers have been attempting to make the rule of institutions replace the rule of the individual."[62]

He is of course fiercely opposed to the idea of simply emulating Western forms of governance. For him, the form of government is contingent on the culture for which it is designed. He emphasizes, "Neither the government of ancient Greece nor England's style of rule"[63] are appropriate for twentieth-century Iran. Forms of commerce and government each arise from, and are shaped by, an intricate web of specific cultural and geographical factors. Instead of a simple-minded emulation, Shadman advocates that Iranian society must first come to grips with the universal values that are at the root of modernity and its democratic form of government. The appropriate shape of each government can be fashioned only through an integration of these fundamental values with the specific context of Iranian culture and history. Furthermore, such a form can only be found after what he calls a "great debate," an open, wide and earnest discussion, engaging people from all walks of life, a veritable cultural revolution. In other words, he understands that the rule of law, as a principle, cannot be actualized through Jacobin revolutionary fiat. A prolonged process of cultural and political growth is

60. Ibid., 156.
61. Ibid.
62. Ibid.
63. Ibid.

required before the proper forms of government, inspired by universal principles but anchored to local realities, can be fashioned.

Shadman's warnings against emulating Western models are also connected to the third principle that lies at the heart of his vision of modernity. The Iranian discourse on modernity, and the historic debate about its values and dangers, evolved under the long shadow of colonialism. Shadman is well aware of this fact, but does not believe that modernity should be forfeited because of the possible colonial taint. He criticizes the oppressive policies of colonialism on the one hand, and at the same time tries to separate the essential elements of modernity from the question of colonial hegemony. He suggests that, "Persians must doubt nearly every claim made by Farangis," particularly their claim "to support freedom."[65] Europe's greatest sin was, in Shadman's view, "that it has ceaselessly talked about freedom, yet it has not wanted others to have it." He writes of "the days when Europe had power," and "used that power at every turn to oppress others." In non-European societies, they "fostered corruption, bribery and treason," and degraded "anyone who was not of European stock." He admonishes Western powers for becoming "Supporters and allies of traitors and corrupt rulers and an enemy to every patriot." In a rhetorical address to Western powers, he asks, "Why is it that you, who would not tolerate for one day the rule of a corrupt politician, are constantly attempting to make others suffer under corrupt rule?" In Shadman's view, "The West, in collusion with an ignoble nobility, illegitimate entrepreneurs and contractors more corrupt than bandits," have ruined the Iranian economy and saturated it with "useless commodities."[66]

Shadman also writes of the tensions that in his view existed between the United States and Britain. At issue was hegemony over Iran's oil markets and politics. During the early sixties, when United States influence was on the rise, and a new technocratic class, predominantly educated in America, was gaining the upper hand, Shadman warned against too much dependence on the United States. England, he wrote, will—and indeed should—remain a countervailing force to the American monopoly of power.[67]

There was yet another reason why, in Shadman's view, Iran must not blindly emulate *farang*. The dawn of the West, he declares, has already

---

65. Shadman, *Taskhir-e Tamadon-e Farang*, 220-223
66. Ibid., 220-223.
67. For a discussion of this change and Shadman's political reactions to it, see my *Persian Sphinx:Amir Abbas Hoveyda and the Riddle of the Iranian Revolution*, (Mage, 2001). The chapter on the rise of the "Progressive Circle" deals with these developments.

turned into dusk, and Iranians have all but missed the whole cycle. On more than one occasion, he wrote, "The West is sick, and badly troubled."[68] In all of this, he is clearly influenced by the ideas of European philosophers like Spengler and Grosse who wrote about the demise of the West. At the same time, Shadman believes that Iran cannot—indeed should not—escape modernity. Persians must learn to distinguish modernity's genuine promises and accomplishments from its deceptive temptations. Such a path requires a critical and skeptical rationalism, a supple Persian language, a deep knowledge of Oriental and Occidental cultures, a populace engaged in a gradual process of cultural change, and finally, a patriotic intelligentsia at home both in Iran and in the West. Shadman was himself an impressive example of this kind of intellectual.

---

68. Shadman, *Taskhir-e Tamadon-e Farang*, 168.

TEHRAN & MODERNITY*
Ja'far Shahri's Personal Odyssey

Tehran is an oddity. It is a city with a long history and a short memory.[1] As a human habitat, it is almost eight thousand years old, but as a capital city, it is a neophyte. It is that rare metropolis that lacks proximity to water; with its back to towering mountains and its vistas open to tormenting desert winds, it suffers in the metaphor of its own geography. Roaming in those mountains, there is the ghost of Zahhak, the dark and dread foreign force of Iranian mythology. Indeed, another shady figure of the *Shahnameh*, Afrasyab, once pitched his camp near Tehran.[2] As St. Petersburg was for Russian intellectuals like Dostoyevsky the embodiment of an "anti-Christ,"[3] Tehran too, at least in the literary imaginations of some Iranian artists of the last hundred years, has been nothing short of *Dajal*—the false messiah that appears just before the return of the now hidden Imam. From Moshfegh Kazemi's *Tehran-e Makhof* (*Dread Tehran*), to Hedayat's *Blind Owl*, Tehran is yet another version of what Baudelaire called "the infamous city."

But for Ja'far Shahri, Tehran was his Ithaca. To it he felt the special loyalty of a faithful son. With the zeal of a missionary, he set out to chronicle the city's twentieth-century history. In a culture that betrays its ingrained distrust of modern cities by naming its red-light district the "New City," even his surname "Shahri," or its earlier version of "Shahribaf" speaks of the author's deep affinity for the city. The first means "man of the city," the second, "the weaver of the city."

---

*To Parviz Kalantari, who showed me old Tehran.
1. In his article in the fascinating collection on Tehran, Chahryar Adle refers to Tehran as the *ville sans memoire*, or "the city with no memory." See Chahryar Adle, "Le Jardin Habite Ou Teheran de Jadis: des Origines Aux Safavides" in *Teheran: Capitale Bicentenaire*, eds. Chahryar Adle and B. Hourcade (Paris, 1992), 15.
2. W. Barthold, "Tehran," *First Encyclopedia of Islam: 1913-1936* (Leiden, 1987), 715.
3. Kelly Aileen, "Where the Dead Smiled," *New York Review of Books*, 20 February 1997, 43.

During the tenth and eleventh centuries, when Iran was experiencing something of an early, albeit aborted, renaissance,[4] Tehran was a small village that lived quietly, almost surreptitiously, in the shadow of Rey, its grand and towering neighbor. An element of stealth, historians tell us, seemed encoded in the very etymology of Tehran's name and reputation. In thirteenth-century texts, it is described as "a large village, in the vicinity of Rey, rich in verdure and orchards." Caught in the crosscurrents of history, and of marauding tribes and armies, its inhabitants built their homes underground, thus the name "Tahran," or "under-grounder." When an enemy came—as for example the Mongols did in 1220 and all but razed the city of Rey—the wily troglodytes of Tehran "took refuge in their subterranean homes, and came out only when it was safe."[5]

In the sixteenth century, during the reign of Shah Abbas, Iran witnessed another attempt at a native modernity. Isfahan was named the capital and soon its cultural semiotics became a metaphor for Shah Abbas' grand, perhaps grandiose, vision of Iran. The city's Naghsh-e Jahan Square, with its spatial grandeur and name, which means "map of the world," was designed according to the King's astute and carefully enforced calculus of power. The trinity of the mosque, the bazaar, and the crown, the three pillars of power and commerce in traditional Iran, dominated its landscape. The city, and its central square, exuded the self-confidence of the Iranian "We" in the face of the Ottoman or Occidental "Other." The age of Western domination, of an Iranian consciousness subdued and cowed by the progress of the West and its modernity, was yet to come. Tehran, where Shah Abbas had once fallen badly ill, was then nothing but a backwater, a military garrison town with a population of no more than three thousand people.[6]

Even Persian mythology helped underscore the differences between Isfahan and Tehran. Whereas Zahhak's ghost haunted Tehran, his nemesis, the heroic Kaveh, the craftsman who fought Zahhak, found his true supporters in Isfahan.[7]

During the Qajar era, when an enfeebled Iran fell prey to hegemonic colonial forces, Tehran was declared the capital, and ever since its fortune has become inseparably entangled with the "elective modern affinities" of different Oriental despots.

---

4. For a brief discussion of this period of history and its cultural traits, see my *Tajaddod va Tajaddod-setizy dar Iran* [Modernity and its foes in Iran] (Tehran, 1999).

5. "Tehran," in *Kava*, 10 February 1921, 8-9.

6. Barthold, "Tehran," 715.

7. Hossein Ibn-Mohammad Ibn-Reza Avi, *Tarjomeh-ye Mahasen-e Isfahan* [A Translation of a Treatise on the Virtues of Isfahan], trans. Abbas Eghbal (Tehran, 1938), 86.

The first two modern buildings in Tehran, commissioned by Nasir al-Din Shah, the "Pivot of the Universe," are telling examples of these skewed and self-serving affinities. There was Tup-khaneh, a square whose military function and ominous name ("Cannon House"), were reminiscent of what Benjamin calls the "Haussmannization of Paris": an attempt to use urban design to fight "the barricades," to make the city and the citadel more defensible against a popular uprising.[8] The second newly commissioned building was Shams al-Emareh, modern in design, frivolous in function. Prominent in the building's façade was the capital's first public clock. The sound of its bells echoed all over the city, and according to Shahri, frightened the inhabitants. Previously, the sounds of muezzins, calling the pious to prayer three times a day, and the nocturnal cries of a watchman, marking the commencement of the nightly curfew, were the only sounds the inhabitants of the city were accustomed to. Eventually, the government muzzled the sound of the clock by wrapping the bells in heavy fabric. After a while, the clock failed to work altogether, but by then it had become involved in an urban legend; its grooves and niches, people said, had become home to three stray owls. Owls are omens of evil to Persians, and according to the lore of the time, the three owls of the clock emerged from their hideouts only when something ominous was about to happen to the king.[9] Instead of becoming the tool for "quantifying" and measuring time—such quantification being an essential component, indeed a preoccupation, of modernity[10]—Tehran's first public clock was not just a public nuisance, but the locus of occult beliefs of the capital's inhabitants.

Nasir al-Din Shah changed Tehran in other ways as well. After one of his trips to Europe, he ordered the city walled and moated. The wall had twelve gates—for Shia Islam's twelve Imams—and one hundred fourteen crenellations, for the one hundred fourteen suras (or chapters) of the Qur'an. By the end of his reign, Tehran was a city of dirt roads and mud houses, of open sewage and nocturnal infestation by hooligans and bandits. The Shah's final "modern" intervention in the city consisted of an inept attempt at turning teahouses into centers for a panoptic system of surveillance.[11]

8. Walter Benjamin, *The Arcade Project,* trans. Howard Eilan and Kevin McLaughlin (Cambridge, 2000), 120-126.

9. Ja'far Shahri, *Tehran-e Ghadim* [Old Tehran], vol. 1 (Tehran, 1992), 106-107.

10. See Alfred W. Crosby, *The Measure of Reality: Quantification and Western Society* (New York, 1997).

11. On plans for the city see John Gurney, "The Transformation of Tehran in the Later Nineteenth Century," in *Teheran: Capitale Bicentenaire,* 52-54. For the development of the panoptic system in Iran, see the essay in this book, "Narratives of Modernity: Perspectives of an Oriental Despot."

Tehran began to change rapidly in the aftermath of the Constitutional Revolution. In 1921, the three months of Seyyed Zia Tabatabai's short-lived government witnessed a concentrated effort to introduce the city rapidly, and radically, to at least some of the *accoutrement* of modernity. The proposed changes included bringing gas light and public hygiene to city streets, and replacing the clumsily chosen stones hitherto used by shopkeepers with standard measures and weights. In Shahri's novels as well as his *Old Tehran* and his *Social History of Tehran*, we can find detailed accounts of these proposed changes, as well as the popular response to them.

Tehran saw its fastest growth, its evolution from an over-grown village into a metropolis, in the Pahlavi era. In the last years of Mohammed Reza Shah's reign a veritable "urban crisis" engulfed the city, which was by then dangerously divided between the rich and the poor, "the South and the North."[12] It is no exaggeration to claim that the city has had a convoluted, complicated, and often tortured history, and that this history is inseparably linked to the question of modernity. And there, the last century of this fascinating history found more than its match in the character of Ja'far Shahri.

Shahri was a man of myriad talents, prodigious memory and unrelenting stamina for creative work. He was born in 1914 in Oud-Lajan, one of Tehran's oldest and most colorful neighborhoods, and he died in his beloved Tehran in November 1994. By early 1990, he had lost much of his eyesight and was forced to curtail his creative work. Happily, however, his infirmity coincided with a belated recognition of his writing. Though by then he had already written some twenty books, most of them about Tehran, he still felt that he had left much unsaid. In a tone both bitter and woeful, he wrote that "even the little eyesight I had in one eye is now gone. But I still have much more to say. In fact, I have just begun."[13]

In spite of his unusually rich contributions to the social history of Tehran, he was all but ignored by his contemporaries. This strange fact is itself at least partially the consequence of one aspect of modernity's peculiar trajectory in Iran. For at least a century, the common understanding of the concept of the intellectual in Iran was shaped by the Russian notion of the intelligentsia; and Shahri, with his aversion to politics and to the bombast of ideology, his lack of a formal education, his occasional tone of irony and satire, and his proclivity for bourgeois comforts, hardly fit the dour, Procrustean persona of a "committed intellectual."

---

12. Bernard Hourcade, "Urbanism et Crise Urbane sous Mohammad-Reza Pahlavi," in *Teheran: Capitale Bicentenaire*, 207-222.
13. Personal correspondence, 1991.

By his own telling, fate and fortune had been unduly harsh and unkind to him. Born into a family of entitled wealth, his profligate father squandered the family inheritance, physically abused his mother, and then abandoned his young son to his own devices. From a life of relative luxury, Ja'far was suddenly and forcefully exiled into the bowels of the "lower depths." Using his native talent and his unrelenting desire to excel, he became something of an urban nomad, navigating his way through innumerable crafts and odd jobs, gradually fashioning for himself a life of comfort and leisure. He suffered Dickensian indignities at the hands of a jealous stepfather, cruel and cunning stepmothers, pederast bosses, crooked clergy, an adulterous wife, and, finally, ungrateful children.

Throughout his travails, texts were his real homeland, a sanctuary free from the dread of the quotidian, where he lived at least part of his life in dreams. Neither sirens nor Cyclopes could thwart his relentless effort to come home to the text. The words that comforted him as a beleaguered writer now enrapture us as his enthralled readers. They have also become an indispensable compendium of facts, anecdotes, idioms, technical terms, mores and manners, urban geography, popular folklore, and cultural habits of Tehran in the throes of modernity.

What Walter Benjamin tried to do for nineteenth-century Paris in his famous and unfinished *Arcade Project*, Shahri more or less accomplished for Tehran. Benjamin wanted to write the "primary history" of Paris. Instead of focusing on the lives of "great men and celebrated events of traditional historiography," he wanted to represent the city through "the 'refuse,' and 'detritus' of history, the half-concealed, variegated traces of the daily life of the collective."[14] Benjamin's method was to "carry over the principle of montage into history. That is, to assemble large-scale constructions out of the smallest and most precisely cut components. Indeed to discover in the analysis of the small individual moment the crystal of the total event."[15] His was, in short, the gaze of the *flaneur*, the urban detective, at home nowhere and everywhere.

Shahri was Tehran's flaneur. He helps us "interpolate into the infinitesimally small"[16] the grand sweep of history. His eleven-volume history of Tehran is indeed history through montage. He captures, in a language that is somewhat uneven and sometimes unpolished—yet staggeringly rich in detail and precision—the moment that many popular crafts and

---

14. Walter Benjamin, *The Arcade Project,* trans. Howard Eiland and Kevin McLaughlin (Cambridge, 1999), ix. For a brief description of the flaneur, see below page 69, note 27.

15. Benjamin, *The Arcade Project*, 931.

16. Ibid.

social institutions, avenues and neighborhoods in the city of Tehran began to get their first whiff of the modern age. For example, he writes with aplomb and authority about the day that European shoes first appeared in the Tehran bazaar. Then, with uncanny precision and meticulous care, he chronicles the economic, technical, emotional and practical changes brought about as a result of this apparently simple development. His rich description of the shoe trade is more than matched by his no less precise and detailed accounts of hundreds of other aspects of Tehran's social and economic history.

Abundant in his books is the common lore of the people of the city. He captures the linguistic and cultural pulse of the city at different moments. With his help, we overhear an older woman talk to a young girl about abortion around the time of the First World War. "Are you sure you're pregnant?" the urban shaman asks, and adds, "Maybe you just have a cold in your stomach and that is why you missed your period. Maybe it is because of your weight. Heaven knows you have been putting on a new layer of fat every day. Sometimes you might miss a period because you got too much phlegm in your system. Just eat a bunch of celery, and it'll get it running again. Even if you are pregnant, it ain't a big deal. Buy a big bunch of parsley, squeeze the juice and drink it.... Aborting a child is nothing. I was an *attar* [traditional druggist] myself and know all the tricks...there are other ways, too, you know. If you eat a small piece of *Lahuri nabat* [sugar cubes from the city of Lahur], the baby is sure to fall. If you don't like that, drink some red onion juice, or boil some cow dung and drink that. There are even easier ways; take some rabbit shit, and burn it under your dress."[17] In Shahri's opus, more than in that of any other writer, historian, or social critic of our time, we can find the most complete, albeit crudely cut, "crystal" of the total experience of Tehran as it reluctantly slouches toward a new age.

He wrote in different genres, and if we accept Blumenberg's notion[18] that the core of modernity, its central tenet, is the self-assertive individual, then Shahri's metier is a kind of subtle but forceful self-assertion that is concealed in all he writes. Whether he is writing poetry or memoir, novels or short stories, the social history of Tehran, or a compendium on herbal medicine and the Persian occult, Shahri is always at the center of the narrative.[19] Such self-assertion was, as Shahri himself deftly

---

17 Jafar Shahri, *Shekar-e Talkh* [Bitter sugar] (Tehran, 1977), 379.

18. Hans Blumenberg, *The Legitimacy of the Modern Age*, trans. M. Wallace (Cambridge, 1988).

19. His trilogy of novels—*Bitter Sugar*, *Nettle*, and *Fortune's Pen*—are in fact, as he makes clear in the introduction to the third and final volume, the story of his own life. (continued)

reminds us, at odds with the mores of the time. He criticizes the many social forces that worked against his attempt to fashion an autonomous self. "It is not all my fault," he writes, "that ever since I can remember, they have done nothing but cultivate fear in my heart; every time I have tried to say something, they've shouted at me, tried to put me in my place. From my mother and father, to the teacher and the bully on the street corner, and even the local policeman on the beat, they've all been there to frighten the hell out of me; they are my bogeymen; because of them, every time I wanted to say something, even if it was just and reasonable, I would think twice before saying it, and eventually I would end up saying nothing at all."[20]

In describing these inhibiting forces, he has particularly harsh words for the role of organized religion. In fact, a kind of anticlericalism is a common theme in all his books. He considers himself a pious Muslim, yet he had nothing but contempt for the mullahs. In a way, an embryonic, inarticulate Protestantism, a desire to eliminate the clergy as the self-proclaimed middleman for God and gatekeeper for heaven, runs throughout his work. Recounting his pilgrimage to Mecca, for example, he writes that "all of this weeping and wailing in Shiism has made us incapable of asking even the simplest questions.... Look at these *Farangis* [Westerners]; they have no Hossein to weep for, and if their tailor is so much as an hour late in delivering their suit, they raise all kinds of hell and seek a thousand and one kinds of damages."[21] He writes of these "turbaned men" who like "poisoned weeds have grown in the garden of religion, and have sucked it dry of all its healthy nutrients; I am talking of the poisoned weeds who have learned by rote some passion story about Hussein, and with it put on the airs of a scholar." In a language whose biting edge is reminiscent of Chaucer's "Tale of the Pardoner," he describes one clergyman who accompanied him on the pilgrimage as an adulterous lecher, a small-time crook, an opium addict, and a foul-mouthed charlatan.[22]

But he has also written a long narrative poem entitled "My Autobiography" that follows, in verse, much of the same territory covered by the three novels. Surely elements of autobiography are nothing new in the history of Persian poetry. What makes Shahri's poem unusual is the kind of individual detail he provides. We learn, for example, the size of his shirt collar (thirty-seven), his shoe size (forty-one wide), his weight (sixty kilos) and his preference for "young and fat" ladies. In fruits, he prefers figs, apples and pomegranates; he likes pomegranates because they remind him of "a woman's breasts." Beer he dislikes, vodka he abhors, and he never goes without his daily dose of hooka.

20. Shahri, *Bitter Sugar*, 71.
21. Ja'far Shahri, *Haji Dobareh* [Once again a Haji] (Tehran, 1977), 171.
22. Ibid., 141.

Aside from his self-assertiveness, and his demand for a religious Reformation, another important element of Shahri's narrative is the nature of his *episteme*, his theoretical point of departure. It is refreshingly eclectic, personal and Persian, with no hint of Western theory. In recent years, theorists from Foucault and Said to Mignolo, Geertz and Greenblatt have written about the hegemonic nature of theory. They have debunked the myth of the non-intrusive, non-political theory. All theory, for that matter all discursive practices, they have shown, partake of a "regime of truth" that is itself inseparably entangled with power. For those studying the question of modernity in Iran, one of the most vexing questions has long been finding the episteme, the discourse and theoretical vista that is free from the taint of what has been called the "colonization of language and memory," and can at the same time transcend the smug, self-referential and dangerously self-satisfied nativism that tries to pass off its ignorance of the world as a sign of its privileged status. The challenge is finding an episteme that is cognizant of the "cultural dimensions of globalization," one deeply immersed in the specificity of the Iranian tradition, as well as informed about the intricate theoretical and political debates in the increasingly global turn to modernity.[23] The answer, we are beginning to learn, might well lie in what Geertz has called "thick description": in allowing the subjects of our study to speak for themselves. We need, in the words of Walter Mignolo, a "dialogical understanding" which listens as much as it talks.[24] Shahri, in the pristine and primitive quality of his narrative, might have inadvertently come to exemplify the kind of "local knowledge"[25] we need if we are to solve the riddle of modernity in Iran. He is that rare breed of writer whose ignorance of the West and of modern theory becomes the source of his strength as a repository—a living, mental, moveable archive—of Tehran's traumatic encounter with the modern. In him we can find a detailed, bare to the bone account of a thousand and one aspects of Tehran's social history. Neither the grand canvas of imported, mummified theory nor the totalizing temptations of meta-narratives are his domain. Raw, savagely unforgiving details and anecdotes are his forte.

His opulent opus is redolent with the kind of frank carnality that Mikhail Bakhtin finds in the liberating, subversive pleasures of Rabelais' "Carnival." Bakhtin praises Rabelais for familiarizing us with "the curses,

23. For a discussion of the global dimensions of modernity, see Arjun Appadurai, *Modernity at Large: Cultural Dimensions of Globalization* (Minneapolis, 1997).

24. Walter D. Mignolo, *The Darker Side Of the Renaissance* (Ann Arbor, 1995), 19.

25. For a discussion of "local knowledge" see Clifford Geertz, *Local Knowledge* (New York, 1999).

profanities, and oaths—and the...colloquialisms of the marketplace," and of always remaining "with the people."[26] Shahri's novels and his multi-volume history of Tehran are not so much replete with Tehran's "colloquialisms" as formed by them. In Shahri we can even find an exhaustive encyclopedia of Tehrani curses.

Shahri's style, the poetics of his prose, is as idiosyncratic as his stories and his characters. Indeed, there is at first glance a jarring, discomforting, prosaic quality to his writing that can easily be construed as poor, unpolished. Such sloppiness can be seen as a consequence of the fact that he was an autodidact, and never completed formal schooling beyond the fourth grade. On closer reading, however, nearly all of his books appear to have the quality of the experiment that Patrick Chamoiseau's brilliant novels also try to capture. It is a style and a language that treads the unbeaten path "at the frontier of the written and the spoken word." It tries to "evoke a synthesis, synthesis of the written syntax and of the spoken rhythm, of writing's 'acquiredness' and of the oral 'reflex,' of the loneliness of writing and of the participation in the communal chant."[27] Shahri, in most of his works, sings Tehran's collective chant; he captures the echoes of the city's bazaars and barracks, its tenements and tea houses. The exuberance of the voice often defies the constraints of the written page and is decidedly oblivious to rules of proper punctuation. They have the feel of an urban delirium. Read slowly, they are sometimes hard to fathom. Read out loud, they find the flow and the tempo of the marketplace, and the defiant texture of a carnival. Shahri was, in short, a master oral storyteller caught in the constraints of a written literature.

The art of the novel is founded on modernity's epistemological individualism and the hubris of humans partaking of God's privilege of creation. The stuff of its narrative is the creative impulse of the writer. The dying art of storytelling is, in Benjamin's words, "the ability to exchange experiences...experiences which are passed on from mouth to mouth."[28] It is an art dependent on the epic faculty of memory, and Shahri was the quintessential storyteller. The fruit of his mastery of mnemonics has become a major treasure-trove to be mined by those seeking to understand Tehran's travails of modernity.

26. Mikhail Bakhtin, *Rabelais and His World*, trans. Helene Eswolsky (New York, 1984), 152-153.
27. Patrick Chamoiseau, *Solibo Magnificent*, trans. Rose-Myriam Rejouis and Val Vinokurov (New York, 1997).
28. Walter Benjamin, "The Story Teller," in *Illuminations*, ed. Hannah Arendt (New York, 1969), 84.

SADEQ HEDAYAT & THE TRAGIC VISION*
Resisting Modernity

The common lore of literary criticism in Iran has enshrined Nima Yushij as the harbinger of modernity in poetry and Sadeq Hedayat as its herald and pillar in the realm of fiction. Closer textual interrogation of Hedayat's opus, I submit, will undermine this proposition. Hedayat only belongs to the movement of modernity in terms of some of his formal and aesthetic innovations. His epistemology and ontology belong to an altogether different tradition and it is only these aspects of his world-view, and not his formal contributions, that I intend to discuss here.

As a concept, modernity has, in recent years, taken on a rather protean character. Its genealogy and essential meaning have become the subject of much contentious controversy and little consensus.[1]

Milan Kundera claims that modernity began when Don Quixote left the comfort of his home to discover the world.[2] More precisely, modernity is a movement that began in the Renaissance and reached its maturity in the age of the scientific revolution. Rationalism, or what in recent theoretical discourse has come to be called logocentrism, is one of its cardinal elements. It fosters a cult of science and rationalism that is ocular and empiric in its emphasis.[3] At the same time, it is founded on the presumption that myth, superstition, and human suffering will come to an end in the secular kingdom of science.

---

*An earlier version of this paper was read at a conference on Hedayat held at the University of Texas at Austin in January 1991

1. For a general discussion of modernity, see, for example, Anthony Giddens, *The Consequences of Modernity* (Stanford, 1990). For a discussion of the protean character of the concept, see Lezek Kolakowski, *Modernity on Endless Trial* (Chicago, 1990), 3-14.

2. Milan Kundera, *The Art of the Novel*, trans. Linda Asher (New York, 1988), 3-20.

3. For a lengthy and erudite discussion of the theme of the ocular and the centrality of the eyes in the vision of modernity see Jay Martin, *The Downcast Eyes* (Berkeley, 1993); for a briefer version of the argument about the importance of the eye, see his "Scopic Regimes of Modernity" in *Vision and Reality* (Seattle, 1991), 3-10.

Individualism is another key tenet of modernity. In the economic realm, it manifests itself as what C.B. McPherson calls "possessive individualism."[4] Notions about the inalienable rights of the individual—the ultimate new legal and political monad—articulate the new sovereignty of the individual. Another central element of modernity is secularism, or in the words of Shelden Wolin, the process that "detheologizes politics and depoliticizes theology."[5] At the same time modernity champions capitalism by fostering industry, urbanism, and commerce. The city and modernity are, in this sense, coterminous.[6]

And finally, in the realm of art, modernity not only introduces new genres such as the novel, but cultivates new relationships in terms of artistic production and reception. It decrees form as the unbridled expression of individualism, and thus opens the way for perpetual revolutions in form and technique. Ultimately, form itself becomes part of content.[7]

With the rise of modernity, voices of opposition to it also began to appear. Some oppose modernity from the vantage point of tradition. They lament the collapse of the theocentric Middle Ages and the loss of its organic cosmos. The Baroque was one such response. What Foster calls the "postmodernity of *reaction*" is the latter day articulation of this early movement of opposition to modernity.[8]

Others began to doubt and ultimately criticize modernity from a radically different perspective, which Foster calls the "postmodernity of *resistance*."[9] Lucien Goldman, George Lukacs, Raymond Williams, and other critics have called this new perspective the "tragic vision."[10] Many of the greatest thinkers and artists—from Shakespeare and Pascal to

---

4. C.B MacPherson, *The Political Theory of Possessive Individualism* (Oxford, 1962).

5. For a brilliant discussion of this aspect of modernity, see Shelden Wolin, *Politics and Vision* (New York, 1965).

6. For an overall discussion of these aspects of modernity, see Stephen Toulmin, *Cosmopolis: The Hidden Agenda of Modernity* (New York, 1990).

7. The same argument, as it relates to the realm of history, has been made by Hayden White. In his many books on the sources of modern historiography, he points out the similarities between historical and fictional representation. See White, *The Content of Form: Narrative Discourse and Historical Representation* (Baltimore, 1987).

8. For a detailed study of the Baroque see Jose Antonio Maravall, *Culture of the Baroque: Analysis of a Historical Structure*, trans. Terry Cohran (Minneapolis,1986). For a discussion of the two kinds of critiques of modernity, see Hal Foster, ed., *The Anti-Aesthetics: Essays on the Post-Modern Culture*, (Seattle, 1983), ix-xv.

9. Foster, ed., *The Anti-Aesthetics: Essays on the Post-Modern Culture*, ix-xv.

10. For discussions of the tragic vision, see Gregory Lukacs, "The Metaphysics of Tragedy," in *Soul and Form*, trans. Anna Bostock (London, 1977); Lucien Goldman, *The Hidden God: A Study of Tragic Vision in the Pensees of Pascal and the Tragedies of Racine*, trans. Philip Thody (London, 1977); George Steiner, *The Death of Tragedy* (London, 1961); Raymond Williams, *Modern Tragedy* (London, 1966).

Nietzsche and Kierkegaard—are considered pillars of this tradition. And it is to this tradition that I think Hedayat belongs. His is a critique of modernity from within: cognizant of its merits, frightened by its failings.

The tragic vision is a disgruntled child of modernity, and much different from the kind of classical tragedy manifest, for example, in Greek drama.

Classical tragedy depicts the inevitable fate of a tragic hero, a fate shaped and determined by a flaw or failing in the hero's character. The tragic vision, on the other hand, is the lamentation of solitary souls in despair over the contingent nature of existence. It is a quest for the meaning of life in a world wherein secularism and logocentrism have undermined the certitudes of divine eschatologies. It is, in the words of Lukacs, the ultimate encounter of fate and a soul bereft of all its certitudes. It is a struggle against the terror of Time, hauntingly depicted by Nabokov as that cradle which "Rocks above an abyss, and common sense tells us that our existence is but a brief crack of light between two eternities of darkness."[11]

The tragic vision befits a Nietzschean "Over-man" for it is preoccupied with questions and contradictions that seem to have no answers, what philosophers call aporias. It decries the lack of authenticity in this world, yet knows this world to be the sole realm of human existence. It celebrates the insights of modernity's rationalism and science, yet it also bemoans its reductionism and believes that many shades and dark corners of the human reality are beyond the illumination of the Enlightenment. In the tragic vision, man is at once noble and bestial, a master and a slave. Thus, the tragic vision and a melancholic sense of solitude are almost contiguous. In the words of Baudelaire, "A man must have sunk low to consider himself happy." The posture of Dostoyevsky's "underground man" is also congruent with the tragic vision's passion for, and at the same time aversion to, the masses and their immersion in the quotidian. Kierkegaard's depiction of this posture, hauntingly reminiscent of Hedayat's excursions in *The Blind Owl,* poetically captures the essence of this dilemma: "My grief is my castle, which like an eagle's nest is built high up on the mountain peaks among the clouds; nothing can storm it. From it I fly down into reality to seize my prey, but I do not remain down there; I bring it home with me and this prey is a picture I weave into the tapestries of my palace."[12]

This tragic vision has a Janus face: it elegizes the absurd sufferings of existence, and at the same time it exults in the keenly comic aspects

---

11. Vladimir Nabokov, *Speak, Memory: An Autobiography Revised* (New York, 1989), 19.
12. Soren Kierkegaard, *A Kierkegaard Reader,* ed. Robert Bretau (New York, 1964), 35.

of man's predicament. It bemoans the absurdity of our death-haunted lives, yet celebrates existence as our only time in this world.

To counter the contingency of this solitary existence, the tragic vision invariably seeks a "totality" beyond the erosions of time, in which it can anchor its search for meaning. For some, like Pascal or Kierkegaard, that totality remains God; others like Marx and Malraux sought it in the idea of revolution. A large number of artists and philosophers, Hedayat among them, sought their salvation in the realm of aesthetics. The absurdity of existence, the terror of time manifested in death, can only be transcended through creativity, through a life experienced and appreciated aesthetically.

Hedayat's existential pessimism is in sharp contrast to modernity's optimistic cult of progress. He constantly laments the contingent nature of existence, and sarcastically debunks the idea of progress. He assumes the posture of the "underground man" in both his stories (especially *The Blind Owl*) and his personal life. He exhibits a kind of disdain, even "nausea," for what he calls the banality of the quotidian. He seems actually to take pride in his alienation from the everyday world. He was extremely selective of his friends, and rarely allowed anyone into his small, close-knit, like-minded circle. This sense of alienation is compounded by what he deems the inability of language to actualize any genuine human communication. Implicit in many of his stories is a critique of logocentrism and urbanity. Finally, he has a Romantic conception of reality as a continuum equally encompassing the empiric and the poetic, the real and the imagined, the mythic and the mundane. Each of these characteristics testifies to Hedayat's affinity with the tradition of the tragic vision, and to his avowed aversion to modernity. While the tragic vision permeates the whole fabric of Hedayat's texts, *The Blind Owl* becomes the ultimate manifesto, or as he refers to it, the "wine" pressed from the grapes of his philosophic and aesthetic vineyard.

The tragic vision is, interestingly, all but absent from Iran's cultural legacy, thus making Hedayat's role particularly significant in Iran's intellectual history. While the certitudes of traditional Islam left little room for the angst of the tragic, even modern secular ideologies came to Iran tainted with the kind of dogmatism that made them inimical to the celebrated ambiguities of the tragic vision. Hedayat fought against the old certitudes in many of his most famous stories, including *The Pearl Cannon* (*Tup-Morvarid*), *The Islamic Mission* (*Beyat al-Islamieh*), and *Alaviye Khanoum*. Even in his essays, he was careful to write on topics that helped clarify further his critical disposition to some of the foundations of modernity. Of all Iran's rich poetic legacy, for example, he chose Khayyam to write about, one of the few advocates of tragic vision in the history of Iranian letters. Hedayat's introduction to Khayyam's quatrains is an eloquent and comprehensive compendium of the tenets of the tragic vision, and of Hedayat's philosophy.[13]

Totalitarian ideology is another enemy of the introspective searchings encouraged by a tragic perspective. In the years after the Second World War, Iranian Marxism was dominated by the ideology of the Tudeh Party—the most important Iranian version of Soviet totalitarianism. The Party had succeeded in attracting a whole generation of Iranian intellectuals. Hedayat had many friends in the party, but refused to join. Instead, he wrote in those very years another manifesto for his tragic vision in his remarkable essay on "Kafka's Message."[14] It was an introduction to his translation of Kafka's short stories, and every passage in it was shaped by ideas in the tradition of a tragic view of existence.

In it he laments man's loneliness, of his utter estrangement from this world. He writes of life as an "endless nightmare" where the torturer and the tortured are both "men without qualities."[15] He considers Kafka the first writer to "depict humanity's despicable plight in a world without God—an absurd world where no individual can rely on anything other than his own power to determine his fate."[16] Kafka, he writes, was "ill at ease in this world," but was also attached to it. At the same time, he invites the reader to create a "new better world." In one of his characteristically succinct sentences, he offers the essence of both Kafka's message and of the tragic vision: "Our freedom is in our death. But we are also hopeful for this life."[17]

His stories too are no less imbued with this spirit. A recurrent leitmotif of all his works of fiction is a pressing dread of death. Indeed, what most precipitates Hedayat's estrangement from the multitude is their obliviousness to this fear: the angel of death never touches their faces. The masses are immersed in the banalities of the quotidian and of bodily appetites; they are suffused in the the false certitudes of their religious or ideological dogmas. In short, they live unexamined lives, and pay no heed to the more fundamental existential questions of life. Like other

---

13. See Sadeq Hedayat, *Taraneha-ye Khayyam* [Khayyam's songs] (Tehran, 1342/1963). Of particular interest is Hedayat's introduction (pp.1-66), where he talks of Khayyam as a philosopher and a poet.
14. See Hedayat, *Goruh-e Mahkumin: Payam-e Kafka*, [The condemned group: Kafka's message] (Tehran, 1342/1963), 9-75.
15. Ibid., 12-13.
16. Ibid., 31.
17. Ibid., 65.

advocates of the tragic vision, Hedayat has a dual attitude toward these masses. On the one hand, he has a deep affection for them as fellow humans; on the other hand, he disdains their facile happiness. This dual attitude can be found in many of his works. Even those works of his praised by Marxist critics as instances of his "progressive period" have a sharp undercurrent of criticism of the common man and his common ways. Stories like *Haj Agha*, *Alaviye Khanoum* and *The Pearl Cannon* fall into this category. Nietzsche perhaps best articulated the kind of double-bind Hedayat felt in his relationship with his fellow man: "In solitude you devour yourself: in company you are devoured by the many."[18]

The only remedy to this pain, the only "opiate for this tortured soul," is in the world of creativity. In Buried Alive (*Zendeh Be Gur*) we read that, "Only through painting could I find a little solace for my pain."[19] Even Hedayat's deep affinity for the glorious past of Iran is ultimately another wager on the redemptive power of the aesthetic realm. His images of this pre-Islamic Persia are grandiose, sometimes sadly racist constructs that have little to do with historical realities. Iran, he writes, "was this paradise on earth, and it became a dreadful Muslim cemetery."[20] His vision, in short, is his aesthetic creation of a paradise lost.

The Blind Owl, undoubtedly Hedayat's masterpiece, is ultimately an exercise in transcending existential agonies and the coincidence of existence through creativity. Art no longer mimics reality but attempts to master it. Salvation can come to the protagonist only if he can make himself understood to his double, his shadow. And he can make himself understood only by narrating, for the double and for himself, a fiction of his life. For Descartes, we exist because we think; for Camus we exist because we rebel; for Hedayat, as for many who behold the tragic vision, we exist because we create.

The Blind Owl best exemplifies this creativity. It is a set of concentric images that cohere into an enormously complex structure wherein the cosmic and the individual are united.[21] The story transcends the boundaries of time and place, and has in its center the portrait of the artist as a tormented young man trying to bring meaning to his existence.

---

18. For a detailed discussion of this aspect of the tragic vision, see Leo Shestov, *Dostoyevsky, Tolstoy and Nietzsche*, trans. Beman Martin and Spencer E. Roberts (Ohio, 1964). The quote appears on page 308.

19. Hedayat, *Zendeh Be Gur* [Buried alive] (Tehran, 1358/1979), 16. Even the title of this story is reminiscent of Hedayat's account of Kafka's message, and another sign of his tragic vision.

20. For an embarrassing example of Hedayat's romantic and sadly anti-Arab view of the past, see his *Parvin, Dokhtar-e Sasan* [Parvin, Sasan's daughter] (Tehran, 1342.1963), 32.

21. For an impressively informed and thoughtful analysis of Hedayat and the sources of his fiction, see Michael Beard, *Hedayat's Blind Owl as A Western Novel* (Princeton, 1990), 86-89.

Even in *Haj Agha,* one of Hedayat's more "realistic" works, the only character capable of finding meaning for life is the poet, who knows that forsaking worldly attachments is the price he must pay to find that meaning: "You and people like you are stupid creatures who only eat, burp, steal, sleep, make babies and then die away and are forgotten. Several thousand generations come and go before a couple of people can arise out of this forsaken flock...and bring meaning to their lives."[22]

Though Hedayat's suicide is, in one sense, an indication that ultimately even aesthetics could no longer salve the cankerous sores of his soul, it could also be seen as his desperate attempt to give his life an aesthetic meaning authored by himself and no one else. Suicide is, in the words of Camus, "The one truly philosophical problem."[23] Thrust into the open text of a life in which he suffered and "wrote with his blood," Hedayat authored his own death, and thus usurped the privilege often assumed to be a monopoly of God or nature.

For Hedayat, modernity, in spite of all its promises and its cult of progress, has not radically improved the human condition. Some of the essential elements of this critical appraisal are found in *"Sin, Kaf, Lam, Lam"* ("S.K.L.L."), where he draws a rather disturbing image of a modern society: "This progress and the fact that people's eyes are now more open has made them miserable. In spite of all this progress, people are more unhappy.... Lives are gloomy and meaningless."[24]

Furthermore, if we take the city and urbanity as a quintessential sign of modernity, then we discover that throughout his works, the city is, for Hedayat, a nest of loneliness and misery, where mirth and merriment are absent and suffering abounds. In *The Blind Owl,* the city emerges as a cold inhospitable geometric conglomeration of decrepit houses, wherein everyone is felled by a strange death and a yellow cloud haunts the horizon. In another story, the city emerges as "mysterious tall buildings" that are "built of dark glasses" and look "like poisonous mushrooms that had sprouted."[25]

The fact that modernity is, at times, championed in Iran by figures politically despicable to Hedayat added to his disdain for the whole project. In many works, particularly *The Pearl Cannon* and *Khar Dajal*—the title comes from the term for the Islamic version of the antichrist—we find his caustic appraisal of the "official" version of modernity. For exam-

---

22. Hedayat, *Haj Agha* (Tehran, 1358/1979), 89.
23. Albert Camus, *The Myth of Sisyphus and Other Essays*, trans. Justin O'Brien (New York, 1955), 3.
24. Hedayat, *Say-e Roshan*, [Chiaroscuro] (Tehran, 1358/1979), 28.
25. Ibid., 10.

ple, alluding to Seyyed Zia's project for modernizing Iran, Hedayat writes: "Once upon a time, there was a flock of sheep. These sheep, having been educated and…progressed, not only wore pants, but each carried, as memorabilia, an urn, a classic invention of their land."[26]

Hedayat's view of humanity is also at odds with modernity's logocentric vision. Champions of the Enlightenment argue that humanity's attachment to myth, superstition and religion is the result of its ignorance and will end with the advent of the scientific spirit. Hedayat, in concurrence with other advocates of the tragic vision, respects the accomplishments of the new rationalism, yet believes in darker, archetypal forces that will forever hinder man's complete rationalism. In his introduction to *Neyrangestan,* or *House of Tricks,* he writes, "It is the very same superstitions that have led men throughout different historical epochs and created man's prejudices, valors, hopes and fears. They are man's oldest solace and still persistently intervene in the daily lives of both the civilized and uncivilized world. Man can give up everything but his superstitions and beliefs. In matters of belief, man does not rely upon his reason."[27]

The best fictional articulation of these philosophical propositions can be found in *The Blind Owl.* It succeeds in creating what Baudelaire calls "An evocative magic, at once the object and the subject, the world external to the artist and the artist himself." *The Blind Owl* defies the Cartesian duality of subject and object. Even the chronology of time collapses into a moment that not only includes the past and the present but is pregnant with the future—every moment is at once perennial and eternal. Hedayat weaves a masterful tapestry from a world in which memory and desire, myth and reality, form a homogenous, non-hierarchic continuum. It is an epic attempt to cohere in a poetic whole the schism that exists between what John Cheever calls the "retard of observation and the flow of feeling."[28] *The Blind Owl* is a fiction about fiction spurred by Hedayat's perceived sense of existential injustice. The novella is not only the odyssey of his search for salvation, but its instrument. His rebellion is metaphysical and his redemption aesthetic. The lucidity and permanence of his opus is, in a sense, a repudiation of the despair that gave rise to it. Tragic despair leads to tragic redemption through art.

26. Hedayat, *Alaviye Khanoum* [Mrs. Alaviye] (Tehran, 1358/1979), 98.
27. Hedayat, *Neyrangestan* [House of tricks] (Tehran, 1342.1963), 1.
28. John Cheever, *The Journals of John Cheever* (New York, 1989).

THE KING OF SHADOWS

Ebrahim Golestan & the Question of Modernity[1]

There is often wind in Ebrahim Golestan's stories. There is no short-age of wind in his films either. Wind and its many cinematic connotations have long been favorite devices of directors. Some critics have claimed that the narrative structures of Golestan's stories are deeply influenced by cinema,[2] but I think the pervasive presence of wind in the land-scape of his stories has less to do with cinematic influences than with facts of history.

The leitmotif of nearly every work by Golestan is the objective and subjective worlds, as well as the public and private lives, of characters caught in the throes of a changing society. The emotional context of their lives is a society where modernity and tradition, despotism and democ-racy, feudalism and capitalism, sedentary urbanism and nomadic mobility, rebellious individualism and constricted conformism, and finally, criti-cal logos and ambitious imagination are in constant battle. Golestan's own description of the atmosphere in one of his own stories could aptly summarize the contexts of all his works: "Outside the wind was howling again. Like it wanted to dislodge the house. All the noises in the world clashed and collided outside the house and turned onto one another."[3]

1. An earlier Persian version of this article was published in *Iranshenasi: A Journal of Iranian Studies*, vol. xiv, no. 2 (Summer 2002): 249-278. I am grateful to Professor Jalal Matini for his comments on that draft of the paper.
2. In an interview with Golestan, he is asked about the influence of films on his stories and he rejects the notion. See Ebrahim Golestan, *Gofteha* [An anthology of his essays and inter-views covering nearly four decades of his career; the title literally means, "what has been said"] (New Jersey, 1998), 187. The fact that his first short stories were published some fif-teen years before he began directing any films gives some credence to Golestan's claim.
3. Ebrahim Golestan, *Azar, Mahe Akhr-e Paiz* [Azar, the last month of the Fall] (New Jersey, 1994). First published in Tehran in 1327/1948.

Wind is not the only sign of the changing worlds of his stories. Many of their titles also hint at the purgatory of transition. Some deal with time, others with memory and identity. One is called "Narrating the Times Past"; another "A Stranger Who Had Gone to See." Individuals in his stories seem stranded between "Today and Tomorrow," and suspended between "The Tide and the Fog." One has the "Fever of Rebellion," while another, standing "At the Bend of the Road" suffers a sharp rift between his body and soul. All of them are constantly "Hunting Shadows."

Ebrahim Golestan is arguably one of the most important figures in modern Iranian art and literature. He is a man of myriad talents who has reached the apex of creativity in several genres, and he can certainly be considered one of the founders of modern Iranian cinema. He not only built the most well-equipped private film studio of its time in Iran, but his film *Brick and the Mirror* began a new path in Iranian cinema. It helped put Iranian cinema on the international map. Hitherto, Iranian films were local in appeal and essentially defined by a tradition of mediocre movies, repetitious in corny themes, poor in acting, and primitive in style. After Golestan, Iranian cinema would gradually gain an international presence and become the darling of film critics. His *Mysteries of the Treasure at Ghost Valley*—the most politically daring film of its era— is a veritable manifesto about the mangled attempts at modernity during the Pahlavi regime. His documentaries, whether describing the crown jewels or the oil industry, combine beautifully taut prose with often stunning imagery, and his attention to words has its roots in his abilities as a short story writer. In his youth he balanced a life as a champion runner with a highly successful career as a journalist and photographer. Some of the most enduring images of Iran during Dr. Mossadegh's tumultuous era were shot through his lens. Golestan is also a theater director and a highly accomplished translator.[4] His new works, yet to be published, are a fascinating combination of memoir and history.

Golestan is at the same time a man of many contradictions. He was only twenty-two years old in 1943 when he was named the editor of a staunchly Stalinist paper. In 1945, he translated into Persian parts of the *Short History of the Communist Party of the Soviet Union, (Bolshevik)*, generally considered the most turgid of Stalin's many historical fabrications and banal theoretical gibberish. Yet in the same period, in his essays and short stories, Golestan fought such dogmatism. In the days when in the Soviet Union—the Iranian Stalinist's Mecca—thousands

---

4. Aside from introducint readers to *Huckleberry Finn* and Hemingway to Persian readers, he also translated and directed "Don Juan in Hell," from George Bernard Shaw's *Man and Superman.*

of people, including many innocent Jews, were sent to concentration camps on the flimsy charge of "cosmopolitanism," Golestan translated Hemingway and published an essay about him in Stalinist publications of the time. He read Shakespeare and translated—but never published—his *Macbeth* into Persian.

The three epigrams for his collection of essays, published in 1998, are a perfect metaphor for his own erudite cosmopolitanism. He quotes Sa'di, who writes, "be innovative but not verbose." He is inspired by Leonardo da Vinci, who suggests, "Learn how to see." And finally, he quotes Shakespeare—more precisely Iago, the diabolic genius of *Othello*—who declares, "For I am nothing if not critical."[5]

In remembering Golestan's attachment to Marxism, we must keep in mind that during World War II, and even for some years after, many writers and artists saw Marxism as a weapon against colonialism, and the Soviet Union as the only effective bulwark against Nazi barbarism. The stench of the gulags had not yet reached the world. A sacred utopian aura still surrounded the idea of the socialism and helped hide the calamities of the real Soviet Union. But to his credit, Golestan soon realized the vacuity of Stalinist ideology, and the depth of corruption in the ranks of its Iranian followers; he chose to steer away from his erstwhile comrades, yet he also refused to join the ranks of those who in those days wrote about "the God that Failed."[6]

Aside from Russian Marxism in Iran, Golestan was also at the center of many of Iran's most important literary, political, and cultural movements in the second half of the twentieth century. Furthermore, in his private life he crossed paths with many of the more important and colorful personalities of his time. Idle or prurient curiosity about his private life, however, seems to have cast a shadow on a serious analysis of his work. Except for two early enthusiastic reviews by Massoud Farzad and Mojtaba Minovi—arguably two of modern Iran's most erudite critics—of his first collection of short stories, little of substance has been written about him. For some critics, Golestan's wealth was his guilt. Others criticized his relationship with Forough Farrokhzad. One critic cast aspersions on his literary abilities because he offered his guests beer in frosted glasses! In the days when the cult of poverty was the common creed of Iranian intellectuals, Golestan was not only affluent but refused any pretense of poverty. His

5. William Shakespeare, *Othello*, ed. A.J. Honigmann (New York, 1997), 2. 1, 115.

6. At the height of the Cold War, a number of Western intellectuals who had once been enamored of Marxism published a collection of essays called *The God that Failed*, edited by Richard Crossman (New York, 1951). For many years, it was the standard text for understanding why intellectuals joined, and then became disgruntled with, Marxism. It was also an important book in the "culture wars" then ragin between the West and the Soviet Union.

reputation as a distant, difficult, even arrogant man has long afforded him an aura of enigma and inscrutability. Finally, leaving Iran before the Islamic Revolution and choosing a life of exile further distorted his image among progressive critics as a "committed" artist. The cacophony of gossip and innuendo about his private life has created what appears like a conspiracy of silence about his work. This silence, and the array of often banal reasons proffered to legitimize it, can itself be seen as a telling measure of the mangled state of modernity in Iran. Everywhere else in the world, with the rise of modernity, the artist's life—as an element of his private realm— is deemed separate and distinct from his work. Indeed, respect for the "private realm" as an inviolate arena and attempts to expand it are a sure sign of modernity and a healthy measure of democracy.[7]

My purpose here is to analyze Golestan's works through the prism of the question of modernity. There is a consensus among scholars today that modernity is the central problem of twentieth- and twenty-first century Iran. The works of Iranian artists thus, consciously or unwittingly, reflect the centrality of this question. But Golestan's contribution to this debate is unique. His exceptional erudition, combined with theoretical sophistication, artistic creativity, a keen eye for details, and finally the poetic beauty of his prose, have perched him on a rare aerie from which he keenly perceives the contours of modern Iranian culture. Golestan is equally at home in Shakespeare and Hafez. He has delved deeply into both Iranian culture and Western civilization; he has assimilated the best of both but is awed by neither. Indeed he is duly appreciative of the accomplishments as well as weaknesses of both cultures. He views them both from the perspective of theoretical exile.

Ebrahim Golestan was born in Shiraz to one of the city's most prominent families. His grandfather was an esteemed and defiant ayatollah—exiled by Reza Shah—and his father published, for many years, a newspaper of liberal persuasion called *Golestan*. His house was a veritable literary and political salon, and it was there that the young Ebrahim met, for the first time, many of the famous writers and poets of the time. Golestan also began to satisfy his insatiable curiosity about the world by devouring the books his father had collected. At the behest of his father, he learned French and could speak it fluently before he left high school.

He was educated first in Shiraz and then in Tehran. At the same time he was an avid athlete, holding for many years a national record in track. In Tehran he joined the newly-formed communist party and soon rose through its ranks to become the editor of the party paper. From early

---

7. For an excellent discussion of the question of private and public, see Richard Rorty, *Contingency, Irony and Solidarity* (New York, 1980).

youth, he was also keenly interested in photography and once he decided to leave the party, around 1946, he became a professional photographer. By then he had also published his first collection of short stories. Eventually he joined the National Iranian Oil Company, where making educational films was part of his responsibility.

His articles in the party press and the publication of his collection of short stories established his reputation as one of the country's leading intellectuals and writers. His circle of friends included Hedayat, Chubak and Tavalalli.[8] He began an intense relationship with Forough Farrokhzad that lasted until her premature death in 1966, and it is easily the most celebrated love affair in all of modern Persian literature. His marriage to his cousin—and the marriage of cousins, according to Iranian custom, is made in heaven—continued in spite of the fact that the tempestuous affair became the subject of much gossip.

Farrokhzad's death, and the gradual tightening of political screws in Iran, convinced Golestan that he had to leave his homeland. All his life, he had been essentially an autodidact. He felt Iran could no longer satisfy his curiosities. In the late sixties, he took a trip to France and, in his own words, spent some "six months just visiting museums and going to theaters and concerts."[9] He is a music and opera aficionado and one of the attractions of the West has always been its rich culture of concerts and operas. By the late 1960s, he had decided to live in exile. He returned only for a while to make the film *Ghost Valley*. Eventually he sold his studio—which had become very valuable as a result of the oil boom of the seventies—and made his permanent home in England. His wife and daughter still live in Iran. His son, Kaveh Golestan, was a successful photojournalist. In April 2003, while working on a story on the US invasion of Iraq, he was killed by a landmine.

It has often been suggested that modernity was created by exiles.[10] Furthermore, the Renaissance gave birth to the idea of the intellectual who is sometimes geographically but always emotionally disengaged from his native land. The concept of an "intellectual" has also been entangled with the question of nationalism and internationalism.

---

8. For an account of Hedayat and his work, see "Hedayat and the Tragic Vision" in this book, pages 89-97. Sadeq Chubak was a writer of renown in Iran who, like Golestan, migrated to the West—first London and then California—even before the Islamic Revolution. Some of his stories have been translated into English. Fereydoun Tavalalli was an accomplished poet and like Golestan, a member of the Tudeh party. Gradually nothing but a dim memory was left of his youthful radicalism. He died in Iran.

9. Ebrahim Golestan, from an interview I conducted August 9, 2003.

10. For a discussion of this relationship, see Susan Rubin, *Exile and Creativity* (New York, 1996), 2.

Machiavelli, as Golestan acutely observes,[11] was one of the first theorists of modernity. He well understood the crucial fact that the age of divine legitimacy had ended. The modern prince, Machiavelli said, must create and maintain his own legitimacy.

Machiavelli was also the first theorist of nationalism.[12] In fact over the last five hundred years, intellectuals have been the main theorists of the varying hues of nationalism. Intellectuals have also been the architects and beneficiaries of a new kind of internationalism; indeed, the new global republic of letters and rationalism, of empiricism and scientific method, has created a new international community to which every intellectual can belong. Intellectuals, while critical of their societies, are invariably citizens of this republic. They live in the realm of ideas and words. Golestan's views on patriotism, nationalism, and internationalism are a polished Persian embodiment of these global ideas.

"Iran," he says, "is not just a geographical unit; it is a cultural state." He emphasizes that "my exile had taken place even when I lived in Tehran."[13] He believes that "one's country is as powerful and expansive as the culture that thrives inside one."[14] He explains that "cultures are not static; in fact, the realm of a culture is never a small corner of earth, or a dot on a map." He refers to the republic of letters as "the active relations between vital intelligences." He goes on to define culture as "the constant and dynamic" exploration of ideas.[15]

At the same time, he is deeply critical of the cultural fate that has befallen Iran. "Our culture," he says, "has long since fallen into a state of decadence." It has become "warped."[16] Iran suffers from a kind of split personality. In Golestan's view, Iranians neither know their own culture, nor that of the West. In trying to understand either culture, they often suffer either from silly grandiosity or poisonous self-loathing.[17] This schism, he declares, has impacted the Iranian mind and vision of the world. In its encounter

---

11. Golestan writes of Machiavelli as "a great thinker who was, in what he wrote and in his vision, a man of the Renaissance." *Gofteha*, 74. It is interesting that he wrote these words even before the resurgence of Machiavelli scholarship in the West during the last two decades. From Leo Strauss to Isaiah Berlin, many thinkers have in recent years written about the importance of Machiavelli.

12. On the question of Machiavelli and nationalism, see Isaiah Berlin, *The Crooked Timber of Humanity* (New York, 1991), 238-263.

13. Ebrahim Golestan, *Nameh-i be Simin* [A letter to Simin], unpublished manuscript. Ebrahim Golestan kindly provided me a copy of the letter.

14. Golestan, *Gofteha*, 51.

15. Ibid., 51.

16. Ibid., 57.

17. It is interesting to note that Golestan's views here are very similar to those articulated by Shadman. See "Shadman and Modernity" in this book.

with the inevitable modern experience, Iran, according to Golestan, faces a serious crisis of historic proportions. Iranians, however, have been hardly prepared for the implications of this encounter. Instead, they "have clung to appearances,"[18] and lulled themselves with the false comfort of facile answers. They have forfeited the task of arriving at fair, judicious, critical and informed judgments about themselves and the West. Golestan's analytical, emotional and eventually geographical distance from Iran afforded him the opportunity to arrive at radically different judgments.

Golestan maintains this distance even when he is writing about his own work. His introduction to the collection of his essays is a clear example of this tendency. Writing in the first person when offering factual accounts, he suddenly switches to a second person perspective when passing judgment on his life. Oftentimes, when people refer to themselves in this way, it can be construed as a sign of arrogance. In Golestan's case, it indicates his attempt to find an objective theoretical perspective, the requisite distance, from which to view his own work. He describes himself as a "normal man of normal height and average intelligence...in a neighborhood of dwarfs." He says to himself: "You wanted to see correctly; maybe you didn't see correctly, but you saw honestly.... You knew that your attempts to see correctly, and consequently describe correctly, made you a stranger. It made you different and in your own mind it made you proud of yourself. Such pride was rueful; it was a pride that came as a result of the dwarfish nature of your surroundings; the surroundings were short, you were not tall."[19]

The culture of criticism in Iran has been ill at ease with this kind of self-assertiveness. In post-World War II Iran, literary criticism was under the theoretical sway of Russian social realism. Ideas like the "social foundations" of art, the "class struggle," and the "responsibility" of the artist were the shibboleths of the day. Artists like Golestan were derided as decadent and bourgeois while the stories of brave but mediocre writers like Samad Behrangi were praised as commendable examples of committed art. Even a well-read critic like Reza Baraheni, forgetting that after the early sixties Golestan made no commissioned films, referred to him as "the best escapee of our time. He knows that if he talks of politics and society, even if he talks of them eloquently, his words will not be taken seriously because of his wealth. He knows that if he writes against oppression and power, people will not take him seriously, and those in power might become suspicious, and no longer commission him to make films."[20]

---

18. Ibid., 50.
19. Ibid., 22-23.
20. Reza Baraheni, *Gheseh Nevisi* [Writing fiction] (Tehran, 1348/1969). I have heard that Mr. Baraheni is in the process of writing a new essay where he will offer a different reading of Golestan and his work.

While pseudo-critics advocated the virtues of simple writing and simple-minded art, Golestan wrote stories that were as complicated in structure as the worlds they described. He believes that invariably there is just one right way to articulate an idea and image, and it is the responsibility of the artist to "work hard and honestly to arrive at this single form; other forms are characterless, and false."[21] Through experience, he came to recognize that "there is no difference between the shallow views of the Left and the Right;"[22] one makes literature the tool of the party and history; the other wants it subservient to God, the king, the country, or the leader. Golestan often pointed to the clear similarities between dogmatic Marxism and dogmatic faith. He noted that there was "a whole lost generation…[that] needed a father-figure, a Mecca."[23] He realized that both the Left and the Right see art as an instrument of ideology, and refuse to accept its autonomy. Both think content is more important than form, and both invariably prefer a revolutionary content to a creative form. Golestan, on the other hand, offers a different vision of the role of politics in literature. Just as another filmmaker—Jean Luc Godard—declared, "The problem is not to make political films, but to make films politically," Golestan believes that "being a revolutionary has nothing to do with the subject you choose; it has to do with how you develop a subject…. [How you] discover its essence"[24] and give it a commensurate form.

In fighting kitsch, Golestan is unforgiving. He minces no words, even when he is writing about the work of a friend. His review of the paintings of his deceased friend Pezeshknia is a good example of this candid style. In this brief obituary—parts of which seem closely autobiographical—Golestan writes of a generation of artists that harbored high hopes and utopian dreams. They tried to realize this utopia by the use of rancid Russian ideas about committed art. The result was disaster. They neither created art nor arrived at their utopian dream. Pezeshknia was typical of this generation: "he went after shallow ideas; he became an image-maker of the world of appearances; true painting is different from mere imitation."[25]

In a talk given to students at Shiraz University in 1969, Golestan was even more blunt in explicating his views on art and the nature of modernity. In those days, just as today, Iranian students were at the vanguard of the political struggle against oppression. Intellectuals and artists often used public occasions to praise the students. But there was no praise coming

21. Golestan, *Gofteha*, 155.
22. Ibid., 133.
23. Ibid., 131.
24. Ibid., 132.
25. Ibid., 136-137.

from Golestan that day. Instead, he began his talk by chastising the students: "I know well, in fact I am convinced, that not even two percent of you have read the few stories of mine; nor have you seen the few films I have made. And you have come here just as you would go to the circus.... In fact, I don't think you know much of value about prose or stories or films. And poetry is no different."[26] Then eschewing the fashionable slogans of the day about the class nature of art, he emphasized that "art is always individualistic; it has been and will always be the objectification of the subjective experience of an individual."[27] It would, I think, be difficult to find a more apt description of the aesthetic foundations of modernity. In every realm—from economy and religion to epistemology and aesthetics—modernity is based on individualism. In aesthetics, modernity's point of departure is the notion that only the artist can, and should, decide what is beautiful; church or state, aristocracy or secret police, cannot and should not dictate the parameters of the beautiful. Art, in short, is ultimately a means for individual self-expression, and nothing more.[28]

Golestan's candor was not limited to his talks with students. He spoke to those in power no less bluntly. Iranian intellectuals in those days, inspired by the Russian notion of an *intelligentsia*, considered themselves in perpetual and irreconcilable conflict with the status quo. In their public pronouncements—if not always in private practice—they were averse to any kind of cooperation, even contact, with the Shah's regime. Any such contact was considered tantamount to betrayal. Golestan took a different approach and paid for it by becoming the subject of a campaign of gossip and innuendo.

In deciding his attitude toward the Shah's regime, he paid no heed to these attacks, or to the received opinion of the day about the duties of committed intellectuals. Instead, he took a more personal and pragmatic approach, working with those in government he liked, and criticizing those he disliked. In his view, some in the government showed considerable intellectual power and complemented that with respect for human dignity. In spite of being "caught in the straitjacket of their time," they were "committed to the comfort and dignity of the people in their community." In the long run, they were far more effective in serving their country than "the impotent phrasemongers who, in desperation, incurable jealousy and malicious envy,"[29] did nothing other than engage in futile and nihilistic negativism.

---

26. Ibid., 36-37.
27. Ibid., 30.
28. For a path-breaking discussion of the aesthetics of the Renaissance, see Walter Pater, *The Renaissance: Studies in Art and Poetry* (Berkeley, 1980).
29. Golestan, *Gofteha*, 30.

Even though he agreed to work with some of those in power, Golestan never seems to have compromised his intellectual honesty or his rightful critical disposition. In fact he sometimes used his privileged position to offer unusually harsh words or images in his work. His film *Mysteries of the Treasure at Ghost Valley*[30] is the best example of his signally harsh criticism of the highest authority, the Shah himself. But his other works are often no less blunt in their critique. His film on Iran's crown jewels is a good example of his approach. Dictates of political puritanism of the day surely militated against the very idea of making such a commissioned film, but Golestan agreed to make it. He turned it, however, into a sobering meditation on modern Iran and the role of monarchy in its history.

As I've argued elsewhere,[31] the nineteenth century saw a new chapter in Iran's encounter with modernity. The discovery of oil turned Iran into a much coveted prize of the "Great Game." In their futile attempt to domesticate modernity, Iranian despots showed only frivolous curiosity about the West. The glitz of the modern appealed to the despots' craving for kitsch, whereas the philosophical underpinnings of the modern polity—such as the social contract and the rule of law—were inimical to their political disposition. In his film about the crown jewels, Golestan offers a pithy account of this historic encounter:

> In the middle of the nineteenth century, roads to Europe were opened. These [the crown jewels] were souvenirs of a journey to Europe. Souvenirs of a closed mind, besotted by toys. Souvenirs of men bedazzled with glitz and glamour. A world of rubies and diamonds and pearls…yet lost in despair. One hundred bejeweled golden watches. But no one paid any attention to Time, and to the passage of time. Only three pens in the midst of hundreds of thousands of precious artifacts. Every stone from this opulent collection is like a page torn from the history of the Persian people. A history of three hundred years of indifference, written in the glamorous syntax of jewels.[32]

Golestan's rendition of Qajar history is no less fascinating than his description of the jewels. He writes of Europe "experiencing an increasingly fast tempo of change," while the incompetence of Qajar kings left Iran in a devastating slumber. The years turned "desolate and inane."[33]

> The country needed a new order. The heap of precious stones was not a new order. In the dynamic tumult of the eighteenth century when new

---

30. For a political reading of the film, and an attempt to decode its many allusions to contemporary figures and events, See my *The Persian Sphinx: Amir Abbas Hoveyda and the Riddle of the Iranian Revolution* (Mage, 2001).
31. See the chapter in this book on Nasir al-Din Shah and his vision of modernity.
32. This comes from the narration of the film; it also appears in *Gofteha*, 177.
33. Ibid.

vision and thought were scripting a new fate for humanity, here in Iran, the quill was empty. The spirit of Fath Ali Shah's era can be discerned in the pattern of his plates and bowls, in necklaces and enameled boxes, in hookas and jugs and teapots. He built his throne with twenty-six thousand jewels and he signed the Turkmenchai Treaty.[34]

The pith and parsimony of Golestan's descriptions can themselves be construed as an element of his theory of modernity. Renaissance brought with it profound changes in the realm of language. On the one hand, prose became simpler and free from the convoluted medieval style. Another one of the key components of modernity was freeing language from the religious and philosophical constraints about carnality. In other words, in the West, from the fourth century when St. Augustine Christianized Plato's philosophy and in the process decried sexual pleasure as the work of the devil, language in Christian society eschewed any public reference to such pleasures. It was only from the fourteenth century, in the writings of people like Boccaccio, Abelard, Chaucer, and Shakespeare[35] that the body and its desires experienced an artistic renaissance. Painters and sculptors began to depict the sublime beauties of the naked body. Writers and poets began to openly talk of sexual desire and even describe erotic encounters.

One of the most important consequences of these developments was the appearance of a new genre called the novel. A novel is more than anything else the narrative of one individual's life as recounted by another individual. Novels have no tolerance for the Manichean view of the world, but instead explore the labyrinth of each individual psyche, and consider every human being the worthy subject of examination. The language of the novel is democratic; it is polyphonic; it heeds few of society's linguistic solemnities; and more than anything else, it is ultimately a form of dialogue, where absolute judgments have no place.[36] The language of the novel is altogether estranged from the certainties of sermons, and is instead founded upon the relativity of truth.

Concurrent with these changes, the very "meaning" and conception of a text changed. Hitherto, society had lived with the belief that there

---

34. Golestan, *Gofteha*, 177. One of the most notorious treaties in the history of modern Iran, it ceded large swaths of land—thirteen states including Georgia and the present-day republic of Azerbaijan—to Russia. The treaty came after a humiliating defeat in 1828 and is considered a turning point in Iranian history. It heralds the advent of a new age of Western hegemony, and Iranian defeat.

35. Much has been written about this aspect of the Renaissance. For example, see Walter Pater, *The Renaissance: Studies in Art and Poetry* (New York, 1998), 1-9.

36. For a discussion of the language of the novel, see M.M. Bakhtin, *The Dialogical Imagination: Four Essays*, trans. Caryl Emerson and Michael Holquist (Austin, 1990).

was ultimately one text—the Bible in Europe—that it had one meaning, and that its meaning had only one legitimate interpreter. Modernity "opened" the text by accepting the existence of multiplicities of texts and meanings and by making them accesible to more interpreters.[37] Pluralism—in politics, art, and epistemology—replaced the monism of the theocentric medieval world. Pluralism in politics required a new species of humans who were citizens—not subjects—of the state, fully cognizant of their rights and responsibilities in shaping their society's future. Pluralism in art demanded new readers who were not docile recipients of the artist's intended meaning, but worked with the artist in creating and negotiating that meaning.

Golestan's language is the language of modernity. His prose has often been praised for its beauty and precision. Even his staunchest critics concede that his writing is "one of the best examples of modern prose."[38] Some have suggested that Hemingway and Gertrude Stein inspired him. But in my opinion, the significance and innovation of Golestan's language—as well as its genealogical sources of inspiration—should be sought in other, native sources.

Golestan's prose is democratic in nature. On the one hand, he uses the languages of various strata of society, and creates polyphony in his narratives. His prose is also democratic because he demands the active participation of the reader in affording meaning to the text. In a traditional society, people are subjects of the king; in a modern society, they are citizens. In the realm of meaning, too, people in the former case need a supervisor, a shepherd, a leader to find the ultimate meaning, and they themselves are passive subjects. Conversely, in the latter case, people take upon themselves the task of finding meaning. In short, in place of one text with one meaning, authored by one omnipotent and omniscient author, now sit independent readers, who are on the same level as the author, and who set out to discover and create the meanings of each text on their own. Golestan's prose then, with its beautiful silences, its poetic reserve, its luminous enigmas, is precisely one that begets citizen-readers and disdains docile readers, or "subjects." Lazy readers are not welcome in the landscape of these stories. The structures of some of Golestan's short stories are not at times dissimilar to a puzzle. His "Thieves on the Job"[39] perfectly embodies this kind of prose. As the events drag into the

---

37. Umberto Eco, *The Limits of Interpretations* (Bloomington, 1990).

38. Reza Baraheni, Writing Fiction (Tehran, 1348/1969), 450. Houshang Golshiri too, on several occasions, has written about the beauty of Golestan's prose and the influence it has had on modern Persian fiction.

39. Ebrahim Golestan, "Thieves on the Job," in *Azar, Mahe Akhr-e Paiz*, 9.

night, the story, though simple in appearance, becomes more complicated and baroque; only astute and persistent readers might decode it.

Another democratic aspect of Golestan's language can be seen in his
effort to bring written and oral discourse closer together. For about
150 years, many Iranian writers have been trying to eliminate the difference between the language of the street and that of literature. But
the proximity of these two in Golestan's stories is distinct from what
other artists had hitherto achieved. He incorporates the poetry and
music of a conversation, with its crescendos and silences, into the texture of his prose. In other words, the structure of his sentences reflects
the silence, the acts of omission and implication, that are found in a
real conversation. Just as the correct reading of a poem requires both
command and cognizance of its rhyme and meter, the correct reading
and understanding of Golestan's prose requires familiarity with its special rhyme and rhythm. In describing what he calls "clean prose," he
refers to this point, and emphasizes that in writing, the most important thing is "to take as our model the trend of an oral conversation,
that has the effervescence of a living organism, and the liveliness of
effervescence." The point is not, he suggests, "to break words or bring
into our language the transient expressions of the street. No, what I
mean is for us to hear how we talk in private, with what rhythm and
tempo, and what order of words. Then, instead of rolling them on our
tongue, we should roll them off our pen."[40] This he calls the poetics
of language, and emphasizes that Persian writers have been aware of
this trope for a good millennium. That is why he emphasizes that the
real roots of his prose must be sought not in Hemingway, but in the
rich legacy of Persian literature, in writers like Sa'di and Beyhaghi.

There is yet another aspect that renders Golestan's language particularly modern. Following in the footsteps of such early masters as the poet
Nezami, Golestan infuses some of his stories and films with startlingly
frank and surprisingly beautiful descriptions of erotic desire.[41] In one
masterful scene, the rhythm of his prose describing a passionate encounter
between a man and a woman traveling on a train provocatively parallels
the rhythm of the train's motion and sound:

> Suddenly then, she was in my arms, and the warmth of her breath, and
> the salty smoothness of her lips and the dark discs of her vertebrae and
> the abundant warmth of her breasts, and the fever of her entire body, a

---

40. Golestan, *Gofteha*, 224.
41. For an erudite and eye-opening account of the history of erotica in Persian letters—
particularly those belonging to the period I have referred to as the age of Iran's aborted
modernity—see Jalal Khaleghi Motlagh, "Tan Kameh Sarai dar Adab-e Farsi," [Erotica
in Persian letters], *Iranshenasi*, vol. 1 (Spring 1375/1996): 15-55.

spreading fervor of possession in a moment with no limits in time, and when she pulled the handle, the door opened and we entered into a kiss that tasted of blood…. And the rest remained unsaid, in a kiss that rolled, and we rolled, and the bed was too small, and the light shone through the curtain.[42]

In his other stories, Golestan writes of other elements of this carnal power. He describes the passionate intensity of young lovers' desire for one another, and of the persistence of love, and its battle with social and political mores of the time. In one story, he also hints, following in the footsteps of Freud, of the relationship between the repression of sexual desire and the act of aesthetic creativity. Freud believed that civilization begets discontent and neurosis, because it inevitably requires the suppression of our instinctive desires. Such neurosis, in turn, becomes the very sublimated source of art and civilization. The narrator in "Love in Green Years"[43]—whose title conjures Cleopatra's "salad days"[44]—begins to read a story just when he feels his love is rebuffed.

There are of course critics who believe that writing about carnal desire, indeed the whole experience of modernity, is Western in nature. They further argue that such modern genres as the novel and the short story are rooted in the Western cultural landscape. In their reckoning, Iranian artists who want to write a novel or become "modern" have no choice but to learn at the feet of Western writers. Golestan is among the handful of Iranian writers and thinkers who have refused to accept this Eurocentric notion. He believes it to be a mistake to assume that Iranian short stories, for example, began with the work of Mohammad Ali Jamalzadeh and Ali Akbar Dehkhoda in the early twentieth century. This kind of storytelling, he asserts, has existed in Iran from the birth of the Persian language. Stories can be found in every language; in fact, Persians have an unusually rich legacy of them—from the poet Nezami and his *Haft Paikar* to Gorgani, whose eleventh-century story *Vis-o Ramin* is a source of *Tristan and Isolde*— but seem ignorant of their privileged literary legacy.[45]

42. Ebrahim Golestan, *Madd-o Meh* [The tide and the fog] (New Jersey, 1373/1994). First printed in Tehran, 1969/1348.

43. Ebrahim Golestan, *Juy-o Divar-o Teshneh* [The stream, the wall and the thirsty] (New Jersey, 1373/1994).

44. In Shakespeare's *Anthony and Cleopatra* we find the following words referring to her earlier love for Caesar, "My salad days when I was green in judgment." (Act I: V, 3). Golestan, himself, suggests that there is no connection and that he had not been thinking of the Shakespearean lines when he chose the title. Golestan, interview with author, 22 July 2002.

45. Golestan, *Gofteha*, 38-39.

This ignorance is not limited to knowledge of the genealogy of short stories. It is also no mere accident, but an integral part of a larger historical pattern. According to Golestan, Iranian consciousness suffers from a deep schism. Just when the West was posed to take off with the burst of energy that was the Renaissance, Iranian culture "began to stagnate and deteriorate, and in consequence, we became ignorant of both the past and the present. And all we did was to imitate, not to extrapolate."[46] If Iranians ever awaken from this dangerous slumber, they will recognize that not just in the realm of the novel, but in many other areas as well, they need not consider themselves mere mimics of the West. Golestan believes that the meaning of modernity can be summarized in two words: "Being human."[47] He seems to be referring to the commonly accepted notion that secular humanism is the core of the modern experience. He writes that a single line of Sa'di's poetry, in which he talks of the shared essence of humanity, embodies the core axiom of the Renaissance.

Critical self-knowledge has been said to be one of the other pillars of modernity and Golestan laments that Iranians have been singularly remiss in this arena. By way of example, he writes of his own experience, and how he learned about the importance of one of the great mystics of Islam—Sheikh Ruzbehan Baghli (d. 1206)—only through the writings of the French scholar, Henry Corbin. Adding insult to injury, the Sheik was buried down the street from Golestan's grandmother lived. He also bitterly remembers how Sadeq Hedayat made fun of Corbin and his work, implying that the study of Islamic Iranian tradition was worthless.[48] In the West, modernity began, according to Golestan, when people questioned all that was "routine and regular;"[49] in Iran too, we must quit gnashing our teeth because we have fallen behind the caravan of history, and begin instead a process of honest and radical critique and analysis. We must, he says, "become naked, and take a good warm bath" and wash away "all the dead cells—blood must flow normally. We must become ourselves, and not some listless and lifeless statue."[50] Golestan's stories and films are such commendable embodiments of what Persian literature can be when it is true to itself.

---

46. Ibid., 48.
47. Ibid., 45.
48. Ibid., 62. Hedayat, along with many other intellectuals of his generation, had little respect for scholars working on aspects of traditional Iranian culture and language. Hedayat even called them "grave robbers." The only exceptions to his ridicule were those studying pre-Islamic Iran.
49. Ibid., 73.
50. Ibid., 63.

The degeneration into lifeless bodies has brought with it the degeneration of language. Golestan is well aware of the intricate and intimate relationship between language and thought. He knows that, "when the mind is not living…the stimuli and tools of the mind also fall into disuse, as they have in our case. Our language was impoverished by our mindlessness, and this poverty itself led to further mindlessness."[51] Only by transcending the reification[52] of our minds and language can we begin to experience genuine modernity. Many of Golestan's stories and films are explorations into the ebb and tide of this transcendence.

Golestan thinks that the Iranian experience with authoritarian modernity—where "modernizing monarchs" change society at the point of a bayonet—has been, as expected, warped at its roots. In *A Tale of Times Past*, he excavates the early phases of this change, while in *Mysteries of the Treasure at Ghost Valley*, he depicts its joyless, even tragic end. His other stories are equally committed to exploring different aspects of this experience. They are glimpses into one moment or episode in the lives of his characters; at the same time they are parables, pregnant with metaphoric meaning about the historic fate of the characters and the social context of their existence. "The Cripple" is a good example of these two layers of meaning.

The story's title, as is often the case in Golestan's works, is particularly rich and resonant with implications. It refers to the fact that one of the protagonists is physically handicapped, and that another becomes incapacitated by the end of the story. It also conjures the more general historic proposition that the Iranian path to modernity has become somehow blocked. The transition from a feudal society to a capitalist modern polity is captured in the life of a village boy, who comes to the city in desperate search of job and survival. He eventually finds employment in a wealthy household. If in the West the Renaissance brought with it mobility and conquest, and in consequence transformed the geographical frontiers of our world, in Iran the child of this modern family is incapable of ambulation. Even the names of these two young boys hint at the changing nature of the times. One is called Hassan, an Arab name with echoes of Iran's religious tradition; the other goes by the name of Manouch, a shortened form of the pre-Islamic Iranian name Manouchehr, and in its abbreviated form redolent of a kitsch secular culture.

Hassan's job is to carry Manouch around on his back. The hard and torturous work is made more difficult by the daily verbal indignities he

---

51. Ibid., 112-113.
52. For a discussion of reification, see Georg Lukacs, *History and Class Consciousness*, trans. Rodney Livingston (London, 1971), 83-110.

suffers. Yet the day when a wheelchair that "Manouch himself can roll around"[53] appears in the house, Hassan's livelihood, as well as his dreams and ideals are seriously threatened. His anger is aroused; he seeks a solution. In his tormented imagination, "the wheel of the chair became bigger and bigger by the minute, eventually taking over the whole place. He knew he had to break the wheel; he sensed that he would not have peace unless he destroyed it; he will not be himself unless he breaks the wheel."[54] Hassan's angry response repeats the historic experience of the working class in industrial societies. In his magnum opus, *Das Kapital*, Karl Marx observes that early in the development of capitalism, workers naively begin their struggle against the system by breaking the machinery. They believe this will liberate them from the shackles of the capitalist system. Marx argued that with class-consciousness comes the recognition that the worker's real enemies are in fact the capitalist system and private property, not the machines. "The Cripple" thus becomes a tragic and potent metaphor for the experience of modernity in Iran, wherein the bourgeois elements of society—and the supposed harbingers of change—are crippled at birth, and Hassan, who can be seen as a reference to either the youthful elements of tradition, or the country's new-born working class, is only too happy to be a coolie and carry his master around.

But even this mangled modernity is enough to change everything in society. Not only the architecture of the city but the very nature of human relations and the structure of human thought undergoes a transformation. In the novella *A Tale from Times Past,* Golestan traces these dynamic changes in the city of Shiraz, his beloved birthplace. The story's pivotal character is a servant for the narrator's family. He and his elderly wife do not utter more than a few sentences during the course of the novella, but they cast a heavy shadow over the whole narrative.

The narrator's family is among the most influential in the city. The power and the prominence of some in the family are on the rise, while others are falling in social status. Absolute power has been hitherto in the hands of the father, who has a particular affinity for trees and flowers. But soon his omnipotence begins to wane. In the overall historic evolution of modern cultures, patriarchy is usually overthrown or weakened. In Golestan's story, even nature hints at this pattern of change. We read of trees that "were no longer anything other than barren trunks, with no leaves, no fruits, not even branches, nothing."[55] In the fast-changing

53. Ebrahim Golestan, "Lang" [The cripple], in *Shekar-e Sayeh* [Hunting shadows] (New Jersey, 1994/1373), 82.
54. Ibid., 93.
55. Ebrahim Golestan, *The Tide and the Fog*, 43.

society of the day, all that was left of patriarchy, and the omnipotence of tradition, was a barren trunk, an empty form.

The composition of the city too is rapidly changing. In the narrator's neighborhood, the bustle of new houses is rapidly replacing the quiet of farms.[56] Even the bazaar, the center of economic power for the traditional classes, has not been immune to change. Its once rich and colorful labyrinthine alleys, even some of the houses in its vicinity, have been demolished. Social mobility usually implies geographical movement and architectural transformation. The narrator's family, as expected, moves to a new home. In this process, the uncle plays a key role. He bribes his way into Parliament, and then feels compelled to purchase a new house befitting his elevated status.

Moving the entire family to this new abode is of course no simple matter. In order to find the auspicious time to move, they have to consult the Qur'an. Here Golestan is alluding to one of the recurrent problems of societies in transition. Economic foundations, even social institutions, can be altered easily, whereas people's habits and social mores are more resistant to change. The restoration of the *status ante*, a return to the past, threatens all transitional societies, and one of the most potent sources for this "restoration" are the unchanging and stubborn habits of culture and morality. In the latter part of the twentieth century, such movements of restoration have often taken on a religious guise. The Shiraz of the narrator's childhood is no exception to these general patterns.

In spite of the inchoate nature of the transition, every facet of life, including social relations, is undergoing important transformation. As the power of the patriarch declines, the geography of the city and the topography of social classes change. Using a language tinged with melancholy, tapered with parsimony and truncated by ambivalence, Golestan's description of the changing city—of the slow dying of the old and the tenuous birth of the new—is one of the most beautiful parts of the novella. The most important manifestation of these transformations can be seen in the fate of the household servant. He has worked for the family for many years. But as traditional relations begin to shatter, and as the family can no longer afford to keep him, he is sent away, only to end up in a poorhouse. On the other hand, another son of a poor family in the neighborhood has "now found a job in the Ministry of Justice,"[57] one of the most coveted economic niches for the non-propertied urban classes. Modernity is coterminous with social mobility. In traditional societies, social status is unchanging and static. There is a kind of social

56. Ibid., 57.
57. Ibid., 40.

sclerosis precluding, if not indeed prohibiting, upward or downward motion. This stasis, or the recognition of it, also begets a sense of social security; the existing social structure, though unfair, can be relied upon to provide for everyone according to their status. In traditional Iran, the servant would have probably ended up living with the family until the end of his life. But modernity allows for change in social status; on the one hand, such a possibility fosters hope in a better future; that is why modernity brings with it the idea of "progress." The other side of the same coin, however, is social insecurity, the evil twin of the modern age. In the Shiraz of the narrator's childhood, this insecurity begins to chip away at everyone's human dignity, especially those of the lower strata.

These changes also bring with them serious alterations in sartorial style. For example, Reza Shah ordered Iranian women to unveil, and men to wear Western-brimmed hats. The content of pedagogy witnessed equally radical alterations. One of the most crucial signs of modernity is the advent of a new kind of historiography. Medieval history was more hagiographic; it trafficked in panegyrics and offered only praise for the exploits of kings and other eminent people. The Renaissance introduced the idea of a rational, even causal, historiography. Society is henceforth deemed an organism conforming to lawful patterns, discernable to rational inquiry. Furthermore, the everyday lives of common people become a legitimate subject of history.[58] In Shiraz, too, the content of history began to change. Hitherto, students had been taught only a kind of mytho-history. The lives of kings—from Darius to Xerxes—were altogether unknown to them. The new history was "different from the stories of earlier times."[59]

And in *A Tale of Times Past* the town mullah—who also doubles as the school's history teacher—adamantly opposes the new lessons. He is particularly incensed that the new books praise Cyrus, whom he calls "an infidel."[60] Lauding him, he often rants, is tantamount to heresy. Some thirty years after this story was written, the outbursts of Sheik Sadeq Khalkhali—the "hanging judge"—against Cyrus closely mimicked what the mullah rails against in Golestan's fiction.[61]

If the recalcitrant mullah embodies a force against modernity, the narrator's two uncles embody the warped, official modernity endorsed by the Pahlavi regime. The uncle who had borrowed money on the family's house and bribed himself into Parliament soon translates political position into

---

58. For a discussion of changes in historiography in the West, see Michel De Certeau, *The Writing of History*, trans. Jay Conley (New York, 1988).

69. Ibid., 34.

60. Ibid., 39.

61. Sheikh Sadeq Khalkhali, *Kourosh-e Doroughin-e Jenayat-kar* [The false and criminal Cyrus. (Tehran, 1370/1990).

economic power, buying up property and even a factory in town. The two brothers—once victims of the family patriarch's cruelty—gradually become so powerful that no one, "not even father," dares challenge them.[62]

Even this uncle, however, has many views often recognized as modern. On the one hand, he is critical of the proclivity of his family—and of Persians in general—to avoid direct talk and take refuge in honorifics, dissimulation, and a habit of linguistic hints and allusions. He declaims, "you never say what you really mean; you circumvent the word."[63] At the same time, he is a firm believer in the modern idea that man is the architect of his own fate. Our fortunes are not in our stars, he often declares. Even when he is rolling the dice for a game of backgammon, he chides his competitors that "we shouldn't let two little dice decide our fate."[64]

The human consequences of this belief in individual determinism can be seen in the uncle's approach to the fate of the old family servant. The father is still a firm believer in traditional values; he is convinced the old man must be saved, lest the neighbors say that the family has been remiss in its duties to an old servant. The uncle, on the other hand, suggests that everyone should be responsible for his own fate. As the two camps in the family fight over their competing visions, it is the poor servant's lot to rot away and die a lonely death. His fate is a metaphor for the lives of millions of people in societies undergoing similar transitions. The traditional values that offer them some form of old-age security have vanished, and the new welfare system that under many capitalist systems replaces this subtle, voluntary network has not yet been established.

Another curse of traditional societies like Iran is the pervasive belief in a messiah. Disenfranchised people are commonly prone to a deep yearning for a savior who will come and lead them to a promised land. In several stories, Golestan tackles this problem by combining his deep knowledge of Iran—of its history and geography, its literature, and the mores and manners of different social strata—with the writer's keen eyes for details, offering gripping, albeit sad, stories about the pervasive hold of this kind of false hope amongst Iranians. "Waiting means not living in the moment,"[65] he writes. He describes the lingering habit of some Iranians of small towns, who in anticipation of the expected Mahdi, saddle a horse "every day, early in the morning...in case the messiah arrives."[66] In another story, one of the characters laments this long, futile wait, and defiantly declares, "when the messiah forgets to arrive" on time, when he delays his arrival long

62. Golestan, The Tide and the Fog, 76.
63. Ibid., 82.
64. Ibid., 84.
65. Ibid., 173.
66. Ibid.

enough that "his wonted horse" is no longer a means of travel, he too, in return, reserves the right "to doubt his saving powers."[67]

Though critical of the tradition of messianism in Iranian culture, Golestan himself, on one occasion, seems to advocate a modern, secular variety of messianic thought. Marxism, particularly in its Leninist reinvention where the vanguard party takes on the savior's mantle, finds fertile ground in the Shiite tradition of waiting for the Twelfth Imam. In fact, this and other strong structural similarities between Marxism and Shiism—both are messianic, both have a "sacred canon," both believe in the cult of an elite acting as agents of change, both practice forms of asceticism for this elite and for society at large, both want to create a new society based on a model of the "perfect human"—accounts for the relative ease with which Soviet Marxism grew in Iran, and was successful in aborting in embryo any democratic interpretation of Marxism. Remnants of this Bolshevik messianism, a lingering token of his youthful affliction with Tudeh ideology, can be seen in Golestan's definition of democracy. The goal of democracy, he suggests, "means working for the good of the people, not according to their wishes. People's wishes, and people's taste are by and large mediocre and mundane—it is in the interest of the people to reach higher levels, though their wishes and tastes remain stuck in the status quo. 'Great masses' and 'large strata' never determine their own demands."[68] Genuine democracy, however, is precisely when people themselves decide their own interest. From the time of the French revolution, often described as the clearest embodiment of the politics of modernity, there has developed two distinct interpretations of the notion of the people's will. On the one hand Jacobins believed that a vanguard minority knows better than the majority what the people's interests are. Out of this tradition, first embodied in Robespierre's gang of revolutionaries and their bloody Reign of Terror, came modern totalitarian "democracies" like the Soviet Union and China. The second group believed that only the masses themselves can decide and determine their interests, and anyone who claims to speak for the people has only their enslavement in mind. Liberal democracy is the result of this second analysis. Golestan's definition of democracy seems shaped by the first tradition.

In Iran, religion has been the chief source of messianic ideas, and Golestan, despite his youthful dalliance with messianic Marxism, offers a refreshingly bold and daring critique of this role in a novella called "Being or Being an Icon." Surely one of the first signs of modernity in

---

67. Ibid., 174.
68. Golestan, *Gofteha*, 324.

any society is the dismantling of the sacred halo of religion. In the Cartesian paradigm—embodying the quintessence of modernity—all ideas and beliefs, save the existence of a doubting self, are subject to doubt, skepticism, even satire. Faith, on the other hand, particularly in its Islamic guise, is founded on obedience and intolerance for making light of its beliefs and its solemnities. Golestan's "Being or Being an Icon" is a brilliant example of the kind of satire and sacrilege that one can expect from the best of modern secular artists.

In the story—its subtitle, "Puppet Show in Two Acts," is itself a defiant gesture to what the author thinks of religion—two brothers named Hassan and Hossein are waiting in the desert. Their father is waiting with them. After a while the mother, astride a camel and riding with a man, arrives. Soon we learn that the stranger is not a "dirty dog of an Armenian,"[69] but a Frenchman. He turns out to be the inventor of the camera—itself one of the most potent metaphors for modernity. Gradually the intended historic identity of the other characters becomes no less clear. Hossein, constantly complaining of thirst, is an unmistakable allusion to Imam Hossein, who along with his followers was deprived of water by the Caliph. One of the most venerable figures in all of Shiism, Hossein is the ultimate martyr in a religion that defines itself, at least partially, by the power of its martyrs. Hossein, like all Shiites, believed that after the death of Mohammed, the mantle of the prophet, or more specifically the authority over the Islamic community, was vested, by divine intervention, in the male progeny of Ali, the prophet's son in law and Hossein's father. Hossein's attempt to reclaim this authority led to the battle of Karbala in 680, in which Hossein and seventy-one of his followers perished. The story of his battle with the army of Yazid, the ruling Caliph, is the most powerful source of Shia's *ta'ziyeh*, or passion plays. But in the world of Golestan's story, Hassan calls Hossein a "masochist." In one scene, the older Hassan tells his brother, "sometimes you make an ass of yourself, and sometimes you make an ass of others. You have passion, but you don't have brains. It's like you were born only to become a martyr; it makes no difference for what. A professional martyr. You are more of a martyr than a human being."[70] He further emphasizes that Hossein's path has nothing in common with that of their paternal legacy. "This poor father of mine had reached light, had reached passion. He was living with truth. But you're slave to your habits—and you've pulled him away from light. You cast the cold shadow of your world on the circle of his light spirit."[71]

---

69. Golestan, The Stream, the Wall, and the Thirsty, 144.
70. Ibid., 151.
71. Ibid., 175.

Hassan has equally harsh words for the messianic proclivity found among Christians. Instead of waiting for a messiah, he advocates a kind of reformation. One of the central tenets of the Reformation was to make the relationship between humans and God direct, free from individual or institutional mediations. Furthermore, Reformists questioned the legitimacy of any one person's or institution's claim to have a monopoly on truth, or on the words of God. Finally, they doubted the claims of clerics to be the gatekeepers of heaven and hell. Selling indulgences was anathema to how they perceived the genuine nature of spiritualism. Golestan's Hassan offers very much the same kind of advice. He is against the idea, promoted by the rest of the family, of making a business out of religion. He is a true advocate of spirituality, and an individualist, suggesting, "you have to depend on your own mind; your own intelligence; even if it does not fit with that of the others."[72]

Hassan's mother and brother disregard his views. They have a highly pragmatic notion of religion. The only use they have for the photographer is to take a family photo, lest their followers forget them. People "can't understand something unless it is in front of their eyes. They forget. If you take a picture, they will be looking at you all the time, they will remember."[73] One would be hard pressed to find another published work of fiction in modern Persian literature that is more daring in its critique of some of the most sacred ideals and characters of Shiism.

The story is no less interesting in its advocacy of the kind of reformation modernity begets, and requires. Finally, the story is different from the kind of anti-Arab rhetoric one regularly finds in other modern literary critiques of Islam, of which Hedayat's short stories are the best example.

Golestan's most detailed treatment of Iran's encounter with forced modernity comes in *Mystery of the Treasure at Ghost Valley*.[74] Looking back at the film thirty-five years later, one is, I think, still impressed with its breath-taking bravado, and the obtuseness of the censors who failed to understand the film's radical message. Only after the film became an overnight sensation in Tehran did the dreaded secret police belatedly understand its subversive content and order it banned. By then Golestan had already chosen a life of exile and was more or less beyond their redress.

---

72. Ibid., 158.

73. Ibid., 155.

74. Lest the censors not allow the film to be shown in Iran, or confiscate copies of it, Golestan also published the film's script in the form of a book. In this essay, I have used the dialogue from the film. For the book version, see Ebrahim Golestan, *Asrar-e Ganj-e Dareh-ye Jenni* (Tehran, 1353/1974) The book was reissued along with the rest of Golestan's earlier books and stories in New Jersey in 1994.

The film was never shown again in Pahlavi Iran. The new Islamic government disliked its anti-clerical message and proscribed it.

The film was finished in 1971, just as the Shah's modernizing push was reaching a feverish pitch and oil revenues had begun their skyrocketing trajectory. In predicting the fall of the Shah at the height of his power and glory, the film was not just bold, but prophetic.

Ghost Valley is the story of a poor sleepy peasant in a poor sleepy village. The story begins when a band of engineers—whose intent and identity we never learn—arrive on the scene, prospecting for the construction of a new road. In other words, the story happens at the time when change and modernity are inevitably about to engulf the village. But the natural, normal course of events is unexpectedly changed one day, when a farmer, plowing his land with his ox, suddenly unearths a hidden treasure. It is hard to miss the allusion to oil; no less clear is the identity of the farmer. From the syntax of his speech and his taste for gadgets and gaudy buildings to the bash he throws to celebrate his newfound wealth, he is an eerie replica of the Shah.

The farmer's behavior begins to change as his wealth increases. But instead of making real changes to his house and village, he is only interested in changing their appearances. He goes on a shopping spree, only to buy junk, and engage in a textbook example of conspicuous consumption. He buys chandeliers, but the village still does not have electricity. He even orders the construction of a new phallic monument to his own grandeur that is unmistakably similar to the Shahyad building in Tehran.

A cast of characters, each representing Iran's different social strata, are also depicted with Golestan's characteristic pith. Like a master painter who, with the help of a few lines, can offer a full outline of a character, Golestan, too, is a writer of few words, each crafted to give the readers a sense of both the interiority and the outer appearance of his subjects. For example, his depiction of the Iranian technocrats, and their wager of tolerating the idiosyncrasies of the Shah in the hope of bringing about change, is full of fascinating insights, about not just Amir Abbas Hoveyda, the Shah's long-serving prime minister, but many of his other ministers as well.

The only character whose historic role in Iran's mangled modernity Golestan misses is the clergy. In *The Valley of Ghosts*, the mullah is an obsessive master of trivia. Like most modern Iranian intellectuals of the time, Golestan considered the clerics an historic anachronism, unwilling, and certainly incapable, of taking over the reins of power in Iran. The Islamic revolution was at least partially the result of this historic miscalculation.

HOUSHANG GOLSHIRI
The Janus Face of Tradition

Houshang Golshiri was arguably the most influential writer of his generation. On the eve of the Islamic revolution, he was one of the organizers of the famous "Ten Nights of Poetry" at Tehran's Goethe Institute. When his turn came at the podium, he eschewed the customary rousing speeches and fashionable political slogans; instead he talked of fiction; he lamented the fact that, in Iran, writers die young. They bloom early, he said, and then in the cultural wasteland produced by ubiquitous despotism, they wither away at the vine.[2] On that night, he was talking of artistic mutability, but with his own untimely death at the height of his creativity he became, at the age of sixty-three, a tragic example of the woeful pattern he had discovered.

Born into a working class family in Isfahan, he burst onto the literary scene with the publication of his acclaimed masterpiece, *Prince Ehtejab*.[3] He went on to write a number of other novels and collections of short stories. But to his consternation, critics found them all wanting compared with the story of the Prince. Aside from fiction, he dabbled in poetry, particularly in his youth. He also wrote several film scripts

---

1. This chapter is a composite of three earlier papers, presented at three different conferences. One was called, *"King of the Benighted* and the Poetics of Persian Culture" presented at the School of Oriental and African Studies, London University, May 25, 2001. The second was called "Golshiri and the Poetics of Persian Culture," presented at Princeton University's "Conference on Shamloo and Golshiri," October 20, 2001. Finally, the third paper was called "Taming the Shrew: Unveiling the Prince: Women in Golshiri's *Prince Ehtejab*," presented at the University of Virginia's conference on "Iranian Women's Cinema," March 30, 2002.
2. For the text of his talk, see Houshang Golshiri, "Javan Margi dar Nasr-e Moaser-e Farsi," [Premature Death in Contemporary Persian Prose] in *Bagh Dar Bagh* [Gardens within gardens], vol. 1 (Tehran, 1378/1999), 290-307.The collection was published while Golshiri was alive and includes a brief introduction by him to the two collections.
3. Houshang Golshiri, *Shazdeh Ehtejab* [Prince Ehtejab] (Tehran, 1357/1979). There is an English translation currently being prepared by British author James Buchan.

and plays. He was a prolific essayist and an indefatigable editor. He was intimately involved with many of the major literary magazines published in Iran in the last five decades. In his capacity as a critic, he was an iconoclast who often defied the shibboleths of the dominant discourse, and fashioned for himself a language and a theoretical vista that was uniquely independent, informed about the new theories but deeply immersed in the reality of Iran and its literary legacy.[4]

But he was more than anything else a writer. Fiction was for him an instinctive necessity, a primal urge, rooted in the human soul. Our acts of cognition, our communication patterns, our affective responses to the world are all, in their narrative structure, stories. He was himself the best example of his theory. The world made sense to him only through the prism of art. Even the question of modernity was for him interesting only to the extent that it could help him write better stories or better understand the history of Persian fiction. And he was a novelist who did not just write stories, but who had a keen interest in the poetics of fiction. In this arena, he wrote on a wide range of topics, including the narrative structure of the Qur'an and its use in literature, and the impact of Iran's oral tradition on modernist fiction. With a passion reminiscent of Patrick Chamoiseau's brilliant novels like *Texaco* and *Salibo Magnificent*, Golshiri contemplated the influence of *naqqali*[5] and the oral tradition on modern fiction. More importantly, on the question of the genesis of the Persian novel, he parted company with the dominant paradigm that had long argued that the novel, as a genre, is Western in nature and source. This prevalent theory implied that Iranian writers who want to be "modern" must emulate their Western masters.[6] Golshiri tried to debunk this theory, and on the way, perhaps unwittingly, helped to undermine the common Eurocentric notion of modernity as well. At the same time, his belief that traditional Persian literature should be mined by modern Persian writers—from the poetry of Nezami to the prose of religious *hadith*—led him to a new and fascinating reading of some of the past masters of Persian prose.[7]

---

4. For a collection of his essays, and poems, see the two volumes of *Bagh dar Bagh* [Gardens within gardens] (Tehran,1378/1999).

5. *Naqqali* refers to the highly stylized oral performance of Persian epic stories, particularly those from the *Shahnameh* (*Book of Kings*). There is now a beautifully rendered new translation of the *Shahnameh*, exquisitely published in three volumes by Mage. See Ferdowsi, *The Lion and the Throne, Fathers and Sons,* and *Sunset of Empire*, trans. Dick Davis (Washington, D.C. 1998, 2000, 2003). For Golshiri's views on naqqali, See his *Bagh dar Bagh*, particularly the section on fiction.

6. Christophe Balay, *La Genese du Roman Persan Modern* (Tehran, 1367/1998).

7. For his views on the genesis and evolution of Persian fiction, see his *Bagh Dar Bagh*, vols. 1 & 2, particularly pp.307-486 in vol. 1 and pp.559-639 in vol. 1.

His own prose is dense and often metaphoric. There is in his style of writing an elliptical and allusive quality that is based on Plato's theory of Forms. In the Platonic realm, men and women are born with an equal and primordial knowledge of all Forms; acts of cognition, as well as experiences of epiphany, are nothing but a kind of reawakening. I only hint, and make fleeting references, Golshiri said in a moment of self-deconstruction, and I count on the innate knowledge of my careful readers to afford words and stories their meanings. Thus a sparse style, an economy of images, and the masterly crafted quality of every sentence emerge as the characteristic signature of his prose.

From his earliest short stories to his last largely biographical novel, he depicts a society caught in the traumas of transition. Nearly every theme of his other works can be found in *Barreh-ye Gomshodeh-ye Ra'i (Ra'i's Lost Sheep)*, the first volume of an unfinished trilogy. In it, Golshiri writes elegantly about a crisis of identity that has beset Iranian society. The story recounts, with angst and melancholy, the plight of Iran's secular intellectuals: They have not yet grasped the meaning and consequences of modernity, yet they reject the tradition they consider reactionary and retrograde.[8] A whole generation is thus lost in the limbo of this transition.

This crisis of identity, according to Golshiri, is at once new and old. On the one hand, Persians have long carried the heavy cross of bifurcated identities. Golshiri writes of a thousand-years-old battle between the Persian and Islamic forces for the soul of Iran. With poetic poignancy, he suggests that the paisley, so commonly found in Persian art, is derived from the cedar tree, planted by Zarathustra, and then bent by the force of the Arab invasion.[9] Iran's encounter with the West, and its new modern ethos, only added to the confusion of this attenuated sense of self.

Another dominant theme in Golshiri's writing is his unrelenting critique of the messianic tendency so deeply ingrained in Persian history. In his often ignored and undervalued *Ma'sum-e Panjom, (The Fifth Saint)*,[10] published prophetically on the eve of the Islamic Revolution, the narrator uses a rich archaic prose to underscore the idea that the Shiite expectations of the return of a Savior—a "Hidden Mahdi"—and the Marxist hopes of a proletarian revolution are ultimately part of the same beguiling and misguided fabric of false hope and dangerous utopian dreams. Messianism and modernity are of course inseparably and inversely connected, with conspiracy theories the other side of the messianic coin.

---

8. Golshiri, *Barreh-ye Gomshodeh-ye Ra'i* [The lost sheep of Ra'i] (Tehran, 1355/1976). The book was never again allowed to be published.

9. Golshiri, *Lost Sheep*, 171-176.

10. Golshiri, *Ma'sum-e Panjom* [The fifth saint], (Tehran, 1357/1979).

In both messianism and conspiracy theorizing, society is convinced of its own powerlessness; in both, individuals are deemed helpless and insignificant in shaping society's fate. However, as a society begins to accept the idea that individuals themselves are the architects of their own fates and histories, as it feels empowered by the practice of democracy, the passive expectations of a heavenly redeemer and the sinister scenarios about the machinations of master conspirators begin to dissipate. Golshiri's two masterpieces, *Prince Ehtejab,* written in the early days of his literary life, and *King of the Benighted,*[11] completed in the last decade of his life, elegantly dissect the human dimensions of these historic tides and turns. They also offer a bold and honest analysis of the Janus face of Persian tradition: Its patriarchal and religious brutalities on the one hand, and the liberating creativity of its tradition, or more specifically, the precociously "modern" ideas of such progressive thinkers as Nezami, on the other.

Both works were written at crucial moments in the country's encounter with modernity. *Prince Ehtejab* was published in the late sixties, when the Shah's modernizing push was reaching a feverish pitch. It depicts the historic impotence, the incorrigible insularity and incompetence of Iran's traditional elite. *King of the Benighted,* on the other hand, was published when the Islamic Revolution, with its de-modernizing ethos, was working itself into a bloody frenzy. In these stories, it becomes clear that neither utopian zealots nor a consumptive aristocratic class can lead Iran out of its centuries-old impasse.

Prince Ehtejab is a chilling look into the darker side of Iran's tradition. It offers a fascinating perspective on the role of Iranian women in the transition to modernity. The poetic, intricately parsimonious prose of *Prince Ehtejab* tries to capture the dying gasps of an anguished man, cursed with the power of memory, overladen with the weight of a dehumanizing past, and faced with the challenge of a new species of self-assertive woman. The novel is an intricate, maze-like discourse on what Shakespeare calls "sessions of silent thought," summoning up the "remembrance of things past."

Some feminist critics have taken Golshiri to task for what they consider his trivializing rendition of women. But in *Prince Ehtejab*, women are the intellectual, emotional and ethical anchors of the narrative; they

---

11. Manouchehr Irani, *King of the Benighted,* trans. Abbas Milani (Washington, DC, 1991). The manuscript was sent to me in several inconspicuous envelopes. In one, the author asked me to translate the book and publish it under a pseudonym. I chose Manouchehr Irani. After Golshiri's death, according to his expressed wishes, I divulged the true identity of the novella's author.

are the harbingers of modernity, and its incumbent mobility; they foster critical introspection, perpetually de-centering and constantly challenging temporal, geographical and intellectual boundaries. They are the high priestesses of what the German historian Hans Blumenberg calls "secular Gnosticism,"[12] a critical self-knowledge that is the very center of the modern experience. They are interchangeably the subject of reverence and rape; their reverence might lead to self-discovery and liberation for the otherwise lost and tormented soul of the Prince; their rape is tantamount to his self-mutilation.

There is something strange and revealing about the title of the novel. The words *Shazdeh Ehtejab* are in Persian a linguistic oxymoron. *Dehkhoda*, the authoritative encyclopedia of the Persian language, gives two meanings for the word *ehtejab*: the first is "Going under a purdah, going under a *hejab*," or veil. While purdah and hejab can conjure a feminine aura as well as a more gender-neutral meaning of begetting mystery of being bashful, the second meaning given by Dekhoda is even more clearly gender-specific. Dehkhoda describes it as "the act of a woman going under the purdah." But as the first word of the title makes clear, the person of this veiling is a man. Why, we must ask, is a prince assuming the hejab?

The story begins with the Prince walking down a dark, dank corridor. Morad, once the Prince's chauffeur, now wheelchair-bound, awaits him. His handicap is the result of his inability to control the speeding coach he was driving. This erstwhile agent of mobility is now dependent for his movement on a veiled woman. We never learn her real name—she goes by her son's name, Hassani—for patriarchy dictates that a woman's name, like her body, is a part of her "honor," and must be guarded from the intrusive gaze and hearing of "others." Nonetheless, as the Prince approaches, it is Hassani who goads her husband into asking for money from the paupered aristocrat.

The feverish, consumptive Prince then enters the house and retires alone to the sitting room. He sits in a chair placed, rather absurdly, in the middle of a large, dark hall, "now empty of all the antique artifacts"[13] that once inhabited it. He is the ultimate exemplar of a bygone era, the feudal lord of an imaginary domain. He sits brooding, remembering another day in this room, a day in which his wife came briskly in and insisted upon turning on all the lights, despite his feeble objections.

On that long ago night, his wife, Fakhrolnesa, enters, turns on the lights, and then begins to wind the many clocks scattered around the

12. Hans Blumenberg, *The Legitimacy of the Modern Age*, trans. Robert M. Wallace, (Cambridge, 1983).
13. Golshiri, *Prince Ehtejab*, 7.

room—timepieces oblivious, like their owner, to the flow of time. They are clearly meant to be mere decor, but Fakhrolnesa now insists that they be functional. The Prince eventually and reluctantly joins her in winding them, despite his constitutional abhorrence of temporal discipline. The cacophony of the clocks' ticking, combined with the brightness of the lights, turns out to be more than he can bear. He protests, but to no avail. Fakhrolnesa then commandeers a pile of books and sends them to her room. "I want to confiscate the books,"[14] she says wryly. She launches into a sarcastic discussion of the travelogues of their common ancestors, also kept in this room. She vehemently expresses her abhorrence for the frivolity and cruelty of their aristocratic, patriarchal lives. In the book's opening, then, women are identified with at least three essential symbols of modernity: lights, clocks, and books.

The Prince is at once enlightened and frightened, aroused and threatened, by the woman he loves and despises. Like most men of modern Persian literature, he reveals starkly ambivalent feelings toward the beloved, whom he sees as both a whore and a Madonna. Fakhrolnesa—whose name literally means "the pride of women," and whose physical attributes owe much to Hedayat's *The Blind Owl* and to the Platonic ideal of female beauty that the Persian miniature has long tried to capture—is at once the Prince's nemesis and his messiah. Only by taming her honest, searing and relentlessly critical faculties, only by caging her mind and body in the confines of a constraining domesticity, only by himself seeking the purdah—a veil protecting him from the glaring gaze of her intellect—can his threatened identity be saved. Fakhrolnesa's self-assertiveness, her curiosity about the world, her critical disposition toward the past, all combine to make her the most potent symbol of modernity in the story.

The Prince's predicament is the classical case of the tragic "double bind." Following his wife's lead risks forfeiting his fragile sense of self, a self fashioned in large part by the misogynist pathology of his ancestors. And yet his decision to turn a deaf ear to her—eventually going to the length of incarcerating her in order to obtain her silence—results in the murder of that self. When Morad—whose name in Persian conjures utopian hope, but who serves in the novel as a harbinger of death—tells the Prince that "Ehtejab is dead,"[15] it is clear that the Prince's frantic drive to escape from the luminous and liberating insights of his beloved, his grotesque attempt at mutual veiling—his own intellectual and her physical "ehtejab"—has been the ultimate cause of his demise.

14. Ibid., 11.
15. Ibid., 94.

Here, then, is a man incapable of playing the traditional "masculine" role, and yet unwilling to accommodate to the new spirit of the time. He cannot heed the advice of his wife/redeemer about the necessity of fashioning a new self, nor can he adopt a new grammar of interaction with women, and with society at large. As a metaphor for Iran's landed gentry, the story of *Prince Ehtejab* clearly depicts the doomed fate of this class in its historic encounter with the inevitable march of modernity. They are too weak to fight it, and too dependent on traditional privilege to change. They are, in T.S. Eliot's words, "hollow men," and for them, "This is the way the world ends / Not with a bang but a whimper."[16]

King of the Benighted picks up the story of this difficult encounter a number of years later. The old landed gentry is long dead, and in its place now sits a new clerical aristocracy. Like their consumptive predecessors, these clerics too are incapable of embracing change. Agents of progress in this story are not women but "utopian" youths. Their attempt to foster change is just as much a failure as the attempt of the woman in *Prince Ehtejab*.

King of the Benighted is a work of many subtle ironies and myriad layers of meaning and metaphor. In form and content, in moral judgment and aesthetic innovation, in literary style and historical allusion, it exemplifies the original meaning of the Latin word for text, "something entwined." Like a fine Persian carpet, *King of the Benighted* is woven from filaments of varying colors and textures. Posterity may well remember it as the benchmark for the post-revolutionary literature of Iran.

The story's narrator is a poet who laments the scourge of politics in art. He bemoans the fact that both oppressive monarchs and mullahs have forced him to write superficially "political" poems. Even his friends and colleagues expect him to "bear witness," to expose the cruelties of oppression, to be "committed." But he craves to write poetry that is more personal. In images whose pantheistic simplicity is reminiscent of Sohrab Sepehri's poems,[17] he tells us that his inspiration comes from the small statue of an angel in his garden, and from "the pomegranate tree, his consolation of April," especially when it blossoms and looks like bonfires lit atop a green mountain.[18] This point alone is enough to make *King of the*

16. T. S. Eliot, "The Hollow Men," in *The Complete Poems and Plays, 1909-1950* (New York, 1950).

17. Sepehri was a great poet and a celebrated painter. Like Golshiri, he died young, and was known for the simplicity of his poems and for the deeply personal nature of his imagery. His aversion to politics, and to "committed" art made him something of a pariah in the minds of "progressive" critics. Since his death, there has been a resurgence of interest in his work.

18. Irani, *King of the Benighted*, 33.

Benighted a manifesto for the aesthetics of modernity. It reasserts the conviction of all genuinely modern artists that art is an end in itself, and that art is ultimately a form of unbridled self-expression.

But the dominant Persian discourse on art, indeed many of its pivotal ideas of modernity, was forged in the smithy of nineteenth-century Russia. Concepts of "social criticism" and twentieth-century Marxist dogmas about socialist realism came to dominate the culture of literary criticism in Iran.[19] A kind of kitsch that pandered to the lowest common denominator of the reader's sensibility became synonymous with "progressive" or *khalghi* ("for the masses") art. Modernist experimentation with form as well as complex linguistic and narrative structure were dismissed and disdained as "decadent" or "petit bourgeois" frivolity. Such progressive theories have a populist veneer; they claim to address the needs and interests of the masses. They are in fact elitist; they have as their point of departure a highly patronizing disposition toward the very people they claim to serve.

Using a prose whose pith and restraint hint of poetry, *King of the Benighted* subverts these shallow notions about committed art. It is a book that is sophisticated and accomplished in form, overtly disdainful of all who want to force artists to write political tracts, yet deeply political in its content and message. The story also affords us a revealing glimpse at the one important point where the cultural politics of mullahs, many Marxists, and monarchists converge. In politics the ends they seek may differ, but in aesthetics, they share the notion that works of art are only a means toward political ends, vehicles for the propagation of ideology. In other words, they have an "instrumentalized" approach to art and see it as a tool for political goals and for educating the ignorant, malleable masses. A genuinely democratic aesthetic, one that allows for the freedom of the artist and posits the people as architects of their own fates—not lost sheep in need of a shepherd—can be built only on the ruins of such instrumentalized and patronizing notions of art.

King of the Benighted recounts one day in the life of a poet in the Islamic Republic of Iran. It is reminiscent of Stephen Daedelus' journey in James Joyce's *Ulysses*. For the poet, like Daedelus, history is a nightmare from which he is trying to awake.

The story begins in the poet's bedroom. It follows him to prison, and offers an image of prison brutalities that is as gripping as it is dreadful.

---

19. For the Russian setting, and the sources of some of these theories, see Isaiah Berlin , *Russian Thinkers* (New York, 1986).

In prison, as in his days of "freedom," the poet is haunted and per-secuted by Revolutionary Guards, by censors who interrogate him about the meaning of his metaphors, and by the painful memory of a mullah who flogs him in the name of the Qur'an. The ravages of the unrelent-ing war with Iraq rouse in him a strong sense of pity and dread. There is also the tedious grind of everyday life, and above all, the knowledge of death and the terror of time. These factors all combine to create in the poet a debilitating despair—a despair, or "nausea" that typically afflicts artists in the secular modern world. Modernity shatters the sense of a cosmic unity, and deprives the artist of the comforts of a theocen-tric world, where religion offers answers to all questions and affords meaning to life. "Fear and trembling" are the inevitable price paid by modern individuals who want to make sense of the world on their own. That is why Hegel calls this attempt the most heroic in history.

For the poet of *King of the Benighted* memory is both a cure and a curse, a sanctuary and a cauldron of tormenting thoughts. In fact both memory and time become protagonists in the tale. By the end of the story, lines between past and present, memory and desire, dreams and reality become so permeable that, as readers, we cannot decide, with any certainty, whether the time lapsed in the narrative has been only a few hours, a year, or even a millennium.

Tormented by the limits of linear temporality, plagued by his own awareness of death as the ultimate reminder of these limits, the poet chooses to transcend the linear flow of time. In its place, he posits a cyclic temporality, where every minute is at once an eternity. This view of time is in fact not so much a new idea as it is the rebirth (or "renaissance") of an old Persian concept. We know from the history of ideas that patriar-chal monotheistic religions, as well as Marxism, have played a formative role in cementing in our sensibility a linear concept of time. Gnostics, on the other hand, generally have embraced the idea of cycles of time. In pre-Islamic Iran, as Alessandro Bausani argues, the dominant tempo-ral paradigm was "cyclical time…uniting the primordial beginnings with the eschatological end." With the advent of Islam, many age-old Persian ideas were either obliterated or forced to assume an Islamic guise for their survival; the cyclical concept of time was no exception. Of the Persian poets who lamented this breach with the past, and who strove to resur-rect cultural elements of it, few can match Nezami's stature and influence. It is thus fitting to find, interlaced masterfully into the narrative of *King of the Benighted* the story of Nezami's *The Black Dome*.

Like Golshiri in 1981, Nezami in the twelfth century was consciously battling religious fundamentalists who had declared war on all that was Persian and non-Islamic. On a formal level, the narrative tropes of *The Black Dome,* the fluidity of its structure, its multiple and rapidly changing narrators—to be more specific, the fact that within the first one hundred lines the point of view and the time of the narrative change six times—its dreamlike movement in time and space, have much in common with the kind of fiction we call modern, or even postmodern. *The Black Dome* brilliantly vindicates Golshiri's assertion that classical Persian literature, and poets like Nezami, have much to teach Persian writers. This is why Nezami's ghost, like Hamlet's father, haunts the landscape of *King of the Benighted.*[20]

Nezami—with his advocacy of tolerance and rationalism, his proclivity for scientific knowledge, his ability to create female characters of intelligence and power, his defiant celebration of bodily appetites, his Dionysian spirit, his intransigent fight against religious obscurantism, his relentless attempt to revive pre-Islamic kings, his celebration of Bahram (one such king) as someone who, according to one critic, tried to transform his rule "from kingship by will to kingship by law," his critique of utopian ideas, his unabashed self-assertiveness, his celebration of himself, and his eager search for self-knowledge—is a champion of the aborted modernity that took shape in Iran in the eleventh and twelfth centuries.[21] Inspired by early histories, Nezami wrote his poems—according to Sirjani[22]—in order to counter a rising tide of religious fundamentalism.

---

20. Aside from the thematic unities that connect Golshiri with Nezami, there is also an interesting theoretical side to Golshiri's use of Nezami. In his late critical essays, Golshiri embarked on a more far-reaching project of unearthing, in the often forgotten landscape of traditional Iranian prose and poetry, the literary tropes and narrative armature that could be considered the early and native precursors of the Persian novel. His search for these native sources did not obviate his contagious curiosity about the masterpieces of world literature. He read as voraciously in Borges and Bulgakov, Nabokov and Joyce as he did in the writings of the Persian masters. His argument about the sources of the novel challenges the commonly held Eurocentric opinion that the novel, as a genre, as well as its requisite literary tropes and epistemological foundations, is Western in origin. The rich tradition of Persian letters—from epic stories to histories, from *maghamehs* (see "Sa'di and the Kings for a discussion of magameh) to even the religious *hadith* (see "Kafi is Kafi for a discussion of hadith)—was for him a rich repository of fictional tropes. Persian fiction, he argued, can only find its own voice and become universal when it can fuse these local tropes with the techniques of Western novels. He understood that genuine modernity can only emerge out of a radical critique, a "creative misreading," in the words of Bloom, of the Persian tradition. His essays on the poetics of prose are, I think, in themselves sufficient to guarantee him a place in the pantheon of important literary voices of our time.

21. For Nezami's views see Talatoff et al, eds. *The Poetry of Nizami Ganjavi: Knowledge, Love, and Rhetoric* (New York, 2001).

22. For Sirjani's views on Nezami, see Said Sirjani, *Dastan-e Do Zan* [The story of two women] (Tehran, 1370/1991).

Nezami was bent on a critical reading and resurrection of the past, and modernity is always, first and foremost, based on a critical appreciation of the past. Nezami read past histories and poetry, and with them tried to shape a new identity befitting his turbulent time, so in our time, when Iranian modernity and identity are once again in a state of crisis, and when once again strong religious forces are bent on pushing society onto a path of de-modernization, Golshiri uses Nezami to shape a new identity and language, appropriate to the new challenge.

Another crucial indication of Nezami's modernity is his celebration of carnality in both men and women. Echoing stories from *A Thousand and One Nights,* some of his narrative poems fit perfectly Mikhail Bakhtin's definition of the "carnival": a textual attempt, in the spirit of Rabelais, to circumvent social taboos and engage, albeit temporarily and vicariously, in a Dionysian dance of sensuality. Needless to say, Nezami was persecuted in his time for his celebration of erotic pleasures; even C.E. Wilson, his Victorian translator, did not dare translate some of the lines from *The Black Dome* into English. Like R.A. Nicholson in his translation of the erotic lines of Masnavi, Wilson sought refuge for these lines in the safe obscurity of Latin. The poet of *King of the Benighted* is flogged and sentenced to solitary confinement for reciting some of these same daring verses.

Ironically, this telling of the tale of *The Black Dome* is how the poet becomes involved with Sarmad, the pitiful anti-hero of *King of the Benighted*. Sarmad is a *tavvab*, a repenter, yet he delights in these subversive stories. His name in Persian evokes the idea of paradise, yet his life is an inferno. In his fate we see the dangers of utopian politics and the inhumanity of the Islamic Republic's reign of terror.

The narrative's nuanced and complicated treatment of Sarmad might well be the best example of what distinguishes a work of art from kitsch, or what Golshiri himself calls *basmesazi*. Kitsch simplifies and reduces a complex world and is invariably judgmental. It offers a simple, and simple-minded, Manichean view of the world, riven between demonic and angelic forces. It traffics in certitudes. Genuine art, on the other hand, defamiliarizes reality by highlighting the innate complexities of the human condition; it reveals the unique, irreducible quality of things and people. It fosters a kind of gentle relativism, where everyone has a story to tell. By celebrating the complexities of the world, good art renders judgment more difficult.

At first glance, judging Sarmad should be easy. Here is an erstwhile revolutionary who has repented in prison, and as a token of his repentance, has agreed to deliver the coup de gras to his comrades of yesterday. He is, in the perfidy of his work, reminiscent of the kapos in Nazi concentration camps, or the *pridurki* in the Soviet Gulags. Primo Levi, who has written some of the most memorable accounts of life in Nazi camps, describes kapos as prisoners "entrusted with the task of maintaining order among new arrivals…to extract corpses from the chambers, to pull gold teeth from jaws, to cut women's hair, to sort and classify clothes and shoes…to transport bodies to the crematoria and oversee the operation of the ovens."[23] But Levi, who suffered much at the hands of the Jews who joined such "special squads," finds it hard to condemn them. Instead of just laying blame, he tries to understand the motives and the inner lives of those who chose to become kapos. He is surely outraged by their actions, yet he underscores the fact that, in his opinion, the real culprit is the Nazi system. He suggests that organizing these despicable squads was the "most demonic crime" committed by the National Socialists. We too will not understand the nature of the Islamic Republic if we fail to understand utopian dreamers like Sarmad whose hearts have turned to stone. A statistical account of their lives, in the dry antiseptic language of social science, can be found in Ervand Abrahamian's *Tortured Confessions*.[24] *King of the Benighted*, on the other hand, offers a look at their interiorities. It humanizes those dehumanized by the Islamic regime's reign of "spiritual" terror.

Sarmad and his band of tavvabs are no less an affront to our common values of human decency than the kapos. But like Primo Levi, the author of the *King of the Benighted* is analytically insightful, and morally magnanimous, in his treatment of the Persian kapos. He too lays most of the blame squarely on the Islamic regime, which places a young man of eighteen, filled with Utopian dreams, in a position where he has either to embrace death, or live as its treacherous grim reaper. It is a choice more devilish than Mephistopheles himself could dream of.

When prose fails to adequately describe the calamities wrought by the system that makes such demonic offers, then poetry, with its allusive allure and powerful metaphors, is conjured to describe the ineffable. And when it, too, proves impotent, then silence, and its rich language, is the sole salvation. *King of the Benighted* moves in the grey zone between language and silence.

But there is, finally, in *King of the Benighted* a soaring sense of self-transcendence. Hegel has argued that the soul and essence of art is

---

23. Primo Levy, *Drowned and Saved*, trans. Raymond Rosenthal (New York, 1989), 50. For another brilliant discussion of this aspect of Auschwitz, see Girogio Agamben, *Remnants of Auschwitz: The Witness and the Archive*, trans. Daniel Heller-Roazen (New York, 1999).

24. Ervand Abrahamian, *Tortured Confessions* (Berkeley, 1999).

precisely the ability to self-transcend. In art, too, the cherished power of dialectical negation should, he says, manifest itself in a perpetually critical approach, not just toward reality, but toward form, mimetic principles, and the conventions and parameters of genres themselves. While the narrator of *King of the Benighted* laments the onslaught of political kitsch, while he mourns the fact that in the current Iran all are benighted in the loss of their utopian hopes, the book's own masterful form and content, its liberating and optimistic vision, transcends the bleak reality it depicts. It becomes, like all great art, the "diaphanous limbo"[25] in which paralyzed despair becomes joyous epiphany.

---

22. Robert Musil, *The Man Without Qualities* (New York, 1995),

MODERNITY & BLUE LOGOS[*1]
Rediscovering the Feminine

Once upon a time, Victor Emmanuelle III, Italy's last ruling monarch, was scheduled to open an art exhibit. His forte was in military matters; he knew little about the world of painting. The King paused in front of a canvas: a small village perched on the slopes of a towering mountain. Courtiers and councilors all anxiously waited for some royal declamation. The poor king groped for words and finally asked, "How many inhabitants does it have?"[2]

In telling this anecdote, Umberto Eco reminds us that the monarch was clearly not familiar with one of the more obvious rules about the relationship between art and humanity. Critics, following Coleridge, have called it "the suspension of disbelief," and consider it one of the cardinal rules of this relationship. In considering a work of art, we must always remember that the world imagined by the artist is the creation of her, or his, mind. It is an imagined world and thus "unreal." At the same time, if readers find the created world too fantastical to believe, they might suspend not their disbelief but their very interest in the work altogether. Whether, like the Italian monarch, we search for mundane fact in a world of creative fantasy, or whether—following in the footsteps of the "Socialist Realism" of Stalin and the "Islamic Art" of Ayatollah Khomeini—we confuse the boundaries between the world of the real and the world of the imagination, we will in either case inhibit our own ability to appreciate a work of art, and impede the ability of the artist to freely create the world her or his imagination desires.

*For Jean Nyland

1. In January of 1994, Shahrnush Parsipur asked me to write an introduction to her new novel *Blue Logos*. The current essay is a revised version of that introduction. Several people were particularly helpful in preparing the early draft. Ann Janicky worked hard to track down books on alchemy. Jean Nyland was my constant guide through the labyrinth of Jungian psychology.

2. Umberto Eco, *Six Walks in the Fictional Woods* (Cambridge,, 1994), 75.

Implicit in any work of art is an unwritten contract between the artist and the audience, defining, among other things, the substance of the world created in that work. In twentieth-century Iran, some novelists have attempted to recreate the most simple, and often simple-minded, renditions of human life. Following in the footsteps of Soviet realist writers, Iranian writers tried to deny the complexities of their audience's emotional and intellectual lives, turning them into facile narratives, linear in form and mechanically rational in substance. They have disparaged as "decadent" and "formalist," all works that did not conform to their half-baked notions of materialist realism. In spite of the "progressive" and "democratic" pretensions of such critics and writers, their narratives are ultimately and deeply anti-democratic. They demand obedient and passive readers who read and accept the text for its "message." Such artists are in fact aesthetic terrorists. Using slogans about the sufferings of the masses and relying on human compassion for the plight of others, they take hostage society's literary taste. Furthermore, by their implicit claim to know the truth they deny their readers a chance to appreciate and live with the inherent ambiguities in the world; the ability to tolerate this ambiguity is the precondition for a developed sense of the self and for a democratic polity and citizenry.

On the other hand, for some artists and novelists, the measure of reality has been the labyrinthine complexity of human existence. In their narratives, as in human consciousness, the real and the imagined, myth and logos, natural instincts and learned habits, cohabit in a complex yet surprisingly homogenous world. Such artists demand active readers who will use their own critical and rational faculties to deconstruct the elements of each narrative, and along with the artist, create the meaning of a text. In this process of creation, the artist is not a godlike architect of textual meaning, but a fellow traveler in the imagined world. In spite of the "elitist" appearance of such works, they are in fact deeply democratic in their dispositions, and in the influence they have on their readers. Among Iranian writers of today, Shahrnush Parsipur is one of the most prominent artists of this persuasion.

One of Parsipur's defining characteristics as a novelist is that she is neither a literary hostage-taker nor a hostage to received opinions and literary dogma. Whether facing the ruling regime or the readers of her novels she is fearlessly frank, and stylistically experimental. In the process, she has created an oeuvre that is uncommonly creative and varied in form and content. The world of Parsipur's novels has a texture all its own, and few Iranian modern writers have expected as much suspension of disbelief from their readers as Parsipur. Nevertheless, readers have not only understood her world, but have shown an affinity for it in record numbers.

The leitmotif of Parsipur's fiction is the battle of self-assertive and free souls, usually women, against the conformist ethos of their time. In *Dog and the Long Winter*,[3] one such self-assertive young woman comes back from the dead to recount the tale of her melancholy, aborted life. The roaming of her introspective consciousness is used to sketch a moving account of her rite of passage into womanhood. The novel shows how her attempts at self-assertion and self-consciousness bring her agony, how the constrictive labyrinth of a society dominated by traditional cultural mores has no tolerance for the liberated woman. The narrative masterfully unravels the tyranny of this tradition and how it manifests itself as sympathy and solace for the docile, and as brutality and banishment for insolent mavericks like the heroine.

In *Women without Men*,[4] we read about Zarin Kolah who "took her husband by the hand, and they went and sat on a lotus. The leaves of the lotus soon enwrapped them. Together, they turned into smoke and went up in the air." In *Tea Ceremonies in the Presence of a Wolf*,[5] characters travel to a mythical world of the past. And finally, Touba, once a tree in Paradise where the mythical bird Simorgh liked to perch, and now the indomitable heroine of an epic tale, sets out to find the meaning of the night; the narrative of her search becomes the stuff of Parsipur's most famous novel, *Touba and the Meaning of the Night*.[6]

In *Blue Logos*, all the narrative tropes and historic insights of these past novels have come together to create an uneven but fascinating work of art. The formal strategies and substantive core of *Blue Logos* is an amalgam of all of Parsipur's novels. The historical context of the story is a society in the throes of modernity. The locus of the narrative is the emotional, rational, physical, and erotic lives of women in a society estranged from the feminine, a society that at times shackles, at other times fights, but most of the time altogether ignores women. The author attempts a task worthy of Athena[7] herself; she wants to reconcile Iranian society with the feminine side of its soul. At the same time, the novel wants to

---

3. Shahrnush Parsipur, *Sag va Zemestan-e Boland* [Dog and the long winter] (Tehran, 1355/1976).

4. Parsipur, *Zanan-e beduneh Mardan* [Women without men] (Tehran, 1369/1990). There is now an English translation of this collection of short stories available. See *Women without Men*, trans. Kamran Talatoff (Syracuse, 1998).

5. Parsipur, *Adab-e Sarf-e Chay dar Hozur-e Gorg* [Tea ceremonies in the presence of a wolf] (Los Angeles, 1994).

6. Parsipur, *Touba va Ma'na-ye Shab* [Touba and the meaning of the night] (Tehran, 1367/1978). An English translation of this book is set to be published this year.

7. Zeus' favorite daughter, the goddess of wisdom, and Ulysses' mentor in both the *Iliad* and the *Odyssey*.

bring Iranian women closer to the masculine elements of their own psyches. For centuries, they suffered under the weight of a humiliating image of womanhood. Worse still, they frequently internalized the image. The unstated goal of the novel is to lift this burden of the past.

Blue Logos is also a retelling of the story of Adam and Lilith. In the narrative tradition which predates and provides a source for the Old Testament, Lilith is Adam's defiant first wife, who is banished from the garden for refusing to perform her wifely duties. To replace her God creates Eve from Adam's rib. In the place of paradisial comfort and tranquility, the purgatory of war and the contingent anxieties of life provide the backdrop to the encounter between man and woman. Lilith has come not to tempt but to offer a way to salvation. Messianism is indeed a central component of Iranian history; but the messianism of *Blue Logos* is of an altogether different hue. Contrary to the tradition of Iranian messiahs, who often appear in the guise of a knight, an Imam, a political party, or a mullah, and use force and violence to establish the promised utopia, the goal of Parsipur's messiah is not some promised land, but a state of mind. The peaceful unity and inner harmony of the soul is all she offers. Furthermore, the novel clearly implies that our messiah is within our battered selves. Our liberation will come when we learn to heed its voice. The German historian of ideas Hans Blumenberg defines modernity as a form of "secular Gnosticism,"[8] and *Blue Logos* is an attempt at just such a gnosis.

Blue Logos is, in several ways, a work of liberation. Most importantly, the novel delivers the inspiring image of a powerful heroine. In every society, woman's freedom is the ultimate measure of liberation and progress. Parsipur has been the voice of the kind of Iranian woman who is at once deeply attached to tradition, and to the idea of fashioning a fresh, liberated self. Her novels provide women with a new and deeper understanding of the feminine principle, and of the complexity of their relationship with men. As Jung often reminded his modern readers, a clear gnosis of *anima* and *animus*—or the masculine and feminine principles— is the first step in creating relationships that are mutually liberating for both genders. *Blue Logos'* long, sometimes meandering (and unfortunately uneven) narrative is a call to arms for just this growth of consciousness.

The novel's message of liberation is not limited to women, for it is not just women who have suffered from patriarchy. In the landscape of *Blue Logos* lives the generation of the heroine's grandfather who, in his own

---

8. Hans Blumenberg, *The Legitimacy of the Modern Age*, trans. Robert M. Wallace (Cambridge, 1987).

words, "had a big problem. It was our custom to marry a wife/servant and worship a lady/lover. The sad thing was that most of the lovers were imaginary." He laments his own sad fate, lost in the "labyrinth of sexual relations. I never made it through. I remained a young boy all my life."[9]

On the other hand, we read the haunting tale of a beautiful woman and her estrangement from her husband:

> We were on our way to attend the wedding of a relative in a city not far away. It was in the transparency of darkness that I first saw him approach me. He was the same man sitting next to me, like a flicker of fire on a dry heap of wood, in an oven ready to burn. He was both near and distant. He brought the tip of his toes near mine. Suddenly I began to shake. Body heat began to consume me.... I smiled reflexively. I put my hand on his. I turned and gently kissed one of the throbbing vessels on the left side of his neck. He turned red. He pulledback his hand violently.... My self began to hide from his self. Rapidly he was descending into the depth of the ocean, never to return again.[10]

The economy of words in this parable is an example of some of the finest narrative of the novel; one would be hard put to find a single superfluous word. There are also echoes of Camus' masterpiece, "The Adulterous Woman,"[11] in which a married woman leaves the bed she shares with her husband, walks to the balcony, and experiences ecstasy at the sight of the endless, calm desert.

If men can only fall in love with imaginary lovers, as the novel clearly implies, then *Blue Logos* is an elegy to the lost paradise where man and woman lived in harmony.

Of course men dominate not only Iran's profane, temporal world but also the sacred realm of its heavens. *Blue Logos* wants to reclaim the presence of the feminine principle in this sacred world. In the novel, the woman's main interlocutor is a lieutenant, and his liberation lies in his recognition that in him resides a feminine side. In Iranian society, too, liberation will only come if the reality of its male-dominated history gives place to a consciousness whose aim is the unity of masculine and feminine, rather than the incessant battle for dominance.

To create a new symbolic "capital" of social intercourse and artistic discourse, Parsipur claims new territories and mines the Persian tradition of letters. Sohravardi, one of the most famous, and enigmatic, Iranian philosophers of the Illuminationist school, wrote a beautifully

9. Parsipur, *Aghl-e Abi* [The blue logos] (Los Angeles, 1372/1994).

10. Parsipur, *Blue Logos*, 70.

11. Albert Camus, "The Adulterous Woman" in *Exile and the Kingdom*, trans., Justin O'Brien, (New York, 1957), 3-34.

dense parable called "The Red Logos."[12] In it, every night, the mythical bird, Simorgh, "who nests atop the Touba tree," leaves the tree and
"spreads its wings across the world." In our time, the Simorgh is none
other than the heroine of *The Blue Logos,* who comes each night to meet
the lieutenant and guide him to his salvation.

Indeed, in the landscape of the novel, women have already reclaimed
their long-lost power. Parsipur is both the "empirical author" and the
woman narrator, and in both roles she acts like an omnipotent goddess,
creating the world of the novel. The women in the story are always at
least as powerful as the men. It is a woman who reads the man's mind,
who accurately predicts the future, who knows the past. She never allows
herself to be humiliated, nor is she given to humiliating others. She does
not give or take orders. To women, she declares, "You are the seeds of
existence, hold your head high, be proud of yourselves. The world must
show deference to you, as you must show deference to the world."[13]

Of all her novels, *Blue Logos* resembles Parsipur's life the most. In her
own words, she was conceived "in the same month as the atomic explo-
sions in Hiroshima and Nagasaki." She comes from what she calls "a poor
aristocracy," rich in titles and genealogy, poor in economic possessions
and performance. Of her mother's fine family lineage, all they inherited
were eccentric relatives, economic poverty, and the necessity, dictated by
demands of the class system, to hide their poverty from everyone. Parsipur
was, for a while, a government employee. She married early, had a son,
then got divorced. She attended college in Iran and in France. Both were
relatively brief educational forays; neither ended in an academic degree.[14]

She began writing when she was a young girl. Literature was her passion and politics only a necessary nuisance. Yet under both the *ancien
regime* and the Islamic Republic, she spent time in prison for political reasons. The last time was for more than five years. The memoirs of her prison
experience have been published, and they offer a chilling account of that
experience. All her life she has pursued an avid curiosity about the occult
and Eastern philosophy. In Paris, where she lived for about two years, she
studied Chinese culture and language. In Iran, she translated a book about
the *I Ching.* There is, in her very demeanor, that rare, poetic combination

---

12. For an informed and informative account of the school, see, for example, Henry Corbin,
    Spiritual Body and Celestial Earth: from Mazdean Iran to Shi'ite Iran, trans. Nancy Pearson
    (Princeton, 1977).
13. Parsipur, *Blue Logos,* 161.
14. For a brief autobiographical sketch of Parsipur's life, see "The Identity of an Author,"
    in *Adab-e Sarf-e Chay dar Hozur Gorg* [Tea ceremonies in the presence of a wolf] (Los
    Angeles, 1993), 225-243.

of epic thirst to know the world and an amused disdain for the demands of the dull quotidian. She suffers from manic-depression, as she readily admits, and it is evident that she wrote *Blue Logos* in one of her more effusive manic phases. Writing the book was preceded and succeeded by two serious episodes of depression.

She has a contagious desire to learn about the world. She is as curious about the writings of Rabe'e, the eleventh-century poet and female mystic, as she is about the work of Stephen Hawking and his theory of time. She wants to view the world not from the perspective of a Cartesian *cogito*, but from the epistemological vista of self-conscious femininity. She also wants to think independently. Modern Iranian intellectuals, fascinated as they have been with modernity and the West, seem to have paid far less attention to "theoretical curiosity," one of modernity's cardinal tenets. Rather than trying to make sense of the world on their own terms, they went into a frenzy of translating Western works of theory and literature, and then mechanically offered concepts and categories wrested whole from the Western experience. A concomitant element of this movement was a nihilistic disdain for Iranian tradition. Parsipur has been different. She wants to make sense of the world herself, using her own critical faculty, and incorporating useful elements of the often-maligned Persian tradition.

At the end of the novel, in a moment of postmodernist conflation of subject and object, in an image reminiscent of Akira Kurosawa's film *Dreams*, the heroine walks into the landscape of a painting, "onto the canvas, just on the other side of the river."[15] The canvas is clearly the text of *Blue Logos* itself, and the heroine that walks into it is surely Parsipur: the empirical author and the fictive author of the narrative become one.

While in one sense Parsipur debunks the Cartesian dualism between subject and object, she also has a special affinity for the famous Cartesian postulate. "I write because I have begun to think.... I write because apparently [through thinking] I have become human."[16] The novel is dedicated to Don Quixote; and Don Quixote, Kundera has argued, is a herald for the advent of the modern. He personifies the Cartesian *cogito*, leaving the comfort of his house to discover the world on his own. Other people's descriptions of the world no longer satisfy him. Along with Sancho Panza, he sets out on a journey of discovery, bent on subduing the demons that roam the world of received opinions. Cervantes' masterpiece has also been called the first novel written in the tradition of magic realism, and in this sense, too, there is an affinity between Parsipur and the character

15. Parsipur, *Blue Logos*, 538.
16. Parsipur, *Adab-e Sarf-e Chay dar Hozur Gorg* [Tea Ceremony], 281.

to whom the book is dedicated. The dedication appears even more apt when we remember that Don Quixote's persistent search for his beloved—a beloved, incidentally, fashioned from the filaments of the medieval Romances he voraciously read—can be seen as a subversive celebration of the sacred feminine, the ephemeral anima.

Persian literature is replete with mystical parables whose narrative structures defy the traditional dictates of time and place. In a mode similar to magic realism, they cohere myth and metaphor, dreams and reality, into an "imaginable" world that lurks between the realm of the real and the fantastic. Parsipur is as much indebted to this Persian tradition as she is to Gabriel Garcia Marquez. In her novels, there are as many traces of Persian poets and philosophers—from Khayyam, Hafez, Beyhaghi, and Sohravardi, to Hedayat, Sepehri and Farrokhzad—as there are allusions to Wolfe, Faulkner, and Marquez. Steeped as she is in all of these traditions, she is a simple emulator of none. Indeed, from all of these influences, she creates a world all of her own, a world not unlike a Magritte painting.

As with a Magritte painting, traditional unities of time and space, or assumed homogeneities of "represented" realities, have no place in Parsipur novels. In the world she creates, the dead easily talk to the living, painters walk painlessly onto their own canvases, mythical heroes and heroines live side by side with temporal characters, and events and characters from distant times and strange lands live easily next to one another. In a trope reminiscent of Dante and his discourse with Virgil, and in an atmosphere that hints of his *Inferno*, characters in her novels can have a glass of wine with Hafez; their dreams are easily disturbed by the sound of a deer, scampering in the forest of the author's imagination. It is even possible to talk to the old man who dominates Hedayat's masterpiece, the *Blind Owl*.

From the opening lines of *Blue Logos*, the rich tapestry of her narrative becomes amply evident. The novel begins in a police precinct office in Tehran. It is customary for the officers on duty in such precincts to wear a metal sign, usually in the shape of a crescent that hangs with a chain around their necks. Her choice of words in describing the scene tells careful readers much about the realm they are about to enter. She writes:

> When the door to the office of the guard on duty for the night was opened, the lieutenant looked up with curiosity and anticipation. He was young, but tired. A moon of the fifth night was hanging on his neck, and he could feel the weight of the chain.[17]

17. *Blue Logos*, 45.

Words like door, chain, guard and night all echo a sense of enslave-ment and enclosure. The lieutenant, throughout the novel, is a symbol of the male principle; he is the "guard of the night." In the context of this novel and that of Persian modern literature, night can be understood on two very distinct levels. On the one hand, night is the only time when the heroine of the novel, much like the Lilith of ancient myth, appears. At the same time, in the poetic tradition of modern Iran, night is a metaphor for the dark times of oppression and alienation. In *Blue Logos*, when darkness comes, the woman appears, like an apparition, and at the first sign of "the bird of dawning," like Hamlet's Ghost, she disappears. At the end of the novel, we too are left, like Horatio, to wonder whether the season will ever come when this bird shall "sing all night long," and the nights will once again be "wholesome."

The lieutenant is not happy about his plight. He is "curious" and knows his life is wanting some sense of meaning, thus he is "waiting." The crescent moon is also traditionally an emblem of the Great Goddess. In nearly all mythological systems, the moon is a feminine image, and the Moon Goddess is deemed the ultimate muse of all poetry.[18] Furthermore, the number five is, according to Jung, the number that represents the feminine principle.[19]

In *Seven Beauties,* one of the greatest narrative poems of Nezami (1141-1203),[20] Bahram, the Sasanian king, discovers portraits of seven beautiful women. He falls in love with all seven and marries them. They repre-sent all the climes of the inhabitable world of the medieval imagination. The king builds seven palaces, each with a dome, for his seven brides. Each dome is the color of a different clime, appropriate to the land whence the queen comes. The king spends one night of the week in each of these palaces and listens to a story each of his beloved queens, Scheherezade-like, tells him. The fifth dome is blue in color, connect-ing Parsipur's lexical choice—"the moon of the fifth night"—with Nezami's wonderful epic poem of love.

Of course, every text is, to use Eco's metaphor, like a forest, "a garden of forking paths,"[21] and readers behave differently in it. Some enter the

---

18. Robert Graves, *White Goddess* (New York, 1987), 9. In Persian mysticism, the moon is considered "the feminine principle" of the material world. See Taghi Pournamdariyan, *Ramz-o Raz-e Dastanha-ye Ramzi dar Adab-e Farsi* [Mysteries and secrets in the fables of Persian Letters] (Tehran, 1364/1995). The book is also an excellent introduction to the ideas of Sohravardi.

19. C.G Jung, *Psychology and Alchemy*, trans. F.C. Hull, vol. 12, (New York, 1950), 184.

20. For some discussion of Nezami and his time, see the essay "Golshiri and the Janus Face of Tradition" in this book.

21. Eco, *Six Walks in the Fictional Woods*, 6.

forest only to find as quick an exit as possible. They like the end of the story more than the story itself. They have little time to savor the nuances of the story and soberly contemplate every tree and all its leaves. They also have little tolerance for the complexities of form and content. Such complexities only prolong their much-anticipated moment of exit from the forest. Others want to linger in the "fictional forest," and discover each tree and every byway. The joy of discovering the forest is far more important than the rewards of finding a way out of the woods. For such readers every narrative is an unfinished story. Only their own active participation can bring the story to a provisional end, an end that will change every time other readers enter the same forest, or indeed each time they themselves enter it again. Just as we never swim in the same river twice, so we never read the same book twice. While the popularity of Parsipur's novels indicate that they attract both kinds of readers, they seem to be more hospitable to those who prefer to linger in the woods.

The central events of *Blue Logos* take place in Tehran, during the time of the Iran-Iraq war (1980-89). But the narrative in fact covers a far more expansive terrain, going back as far as the earliest lunar mythologies, and as deep as the farthest recesses of the archetypal mind. Like some of the major works of modern fiction, the novel creates a field of experience, rather than following the expected contours of a plot. As the heroine declares, "I have decided not to let myself go mad, not to succumb to any limits, and allow the free flow of consciousness to go where it wants."[22] Readers too seem to have only one choice. They must suspend disbelief, forgo normal expectations of a tightly knit plot development and instead allow the narrative to wash over them. In the tradition of other postmodern novels, *Blue Logos* has to be experienced as much as it has to be read.

In fact, reading *Blue Logos* can be compared to a mystical experience. Some mystics believe that anyone who is immersed in total isolation for forty days will, at the end, arrive at a kind of epiphany—a lucidity of vision where the normal parameters of time and space all give way to a new numinous unity. European alchemists called this condition *Unio Mentalis*.[23] In the case of *Blue Logos*, the farther we enter the mythopoeic landscape of the novel, the more elements of the quotidian cohabit easily with fantastical images of the mind. Indeed, if in the first half of the novel, the woman shows the way of salvation to the lieutenant, in the second half it is the centaur—traditionally a masculine, "animus" figure—who guides

---

22. *Blue Logos*, 409.
23. For a discussion of some of the key concepts of alchemy, particularly as they were developed or used by Jung, see James Hillman, *The Blue Fire*, ed. Thomas Moore (New York, 1987), 150-160.

the woman on a journey to discover her deepest feminine nature. And then, having attained the transcendental consciousness of "Blue Logos," the promised luminous unity of the mystic, the woman, in collaboration with the centaur, offers a fascinating reading of Iran's history. She reveals, not surprisingly, a long tradition of overt misogyny. At the same time, she sheds light on the forced exile of women from history as one of the consequences of this misogyny.

In the process of arriving at this new consciousness, or indeed as a precondition for it, the woman of the novel becomes the archetypal Mother Goddess. From darkness, she clamors to reach the light of self-gnosis and self-assertion. She declaims, "I want to bear a child." She laments, "I wanted warmth, I wanted love, I wanted light, I wanted presence. I screamed: Why do you keep me at the bottom of the ocean?" And then the woman is with child, and the child is knowledge. "The child was born," she declares, "and this was the child that came into being because I had thought him."[24]

Clearly the child thus born is both literal and metaphoric. Woven into the fabric of the narrative is the ontological premise that a mythical and mysterious unity connects the epiphany of artistic and intellectual creativity to the agonies of childbirth. The novel clearly asserts that the common brutalities of men toward women have made both kinds of creation more difficult for women. With uncanny eloquence, the last image of the novel poignantly articulates this view. There we read about the final encounter of the heroine and the lieutenant. She is about to enter a painting. Descriptions of the painting leave little doubt that it is in fact the same work of art we read about in Hedayat's *The Blind Owl*. The lieutenant has by now experienced the liberating effects of "Blue Logos." In his hand is a broom, and brooms are historically understood as symbols of feminine wisdom and power. As the woman is about to enter the canvas, she asks the lieutenant to sit in such a way as to cover the image of the old man in the painting. In other words, a newly liberated man can finally replace, or at least overshadow, the misogynist patriarch of Persian tradition, best captured in Hedayat's *The Blind Owl*.[25]

In *Blue Logos* the rhythm of Parsipur's narrative has the fast tempo of an uncontainable stream of consciousness. It is as if the mind is working more rapidly than the logistics of writing will allow. While hers is not an exercise in what the surrealists called "automatic writing," it has the rapid-fire feel of an oral effusion, of Sufi rants (*Shath*) in a moment

---

24. *Blue Logos*, 234.
25. For further discussion of Hedayat and *The Blind Owl*, see the essay in this book, "Hedayat and the Tragic Vision."

of transcendent epiphany. This might partially account for why the novel's prose is so far from polished. Even grammatical errors are not hard to find. She clearly does not belong to the Flaubert school of writing, where the author ponders long and hard on every word. Some critics have even accused her of "clumsy writing." She herself seems aware of this quality in her novel, and attributes it to the "inordinate amount of junk I have read. Many of them were bad translations and the shadow of this experience is evident in my prose. In other words, I don't have what you would call a polished prose."[26]

Blue Logos can also be read as a novel of ideas. In her own version of an autobiography, Parsipur writes, "I had always hoped one day to study philosophy."[27] *Blue Logos* is an attempt to fulfill this desire, and this philosophical bent is both one of the novel's strengths and its Achilles heel. On several occasions, her desire to engage in philosophical excursions seems overbearing. Woven into the fabric of every novel is a range of diversions and digressions. Many postmodern novelists have forsaken the constraints of a plot altogether in favor of creating more liberating rules of narrative structure. *Blue Logos* is then a postmodern novel, anti-mimetic in its epistemology, and anti-plot in its form. It even includes long segments of T.S. Eliot's "Ash-Wednesday."[28] These disparate diversions usually cohere into a narrative of enough dramatic tension, but Parsipur occasionally fails to pass the test Kundera set for narrative diversions. They must always, he said, "keep the attention of the reader."

Besides postmodern literary theory, there is another source for Parsipur's unusual narrative mélange. A common characteristic of Persian classical literature is the existence of multiple genres in the same narrative. Philosophical parables, poems, historical anecdotes, aphorisms, and words from Islamic Scriptures often come together to shape the classical narratives of Persian literature.

Furthermore, the desire to engage in philosophical discourse places the heroine of *Blue Logos* in a rare historical position. Of all human intellectual endeavors, none had, until the twentieth century, been as universally monopolized by men as philosophy. In the West the first

---

26. Parsipour offers this view of her writing in an interview with two journalists. See Mahdokhte Sanati, "Moshef-e ba Sharnush Parsipur" [Interview with Sharnush Parsipur], Forough, 2 (1998): 5-22.

27. Parsipur, *Tea Ceremonies*, 228.

28. It is interesting to note that she uses those sections of "Ash-Wednesday" where Eliot is creating an image of Mary. "Lady of silence / Calm and distressed / Torn and most whole / Rose of memory" all the way to these lines, "Speech without words and / Word of no speech / Grace to the Mother / For the Garden / Where all love ends." T. S. Eliot, "Ash-Wednesday," in *The Complete Poems and Plays* (New York, 1967), 62.

woman philosophers only appeared in the twentieth century; in Iran, the situation is even worse, in that there has yet to emerge a single woman philosopher—unless we construe Ghorat al-Ayne's theological interventions as a form of philosophy.[29]

The woman in *Blue Logos* has a rather eclectic concept of philosophy. Her room, also called her "shrine," is adorned with pictures of Beethoven, Buddha, Socrates, Farrokhzad, Dostoyevsky, Plato, Balzac, Rasputin, Jesus Christ, Harpo Marx, Lao Tsu and Virginia Wolfe.[30] In her mind, philosophy is essentially an act of intuition rather than one of cold, rational research, contemplation, and compilation. The heroine declares, "Lieutenant, I don't have a mathematical or philosophical mind. I think about the world intuitively." And in her vision, *Cogito ergo sum* does not apply only to the world of animate objects. "Everything thinks, therefore it is."

This intuitive sense leads her to conclusions that are often astonishing, sometimes for the brilliance of their insights, other times for their sheer banality. An example of the first kind can be seen in the book's description of a marketplace. With no evidence that Parsipur has any extensive reading in Marxist philosophy, we see a beautiful, and radically critical, portrayal of the marketplace: "When I returned to the center of the market, suddenly I saw that everyone who was selling something had, like a frozen image in a film, turned into stone."[31] The Marxist idea of reificaion and fetishism[32] could not find a more succinct image.

In another section, she writes, in a tone full of poetry, "Love, in its journey from the forest to the desert, changed its nature." The book is in fact filled with allusions to the cataclysmic changes that were brought about in human history as a result of *homo sapiens*' migration from the forest to the desert. There is again no evidence that Parsipur ever read,

---

29. She was an unusual woman of much erudition, fearless in her defense of her new-found faith in the Babi movement. She is arguably the first woman in Iranian history to voluntarily take off her veil. Even in a gathering of her religious brethren, the sight of her, defiant and eloquent, was too much for many of the men. One took a knife to his throat on the spot, plunging a dagger in his own heart, and another tried to kill her. Eventually she was executed by the government at the age of thirty-two. For a full study of her life and works, see Farzaneh Milani, *Words and Veils*, (Syracuse, 1992).

30. *Blue Logos*, 211.

31. Ibid., 312.

32. Fetishism is one of the most interesting and important concepts in Marxian philosophy. It has been defined as "phantom objectivity" or when things take on an apparent autonomy and seem "so strictly rational and all embracing" as to appear natural, or permanent. Such a process is a result of alienation, and in turn further strengthens human estrangement from the world. See Georg Lukacs, *History and Class Consciousness: Studies in Marxist Dialectics*, trans. Rodney Livingston (Cambridge, 1968), 83-220.

or knew about Blumenberg. None of his books have been translated into Persian. Yet, in many significant elements, *Blue Logos* concurs with what Blumenberg has written in his monumental study of myth.[33]

In another part of the book, the narrator engages Iran's encounter with modernity. Her conclusions are striking for their pessimism that borders on self-loathing. Human beings from this corner of the world, she writes, "Are about to enter the twentieth century dressed only in rags, a clay pot in hand, with a hand-carved ornamented desk, a hoe and a cow at their feet, a balance, and a few books written in the most obtuse languages" about the "mysteries of esoteric works," and will look at trains, steam ships and cars—and finally computers—in helpless and hapless amazement.[34] But contrary to her claim, there is much in Iran's past that can help Iranians forge a new identity befitting the new times. In the West, the Renaissance was about discovering a long-lost past. For Iran, too, the Renaissance will come only through a rediscovery of Iran's past, with all its warts and wonders. Furthermore, a provocative narrative like *Blue Logos* itself shows that "clay pots" and "esoteric books" are not all Persians have in their quest to meet the challenges of modernity.

The heroine's intuitive sense of philosophy has yet another consequence for the narrative. She "lives in the world of the red," but "thinks in the world of the blue." According to Roman Jakobson, in every text there is what he calls "the dominant."[35] Blue is surely "the dominant" in Parsipur's novel. Another recurring theme in the novel is the symbology of a cross. In both the context of *Blue Logos* and archetypal psychology, blue and the cross are closely linked.

Blue is the color of feminine wisdom; it is the color of the Virgin Mary, and a metaphor for her virginity—her "wholeness" and purity. It is hard to find a medieval image of Mary where she is not in blue. For Jung, blue is the color of the *anima*. Only with the help of blue can the incomplete trinity become a cross. Gold is the color of the Father, red the color of the Son, and white that of the Holy Spirit (a feminine spirit "in disguise," perhaps a reincarnation of Sophia). The fourth arm of the cross, the feminine divinity represented in Christianity by the Virgin Mary, is blue.[36]

---

33. Blumenberg argues that the beginning of humanity's life on barren lands—as opposed to jungles—created the existential angst that is the source of myths. See *Work on Myth*, tr. By Robert M. Wallace (Cambridge, 1990).

34. *Blue Logos*, 134.

35. Roman Jakobson, "The Dominant," in *Readings in Russian Poetics*, ed. Ladislav Maejka and Krystyna Pomoska (Cambridge, 1971), 82-87.

36. Erich Neuman, *The Great Mother*, trans. Ralph Manheim (Princeton, 1991); also Emma Jung and Marie-Louise Von Franz, *The Grail Legend*, trans. Andrea Dykes, (New York, 1920).

In alchemy the condition called *Unio mentalis* is the rare moment when subject and object, narrative and narrator, the world of the real and of the imagination, achieve a unity and deliver a much-coveted lucidity of vision. Blue is the color of unio mentalis.[37] And the mandala, the ultimate geometric symbol of unity, is a circle "squared" by a cross.

The color of melancholy is also blue. It is the color of angst, and of the joy that invariably accompanies wisdom of the world. At the same time, blue is the color of the ocean and of water, and water is mythically understood by human beings to be itself a metaphor for utopia, for change, for fecundity, for cleansing, and, of course, for the Feminine. Blue is the color of the sky, and the sky is where Zarathustra's defiantly independent eagle flies.[38]

In the literature on the curative magic of stones, blue is the color of the stone that helps humans in their thinking, augments their valor, and heals their old wounds.[39] The stone of Hermes, yet another incarnation of the Holy Grail, was first red in color and gradually turned blue.[40] Persians, Indians and Egyptians all believe that blue stones possess magical powers. Such stones, the ancients believed, keep away bad omens and alleviate pain.

Blue is the color of intuition. Indeed it has been suggested that the androgynous soul of all humans is blue in color.[41] Even the Mother Goddess of Babylonian mythology has a cup, filled with blue blood. In the Old Testament, the color of God's throne is blue, and in Persian mythology, blue is not only the color of royal thrones but also the color of mourning.[42] Most of these ideas can be found in Yeats' "Lapis Lazuli."[43]

Parsipur insists that she knew none of these far-flung associations when she first wrote the novel. Their appearance and creative use in *Blue Logos*—and world mythology—can perhaps best be accounted for by Jung's ideas about the "collective unconscious." Like Jung, Parsipur knows that "red is the color of warped emotions," and blue the color of

37. Hillmann, *The Blue Fire*, 150-160.
38. In Nietzsche's *Thus Spoke Zarathustra*, Zarathustra has two favorite animals—a snake for its wisdom and an eagle for its defiance.
39. For the curative powers of blue stones, see E.A Budge, *Amulets and Superstition* (New York, 1978), 86-87 and 323-325. Also, A. Layman's *Compendium of the Healing Stones: A Guide to their Metaphysical and Holistic Uses,* (Palo Alto, 1993).
40. Emma Jung, *The Grail Legend*, 160-166.
41. Starhawk, *The Spiral Dance: A Rebirth of the Ancient Religion of the Great Goddess* (San Francisco, 1987), 42.
42. Robert Graves, *White Goddess*, 269.
43. W. B. Yeats, "Lapis Lazuli," in *The Collected Works of W. B. Yeats*, vol. 1 (New York, 1983), 294.

liberation. She declares, "Christ is the ocean."[44] If we are ever to cure the contingency of our lives, she writes, then we must heed the blue of our soul, and strive for our own lucid moment of unio mentalis.

But language is of the world of dualities and tensions. To convey the experience of unity through the use of words rooted inevitably in duality is indeed a Sisyphean task. We live in the realm of the "Red," and knowledge of the "Blue" can only be ours if we "resolve the tension of opposites" in this world, and reconcile the *anima* and *animus* into the united couple which Jung calls the "divine sygyzy."[45] It is through their intercourse— the universal symbol of transcended duality—that the "divine child" is born.[46] And the child is the herald of a new age of harmonious enlightenment. Blue Logos aspires to be nothing short of the the "divine child," born of perfect symmetry, in a deeply unharmonious world.

---

44. *Blue Logos*, 482-484
45. C. G. Jung, "Aion," in *Collected Works*, vol. 9ii (New York, 1959), 12-22.
46. Emma Jung, *The Grail Legend*, 257.

THE PURGATORY OF EXILE
Persian Intellectuals in America[1]

Woe unto him who has no country.
—Friedrich Nietzsche

Exile is when you live in one land and dream in another. From Iran—the landscape of my dreams—no land is farther away, geographically and metaphorically, than the America where I now live.

America is, in the words of one of its more astute political observers, the "First New Nation."[2] It is a country with little history, and even less patience for indulging the past. Iran, however, is a land where the past both haunts and enriches the present; it is a country where, in the words of Hegel, the light of reason first began to shine: "The Persians are the first Historical people."[3] As a nation, America is the land where the Frontier has been the formative myth of its history, where mobility and exile have been central to the country's collective memory. Iran, on the other hand, though first peopled by exiles (the Aryans some 3,500 years ago), and despite the fact that its Islamic calendar commences with the prophet's exile from Mecca, has for centuries been characterized by the insularity of its national experience. Iran, as an idea, seems almost synonymous with the sense of a protected plateau, walled and shielded by towering mountains and forbidding seas. For Jews, exile has been a constitutive component of their five-thousand-year history. Living in diaspora has become, for them, all but second nature, whereby, in the words of George Steiner, "the text" has become a home and an "instrument of exilic survival."[4] For Iranians, living in diaspora was, until two decades ago, a rarity, an oddity commonly experienced only by radical intellectuals, the economically marginalized, or stigmatized religious minorities.

1. An early draft of this chapter was read at "Litera-Tour: Mainz, 2000." I owe a special thank to Ms. Nasrin Amirsedghi for her tireless effort in organizing the conference.
2. Seymour Martin Lipset, *The First New Nation: The United States in Historical and Comparative Perspective* (New York, 1969).
3. Georg V. Hegel, *The Philosopher of History*, trans. J. Sibree (New York, 1991), 173
4. George Steiner, "Our Homeland, the Text," in *No Passion Spent* (New Haven, 1996), 305.

The etymology and the variegated connotations and denotations of *ghorbat*, the common Persian word for exile, eloquently conveys the culture's troubled relationship with the exilic experience. In English, as well as in the French and German languages, a touch of romance, of affirmation, is attached to the very word . Its dual meanings and genealogy—"creating and coming forth" and "banishment"[5]—afford it an air of heroism. Ghorbat, on the other hand, itself an exile from the Arabic language, has the same root as the Persian word for "dusk"; it shares its genealogy with *maghreb*, Persian for "the West," and for the land where the sun eternally sets.[6] Nasser Khosrow, the acclaimed eleventh-century Persian poet, traveler and theologian, writes of exile as "a tarantula," and the poet Sa'di thought that a quick death at home was surely preferable to a long life in exile.[7]

Indeed, as if to underscore the inevitable melancholy of exile, one of the secondary meanings for the Persian word for exile is "silent weeping." One of the derivatives of the word ghorbat is *ghorbati*, ostensibly meaning anyone who is away from home. It has, however, taken on harshly pejorative connotations. As a culture that has historically privileged the sedentary over the mobile, a culture whose traditional architecture eschews windows to the outside world in favor of enclosed, high-walled gardens and yards, it is then not surprising that ghorbati is used as a derogatory word, synonymous with a Gypsy, a barbarian, or even a harlot.

Mohajerat, the other word commonly used for exile in Persian, is no less unequivocal in betraying the culture's attitude toward the affliction of exile. *Hejrat*, or the act of leaving home, not only refers to the prophet's forced departure from his birthplace, but can also be used to refer to death.[8] In the unconscious of the Persian language, then, death and exile are part of the same continuum of rupture and departure.

---

5. For a discussion of the meanings of the word exile, see Christine Brooke-Rose, "Exsul," in *Exile and Creativity: Signposts, Travelers, Outsiders, Backward Glances*, ed. Susan Rubin Suleiman (Durham, 1996), 10-24

6. Nader Naderpour writes of this shared genealogy in the introduction to his last collection of poems. The piece is called, "The Exile of Poetry, and the Poetry of Exile." See Nader Naderpour, *Zamin-o Zaman* [Time and the earth] (Los Angeles, 1996), 7-28.

7. As I have argued in the chapter "Sa'di and the Kings" Sa'di was a first-rate mind, capable of simultaneously holding two opposing views. The emotionally charged question of exile was no exception. He was himself a tireless traveler, spending some forty years journeying to far away places. Furthermore, in one poem, he describes the emotional limbo of those who can no longer tolerate the indignities of home, yet they also lack the heart to leave it. In yet another poem, he declares that exile is preferable to a despondent and degrading life at home.

8. All points about the roots and uses of the Persian words for exile are from *Dehkhoda*, the grand encyclopedia of Persian language.

And yet today, at least two million Iranians, from all walks of life, live in ghorbat. Close to a million of them are in America and since the "international context" of exile is one of the themes of this conference,[9] I would also like to search for some points of convergence and contrast between the Iranian intellectual's experience of exile and the fate of German intellectuals in the 1930s who fled Nazism and landed somewhere on the vast American continent.

The comparison is in one sense unfair, if not indeed untenable. Half a century has passed since the arrival of the large contingent of German intellectuals in America. Temporal distance has allowed for a full and dispassionate appraisal of their genius and accomplishments, as well as their foibles and failures. The fact that German intellectual émigrés of the 1930s included an almost endless litany of towering twentieth-century figures—from Albert Einstein and Bertolt Brecht to Thomas Mann and Hannah Arendt, from Theodor Adorno and Ernest Cassier to Arnold Schoenberg and Walter Gropius[10]—the fact that they helped change the very fabric of social and natural sciences, as well as architecture and urban design in America, and finally, the fact that a majority of this group were Jews, and as such were not only exiles in Germany but suffered some of the pangs of anti-Semitism in America, have all worked to facilitate and encourage a large number of studies on the nature of their experience. The history of Iranian intellectuals in America, on the other hand, is a work in progress. The landscape of their accomplishments and failures has yet to be rigorously surveyed, let alone seriously analyzed or studied. Furthermore, it is a landscape that is still constantly evolving, changing as we speak. Any account of what they have sown and harvested can be at best partial and anecdotal.

Exiles, at the existential level, are bifurcated beings. In the post-colonial lexicon, they have "hybrid identities." For Iranian exiles, language provides the first clue to the ambiguities of this hybridity. Twenty-four years after the surge of Iranians arriving in America, there is still no consensus on what we should call ourselves. Are we to bank on the romance the word Persia conjures and call ourselves Persians? This problem has

---

9. The "Litera-Tour" conference was organized by the city of Mainz, Germany. Artists, teachers and scholars from a number of European, Asian, American and African countries were invited for three days of discussions and events.

10. Much has been written about the role of these intellectuals in changing the very fabric of science and social theory in America. For example, see Anthony Heilbut, *Exiled In Paradise: German Refugee Artists and Intellectuals in America from 1933 to the Present* (New York, 1997); Robert Boyers, ed. *The Legacy of the German Refugee Intellectuals* (New York, 1972); Donald Flemming and Bernard Bailyn, eds., *The Intellectual Migration: Europe and America, 1930-1960* (Cambridge, 1969).

been made more acute by the continued malignancy of Islamic politics in Iran. If an Islamic firing squad, or warrant of arrest, haunted the Iranian intellectuals at home, in exile, not just the malfeasance of the same Islamic regime haunts them halfway across the world.

In the anxious wait of such troubled times, the safest path for Iranians was either to become "invisible" or to opt for the relative safety of a new, hyphenated identity such as Persian-American, or Iranian-American. Such names tried to emphasize, by their very morphology, an emotional detachment from Iran. They posited political distance from the regime at home: hyphenated names for bifurcated identities.

Theodor Adorno, the German philosopher and musicologist, and the gloomy poet of exile, considers this bifurcation, this suspension of attachment to a permanent home, the essential component of exile. For exiles, he writes, "homeland is the state of having escaped."[11] Exile is coterminous with awaiting and transience,[12] and with the solitude of the stranger; it begets and breeds a near neurotic dependence on news from "home." Exiles refuse to recognize the permanence of the status quo; they endlessly engage in the Sisyphean task of trying to forge a cohesive narrative to surmount the real and imagined travails and torments of their present purgatory, while at once also nurturing utopian dreams of an edenic homeland. And thus exiles everywhere emulate the Jewish experience and seek the same kind of panacea for their plight as pariahs. A text, a language, an imaginary homeland, become tools of survival. Speaking Persian, for example, becomes a momentary escape from the constant feeling of disenfranchisement. It is a gesture of communion, of solidarity. It is an act of defiance, with elegiac qualities.

Exiles are, in the words of Elias Canetti, custodians of a dead treasure. Adorno, too, seems to be suggesting the same idea by writing about what he calls his "damaged life" in exile. Infusing into his narrative of exile his deep disdain for America, and his pioneering work in criticizing "the mass deception" of the "late capitalist era,"[13] he writes that here in America "the past life of émigrés is, as we know, annulled. Earlier it was the warrant of arrest, today it is intellectual experience.... Anything that is not reified, cannot be counted and measured, ceases to exist."[14] In other pas-

---

11. Theodor Adorno, quoted in Anthony Heilbut, *Exiled in Paradise*, 162.

12. Mary McCarthy, "Exiles, Expatriates, and Internal Émigrés," *The Listener*, no. 25 (1971): 705-708.

13. Theodor Adorno and Max Horkheimer, *The Dialectic of Enlightenment*, trans. John Cumming (New York, 1999), 153.

14. Theodor Adorno, *Minima Moralia:Reflections from a Damaged Life*, trans. E.F.N. Jephcott (London, 1999), 46-7.

sages, he offers an even gloomier image, suggesting that the problem of exiles might have little to do with the kind of reification endemic in capitalist structures. "Every intellectual in emigration is," he writes, "without exception, mutilated, and does well to acknowledge it to himself.... His language has been expropriated, and the historical dimension that nourished his knowledge, sapped."[15] Adorno even abhors the American natural landscape, for "it bears no trace of the human hand."[16]

Nader Naderpour, the recently deceased and laconically embittered Persian poet who had for many years lived in Los Angeles, captures much the same sentiment in his last collection of poems. His anguished voice laments the fate of an older generation of intellectuals who stubbornly refuse to accept the dictates of the exilic experience and assimilate into any aspect of the host country. They prefer the comforts of the intellectual ghetto—real, or imaginary—where they can rest on their past laurels. Here in America, "a landscape without a history,"[17] cities are, for him, "full of noise, empty of words."[18] All that is left of him, he laments, is the "joyless ruin" of his soul.[19] Everywhere he turns, he meets only the "black shadow" of his own loneliness.[20] Indeed, in the desolate landscape of his exilic poetry—a "land as vast as grief and waiting"[21]— everything is bereft of magic and affect. "In the night of this exile," he writes, "there are no stars."[22] Even the moon, the eternal muse of all poets, is dead and lifeless in America, only appearing as "food for vultures." His new abode, Los Angeles, "this city of angels," is "an inferno as beautiful as paradise itself,"[23] and its soulless and greedy inhabitants are only in search of a new forbidden fruit. Here, houses, opulent or modest, streets, busy or quiet, harbors and seas, serene or stormy, all conjure no memory, arouse no emotion. Here, he says, with no memory, and no trace of his accomplishments, he rides time towards the ultimate destination.[24]

The exilic laments described in these poems are certainly not unfamiliar to the Iranian intellectual community. For one thing, ever since Plato tried

15. Adorno, *Minima Moralia*, 33.

16. Ibid., 27.

17. Ibid., 81

18. Nader Naderpour, *Time and the Earth*, 74.

19. Ibid., 93

20. Nader Naderpour, "Blood and Ashes," trans. Michael Hillmann, in *The Literary Review*, vol. 40, No. 1 (Fall 1996) (special Issue: "Iranian Diaspora Literature Since 1980"): 186.

21. Ibid., 86.

22. Ibid., 127.

23. Ibid., 127.

24. Ibid., 125.

to banish poets from his Republic, poets and intellectuals have returned the favor, and felt like exiles at home. Exile in this sense is more a state of mind and psychology than a fact of geography and politics. Cervantes, whose novel *Don Quixote* heralded the advent of the modern age, knew this well. His Don Quixote is the sublime image of an exile: at home neither in his native land, nor in the wilderness of his imagination. To this condition of *existential* exile, geography and locality are but a mere backdrop. Naderpour captures the same sentiments in his essay "The Poetry of Exile and the Exile of Poetry." There he writes that all poets are always exiles, and "all genuine poetry of the world is the poetry of exile."[25]

But aside from this metaphoric exile, past generations of Iranian intellectuals have had some, albeit limited, experience with banishment. The history of that experience can, I think, be divided into three distinctive phases. While there is much that separates the three phases, they nevertheless converge on two important points. Each has occurred in crucial moments of Iran's encounter with modernity, and in each phase, language has been a central problem and panacea.[26]

The first large-scale exodus of Iranian intellectuals created the Hindi School of Iranian poetry and criticism. Just around the time when Cervantes in Spain, Shakespeare in England, and Martin Luther in Germany were contributing to the creation of national languages, and thus preparing the ground for nationalism and other constitutive elements of modernity, and just as Iran's attempt to enter the modern world, orchestrated by Shah Abbas, was aborted, many of the brightest Iranian artists and philosophers, rightfully fearing the frenzy of the Shiites and the chaos of a war unleashed by Afghan invaders, fled Iran and sought a safe haven in India. In exile, they created what has since been called Sabk-e Hendi, or the Indian School.

---

25. Ibid., 8

26. After the coup of 1953 in Iran, a large number of leading cadres of the Tudeh Party, the pro-Soviet Communist party of Iran, were forced to flee the country. Most of them ended up in Eastern Europe and the Soviet Union. A large contingent lived in what was then East Germany. As a group, they were consumed by party politics and sectarian machinations. The sterility of their ideology and their willingness to put reason in the service of dogma, has given the published fruits of their labor a uniformly gray and grim texture. New documents from the Soviet and East German archives are beginning to be used by scholars in attempting to figure out the texture of life for these exiles. Early evidence betrays lives of constant bickering, brooding, sniping and spying. I have seen documents from the Stasi showing the reports of one member of the central committee code-named Charly. Charly leaves nothing to his handlers' imaginations and gives them details about party life that would be of interest, and recorded by a German bureaucrat. For an overall appraisal of this exilic experience, see Babak Amir Khosravi and Mohsen Heydariyan, *Mohajerat-e Sosiyalisty va Sarnevesht Iranian* [Socialist exile and the fate of Iranians] (Tehran, 1381/2002).

Hazim, whose poetry is undergoing something of a revival in Iran today, represented perhaps the quintessence of this first generation of exiles. For him and his compatriots poetry was the narrative form of choice, and in their verse, poetic techniques, words, and metaphors all implode into themselves. A concentric cacophony of metaphors, with no "objective correlative" other than the poet's ability to construct ever more arcane, more obtuse, albeit beautiful, metaphors was one of the main accomplishments of their exilic experience.

But this obsession with language had another, unexpected result. It helped foster a refreshingly modern, even postmodern, hermeneutics. Much along the lines advocated by Nietzsche in the late nineteenth century, Persian poetry of the seventeenth-century Indian School arrived at notions about the ephemeral nature of meaning in a text, and about the contingency of language, and truth itself.[27]

The second wave of exile came in the wake of Iran's constitutional revolution of 1905-1907. When reactionary forces tried to resurrect oriental despotism in Iran, many of the most prominent advocates of democracy and rule of law, fearing for their lives, fled the country. In yet another sign of the ascendance of the West, as compared to the descending East, this time the safe haven Iranian exiles sought was not India, but Europe. Most of them ended up in Berlin. Germany was a relative newcomer to the "Great Game" of colonial domination. It in fact had no foothold in the Middle East, and was thus more than willing to support the efforts of the Iranian nationalists against Russian and British domination. In their attempts to form an alliance with the Muslims, the German propaganda machine, helped by the Iranians, even fostered the myth that the Kaiser had become a devout Muslim. During World War II, Germans used the same gambit, this time offering Hitler as the new epitome of Islamic piety!

In 1919, the "Berlin Committee" could count as its members a truly impressive group of Iranian writers, poets, and scholars. Together, and initially with financial help from the Kaiser's coffers, they published the journal *Kaveh*. By nearly every conceivable measure, it turned out to be one of the most important publications of Iranian intellectual life in exile. Ultimately, it would also help change the intellectual landscape in Iran. The first modern Persian work of fiction, *Farsi Shekar Hast* (*Persian is Sugar*), as well as the first scholarly texts in economics and diplomatic history, were all published in this journal. In every issue,

27. For an erudite account of this school, and its accomplishments, see Mohammed Reza Shafi' Kadkani, *Shaeri dar Hojumeh Montaghedan: Naghd-e Adabi dar Sabk-e Hendi* [Poetry under critical attack: the Hindi School and literary criticism] (Tehran, 1999).

there were also articles about the inadequacies of the Persian language in facing the challenge of modernity, a challenge that was, in the mind of *Kaveh*'s writers, as inevitable as it was welcome.[28]

In articulating these views, one of the main contributors to the journal, Seyyed Hassan Taghizadeh, wrote words that he would later rue. Iranians must, he said, in their blood and bone, become Western. Shedding all that is Persian and retrograde, and embracing all that is Western and progressive, was for the young Taghizadeh the sole path to salvation. Though he would later repeatedly modify and retract this statement, the damage to his reputation, even to Iran's quest in incorporating modernity, proved permanent.[29] The ill-advised words provided the enemies of change and democracy in Iran with an easy target. It helped legitimize their sinister claim that democracy, rule of law, rationalism and individualism—in short, all we call modern—are nothing other than colonial commodities, and instruments of a political ruse meant to lull Muslims submission.

But Taghizadeh's words at the same time echoed an important historic fact about Iranian intellectuals of the time. By then, for a whole generation of writers, poets and thinkers, Europe had become a beacon of progress and hope. As a historic force, these intellectuals were all children of the Age of Enlightenment. The messianic propensity of Iran's culture, ever awaiting a redeemer, was in perfect congruence with the Enlightenment notion that intellectuals are the very repository of light and reason. Furthermore many of these modern ideas traveled to Iran through Russia. In Russia, modern ideas were often reshaped, if not marred, by the despotic and messianic tendencies of Russian history. The concept of the intellectual is a good example of this transformation. In trying to explain the intellectual climate in nineteenth-century Russia, Isaiah Berlin has offered a useful taxonomy of intellectuals. French intellectuals, he suggests, consider themselves "purveyors" of ideas and images, and accept no responsibility other than producing the best possible works. Russian intellectuals, on the other hand, require "total commitment" and think of themselves as "a dedicated order, an almost secular priesthood."[30] It was the Russian notion of the "intelligentsia"—and not the French idea of an "intellectual"—that

---

28. For a discussion of the journal and its views on modernity, see my "*Kaveh* and the Question of Modernity in Iran" in *Tajaddod va Tajaddod Setizi dar Iran* [Modernity and its foes in Iran] (Tehran, 1999), 173-193.

29. Taghizadeh wrote these controversial lines in an editorial for the journal *Kaveh*. It appeared on 22 January 1920. All issues of Kaveh were published in one volume in Tehran in 1981.

30. Isaiah Berlin, *Russian Thinkers* (New York, 1978), 117.

came to dominate political discourse in Iran. The acceptance of this elitist and messianic Russian ideal was made easier by the fact that it neatly matched the Shiite idea of a Mahdi, or savior, and his small band of pious followers. In other words, modern intellectuals became secular versions of the Imam; they became warrior-knight messiahs, steeped in a Promethean sense of social responsibility and self-declared social esteem.

The Pahlavi regime strengthened the intellectual's sense of self-importance. On the one hand, the Pahlavis craved intellectual support; and on the other, they jailed, censored, and occasionally killed prominent intellectuals.

With the fall of the Pahlavi regime, the self-declared Prometheans of the age became pariahs. They were now stranded on the hard rock of shattered hopes, miscarried ideas, and dissension and division among the ranks. Furthermore a disillusioned public had become disappointed with the role intellectuals had played in the revolution. A budding totalitarian power structure had only distrust and animus for secular intellectuals. Part of this distrust was political in nature: Many intellectuals had been at the forefront of the fight against the new Islamic despotism. But there was also another historical and epistemological source to this tension. Throughout the centuries, the clergy had considered themselves the sole and ultimate source of sacred and profane truth. They cherished their self-proclaimed title as the *Ulama* (learned). The genesis of modern intellectuals was clearly a direct threat to the clergy's lucrative monopoly of "truth" and learning. The Islamic regime's systematic policy of eliminating—sometimes physically, other times, politically—the role of the intellectuals led to the third wave of migration in Iran's history.

Iranian and German intellectuals who came to America at different times had important points in common: they had both fled their countries after calamitous upheavals and the rise of new and menacing social forces. Both had, in their respective countries, witnessed the development of a kind of character among their countrymen they could not fathom. The thought and sight of "Hitler's Willing Executioners"[31] in Germany, the presence of hundreds of thousands of religious zealots willing to kill and die for their faith in Iran, provided the intellectuals of the two countries with a disheartening image of their two nations. In each case, their response was to heed the advice of the Oracle at Delphi to "Know thyself." Each group turned inward; each tried to lay bare the collective unconscious, the unadorned histories, of the nations they had left behind.

---

31. For the controversial account of the collective responsibility and complicity of the German people in the crimes of Nazism, see Daniel Goldhagen, *Hitler's Willing Executioners* (New York, 1998).

Trying to map out the psychological and social roots of the Nazi appeal, Adorno and his colleagues began their monumental study, *The Authoritarian Personality*. Leo Lowenthal, who ended up teaching for many years at the University of California at Berkeley, engaged in an in-depth analysis of German mass culture during the years before the rise of Nazism; social critics, he believed, had hitherto focused too much on high art and middle- and upper-class lives; their disdain for the habits and beliefs of the "lower depths" had caused these mores and morals to remain a mystery to them, and it is in that uncharted territory that the roots of Nazism can be found. Thomas Mann's *Doctor Faustus*, Eric Fromm's *Escape from Freedom*, Hannah Arendt's influential study, *The Origins of Totalitarianism*, Franz Neuman's *Behemoth* and its description of the Nazi economic system, and finally Leo Strauss' studies on the origins of tyranny are only a few examples of studies by German exiles that tried to come to theoretical grips with the unfathomable fact that Goebbels and Hitler had come to power in the land of Beethoven and Hegel.

A similar historical turn, a critical appraisal of Iran's past, a vigorous attempt to criticize, and when necessary debunk, the dominant ideological discourse, has been evident in the works of Iranian intellectuals in America. A veritable, albeit belated, Renaissance has been taking place. *Encyclopedia Iranica*, a project whose genesis predates the revolution by a few years, could easily be considered the most ambitious modern effort at a full appraisal of Iran as a civilization. Housed at Columbia University in New York City (not far from the New School for Social Research where many of the German intellectual exiles landed), it attempts to describe every major and minor historical event and personage, every town and village, every writer and river in Iran.

Furthermore, two journals, one called *Iran Nameh*, the other *Iranshenasi*, have been regularly published in America for some time now. They are considered the most respected Persian journals in the world. *Iran Nameh* is about to enter its twenty-fifth year of publication, while *Iranshenasi* nears the fifteen year mark. There are also two oral history projects, one based at Harvard University, the other at the Foundation for Iranian Studies in Washington, DC, which have attempted to save for posterity the recollections of some of Iran's most influential intellectuals and politicians.[32] A third oral history, centered in Los Angeles, is devoted to chronicling the

---

30. Both have begun to put some of their material on line. They are also trying to publish some of the most important interviews in their respective series. For example, see Habib Ladjevardi, ed., *Memoirs of Jafar Sharif Emami*, Iranian Oral History Project, Center for Middle Eastern Studies, Harvard University, (Cambridge, 1999).

life of Iranian Jews. There are several theoretical and literary journals of various political persuasions as well—from the Socialist *Elm-o Jame'eh*, to the literary *Persian Book Review*. There are at least two distinct organizations of scholars (Iranian Studies and CIRA) whose work is concerned solely with Iran. There are a number of feminist organizations that regularly host conferences and talks. For many years, one of these groups helped publish a quarterly called *Nimeh-ye Digar* (*The Other Half*) that had to stop publication in 2001 due to financial constraints.

Many of the bigger cities in America have their own Persian theater groups. Sometimes—as in the case of the Darvak group in Berkeley, whose productions have toured much of Europe over the last decades—they stage avant-garde productions; other times they perform the more traditional fare of comical or classical plays. The question of exile, the battle of assimilated youth with its stubbornly unchanged parents, and comedies of manners are dominant leitmotifs of these theatrical productions. And rare indeed is the American college or university without at least one Persian who holds an important faculty position.

Even a cursory look at the collective portrait of Persian exiles in America will reveal that in their ranks, there is now a new breed of intellectual who has opted for some measure of assimilation and immersion in the host culture. They have mastered the English language, and often publish their works in both Persian and English. They are as comfortable with Shakespeare as with Sa'di; in contrast to Taghizadeh's generation, they are neither awed nor intimidated by the West; nor are they oblivious to Iran's rich cultural legacy. The poet Ali Zarin speaks for this generation when he writes, "America / in the poems of Walt Whitman / Langston Hughes / Allen Ginsberg/ the songs of Woody Guthrie / and Joan Baez / I made you mine."[33]

Over the last few years, an impressive number of these intellectuals have published acclaimed literary anthologies, novels, memoirs, collections of poetry, and innumerable works of scholarship, all written in English. Taghi Modaressi was that rare Iranian who was already an accomplished novelist in Iran before he arrived in America. Here he reinvented himself by writing and publishing novels in English. His novelistic ruminations dissect the agonies of the exilic mutilation, and yet are not despairing in their final effect. Nahid Rachlin is another successful member of this generation of writers. Her forte is describing the plight of Iranian émigré women. And finally, if a book's gross sales are to be taken as a measure of success, then Gina Nahai's *Moonlight on the Avenue of*

33. Ali Zarin, "Made You Mine, America," *The Literary Review*, vol. 40, no. 1 (Fall 1996): 216.

Faith, an acclaimed magic realist account of women's lives at the turn of the century in Tehran's Jewish ghetto, is clearly the most successful novel written by an Iranian in exile.

For Iranian women in exile, 2003 was a year of unusual productivity. Three successful novels and memoirs have been published in the first six months of the year. Azar Nafisi's *Reading Lolita In Tehran*, Marjane Satrapi's *Persepolis*, and Firouzeh Dumas' *Funny in Farsi* use three different genres—fictional memoir, cartoon novel, and the more traditional memoir of exile—to offer different views of the plight of women in Islamic Iran.

Successful as these works have been, they all pale in comparison to the giant strides made by Iranian films in America. A number of critics and scholars have made careers out of chronicling the evolution of this cinema and articulating its theoretical place in the context of recent cinematic trends and theories.[34] It has become fashionable to show and praise Persian films.

Even Persian cooking has been reappraised and found its rightful place in the gourmet pantheon of America. The popularity of this cuisine, aside from its intrinsic tastiness, is to no small measure the result of the untiring work of Najmieh Batmanglij, who has established herself as a world-class aesthete and culinary maestro. Her books have transformed the Iranian cookbook genre from a simple manual of a craft to a sublimely beautiful representation of an art. Mage Publishers, which publishes her books (and all my hitherto published works in English) has been devoted to publishing books about Iran in the English language for two decades. It has succeeded in not just surviving, but establishing an impressive reputation in the highly competitive publishing world of the United Sates.

There are hundreds of sites on the Internet devoted solely to Iranian issues. Everything from the songs of the popular female singer Googoosh, to Qur'anic verses, from soccer memorabilia to the latest news from Iran, can be found on the Net. So vast are the number of Iranian sites that there are now special search engines that can help you find everything from photos of celebrities to old stamps from the Qajar dynasty; Iranian chat-rooms and a burgeoning list of web logs also abound.

Persian music too has been transformed by this new genus of exiles. A promising musical trend has been created by some young, second-generation, Iranians. A refreshingly eclectic mix of Spanish chords, used in counterpoint with new interpretations of Persian modes, or *dastgahs*, give this new music a delightful timbre, at once familiar and altogether strange.

---

34. One of the most prolific of these critics is Hamid Naficy. See his *The Making of Exile Culture: Iranian Television in Los Angeles* (Minneapolis, 1993).

But the creative and critical work of this vast army of old and new exiles has not been without its obstacles. Nostalgia is the narcotic of exile, and the nemesis of sober and critical appraisal of "home." Catering to this affliction has become, like much else in America, a big business. Numerous companies produce the sights, sounds, smells, and tastes of the old country and sell them at often hefty prices. The plethora of Persian newspapers, magazines, radio stations, television channels and cultural groups that exist in many towns and cities afford the exiles a fleeting glance at the imaginary homeland they crave. There are, for example, no less than ninety magazines and newspapers in Los Angles alone. Furthermore "over one hundred thirty feature fiction films made in Iran before the revolution" bring home to "ravenous [audiences] sights and sound of the homeland."[35] A mercilessly long litany of singers, many of them mere novices, with more bravado than singing talent, caters to the exiles' endless appetite for sounds of Persia. Much of what they produce is a strange, discordant mix that combines somber and melancholic verse with jubilant and ecstatic music. Their songs are an awkward combination of kitsch and pathos, sentimental lyrics and heartfelt laments for the lost home. This incongruity is also observed in their music videos, where "the incoherent and fragmented style" of the visuals is "accompanied by 'cohering' ballads whose oft-repeated refrain is 'I am afraid.'"[36]

A far more important obstacle on the road to intellectual and aesthetic consummation for Iranian exiles in America continues to be the events that have taken place in Iran over the last decade. For nearly all of the last century, cities in the West, from Berlin and London to Paris and Berkeley, have been the intellectual Meccas for most of Iran's secular intellectuals. Oppression at home—a constant fact of twentieth-century life in Iran—had meant that those who suffered the pangs of exile were at least rewarded with the feeling that their ideas, thoughts and theories were the cherished vanguard of cultural, literary and political developments in Iran. It was generally assumed that the West was the smithy where the finest, and the most sophisticated, ideas and theories about Iran could be fashioned. Exiles, in short, were in a privileged theoretical position. What they lost in authentic "living at home" they more than made up for by their mastery of theory and their ability to speak freely, without fear of retribution and jail. The advent of the computer age and the inability of oppressive regimes to control cyberspace promised to increase the privileged status of exiled intellectuals. They could, unchallenged by native Procrustean

---

35. Naficy, *The Making of Exile Culture* , 42.
36. Ibid., 178.

authorities, enlighten the minds of Iranians back home. The advent of the information revolution held out the promise that exiled Iranians would become a forceful presence in Iran. The global village was no longer a trite cliché, but an almost tangible reality.

But something uncanny has happened in Iran. Relative freedom of the press came, and soon Iranian intellectuals at home began to write with such bold vigor and innovation that the creative texture, the immediacy, and the theoretical depth of their writing eclipsed nearly all that the exiled intellectuals had to offer. And so a change of historic dimension is taking place today. The main arena for new ideas about politics and democracy, civil society and reform, even modernity and tradition, is no longer located in Persian intellectual circles exiled in the West, but in Iran. The world of scholarship, with its requisite long years of research and rumination, and its dependence on archives and libraries, seems to be the only arena where the exiles can still claim to enjoy a privileged position. Prometheus is now doubly bound: estranged from his home, stranded halfway across the world, he is also exiled from his self-declared and self-affirming role as the ultimate source of light. That light is now in Iran.

In the quintessentially Persian story of Simorgh, some birds set out on a journey of discovery. They are searching for the mythical bird Simorgh, the ultimate embodiment of wisdom. After a long search, they realize that the Simorgh is in fact their own collective wisdom. The wisdom they had been seeking in distant places turned out to be, all along, within themselves.

Democracy, too, is about affirming the fact that wisdom lies not in promised messiahs, exiled intellectuals, or imaginary Meccas, but in the reasoned and collective action of the popular will. Iranian society is finally realizing this native source of democracy, just as in the age-old parable of Simorgh. And every step toward that rediscovery chips away at the need for, and the power of, intellectual messiahs—whether in geographic exile in America or in affective and epistemological exile at home.

ACKNOWLEDGMENTS

The articles included here had their first incarnations in the form of papers or talks given at different academic conferences and institutions. I owe debts of gratitude to Amir A. Afkhami at Yale University, Ahmad Karimi Hakak of the University of Washington, Firouzeh Khazrai of Princeton University, Farzaneh Milani of the University of Virginia, Nima Mina at the London School of Oriental and African Studies, Ali Nayeri of MIT, Michael Shapiro of the University of Hawaii, Ms. Mirsedghi of Litera-Tour, city of Mainz, and finally Nazar-al-Sayyad, of the University of California's Center for Middle Eastern Studies where I have been a Visiting Scholar for eight years.

Students in my class on Iran and modernity at Stanford University provided the first spark for collecting these articles into a book.

A number of friends took time out of their busy schedules to read the completed manuscript and avail me of their insights and comments. I am particularly grateful to Leonardo Alishan, Hamid Moghadam, Mike McFaul, Mohsen Milani, and Hamid and Parviz Shokat for their help.

My debt to Ebrahim Golestan goes far beyond his generosity to me regarding this book. He agreed to read *Lost Wisdom* under trying circumstances; his extensive comments were, nevertheless, keen, discerning and attentive to every detail.

My sister, Farzaneh Milani, read the entire manuscript several times, and brought to every reading her careful precision, her unfailing sense of justice, and her insights as a feminist critique and scholar.

Joanne Kaczor, of Notre Dame de Namur University, kindly agreed to navigate through the many almost illegible notations on margins of early drafts, and to type the first full version of *Lost Wisdom*. She was as always careful, resourceful, and congenial even under stress.

Mohammad Batmanglij of Mage Publishers brought his usual intellectual savvy and aesthetic sense to the editing of the book, while Hugh MacDonald was as careful, cautious, congenial, and consistently watchful a copyeditor as one could hope for.

Last and most, I owe a special debt to Jean Nyland. I read to her every article in its different incarnations, while she read the entire manuscript at least three times. Her vast erudition, and her contagious passion for the world of words and ideas, have been invaluable in providing inspiration and support for *Lost Wisdom*.

Needless to say, none of these people are in any way responsible for the contents of the book. That responsibility rests solely with me.

Abbas Milani
October 2, 2004